Series Editors:
Robert C. Pianta
Carollee Howes

Effective Early Childhood
Professional Development

Also in the *National Center for*
Research on Early Childhood Education Series:

Dual Language Learners
in the Early Childhood Classroom
edited by Carollee Howes, Ph.D.,
Jason T. Downer, Ph.D., and Robert C. Pianta, Ph.D.

Foundations for Teaching Excellence:
Connecting Early Childhood Quality Rating,
Professional Development, and Competency Systems in States
edited by Carollee Howes, Ph.D., and Robert C. Pianta, Ph.D.

The Promise of Pre-K
edited by Robert C. Pianta, Ph.D., and Carollee Howes, Ph.D.

Effective Early Childhood Professional Development

Improving Teacher Practice and Child Outcomes

edited by

Carollee Howes, Ph.D.
University of California, Los Angeles

Bridget K. Hamre, Ph.D.
University of Virginia, Charlottesville

and

Robert C. Pianta, Ph.D.
University of Virginia, Charlottesville

·P·A·U·L·H·
BROOKES
PUBLISHING Cº ®

Baltimore • London • Sydney

Paul H. Brookes Publishing Co., Inc.
Post Office Box 10624
Baltimore, Maryland 21285-0624
USA

www.brookespublishing.com

Typeset by BLPS Content Creations, Chilton, Wisconsin.
Manufactured in the United States of America by
Versa Press, Inc., East Peoria, Illinois.

Supported in part by the Institute of Education Sciences, U.S. Department of Education,
through Grant R305A060021 to the University of Virginia. However, the content does
not necessarily reflect the position of the U.S. Department of Education, and no official
endorsement should be inferred.

Library of Congress Cataloging-in-Publication Data

Effective early childhood professional development : improving teacher practice and child
outcomes / edited by Carollee Howes, Ph.D. University of California, Los Angeles, Bridget K.
Hamre, Ph.D. University of Virginia, Charlottesville, and Robert C. Pianta, Ph.D. University
of Virginia, Charlottesville.
    pages   cm. — (National Center for Research on Early Childhood Education series ; 4)
This volume is based on the National Center for Research on Early Childhood Education
(NCRECE) annual leadership symposium.
Includes bibliographical references and index.
    ISBN-13: 978-1-59857-237-7 (pbk.)
    ISBN-10: 1-59857-237-7 (pbk.)
    1. Early childhood teachers—In-service training—United States.   I. Howes, Carollee.
    II. Hamre, Bridget K.   III. Pianta, Robert C.

LB1775.6.E43 2012
372.110973--dc23   2012006167

British Library Cataloguing in Publication data are available from the British Library.

2016   2015   2014   2013   2012

10   9   8   7   6   5   4   3   2   1

Contents

Series Preface

The National Center for Research on Early Childhood Education (NCRECE) series on the future of early childhood education addresses key topics related to improving the quality of early childhood education in the United States. Each volume is a culmination of presentations and discussions taking place during the annual NCRECE Leadership Symposium, which brings together leaders and stakeholders in the field to discuss and synthesize the current knowledge about prominent issues that affect the educational experiences and outcomes of young children. Most important, it is the aim of these symposia, and the related series volumes, to be forward looking, identifying nascent topics that have the potential for improving the quality of early childhood education and then defining, analyzing, and charting conceptual, policy, practice, and research aims for the future. Topics to be addressed in subsequent volumes include the nature and quality of publicly funded preschool programs and the integration of quality rating systems, early childhood competencies, and models of professional development.

The series is designed to stimulate critical thinking around these key topics and to help inform future research agendas. The series should be of interest to a broad range of researchers, policy makers, teacher educators, and practitioners.

Robert C. Pianta, Ph.D.
Carollee Howes, Ph.D.

About the Editors

Carollee Howes, Ph.D., is Director of the Center for Improving Child Care Quality, Department of Education, and a professor of the applied developmental psychology doctorate program at the University of California, Los Angeles. Dr. Howes is an internationally recognized developmental psychologist focusing on children's social and emotional development. She has served as a principal investigator on a number of seminal studies in early child care and preschool education, including the National Child Care Staffing Study; the Family and Relative Care Study; the Cost, Quality, and Outcomes Study; and the National Study of Child Care in Low Income Families. Dr. Howes has been active in public policy for children and families in California as well as across the United States. Her research focuses on children's experiences in child care, their concurrent and long-term outcomes from child care experiences, and child care quality and efforts to improve child care quality. Dr. Howes is the editor of *Teaching 4- to 8-Year-Olds: Literacy, Math, Multiculturalism, and Classroom Community* (Paul H. Brookes Publishing Co., 2003) and the coeditor of *The Promise of Pre-K* (Paul H. Brookes Publishing Co., 2009); *Foundations for Teaching Excellence: Connecting Early Childhood Quality Rating, Professional Development, and Competency Systems in States* (Paul H. Brookes Publishing Co., 2011); and *Dual Language Learners in the Early Childhood Classroom* (Paul H. Brookes Publishing Co., 2011).

Bridget K. Hamre, Ph.D., is Research Associate Professor and Associate Director of the Center for Advanced Study of Teaching and Learning at the University of Virginia, Charlottesville. After spending a few years as a first-grade teacher in Berkeley, California, she received her doctoral degree in clinical and school psychology from the University of Virginia. She works on a variety of projects related to understanding the components of teachers' interactions with students that promote positive academic and social development. This work includes consulting with teachers as a part of the innovative professional development intervention study MyTeachingPartner. Dr. Hamre also is interested in educational policy, an interest that was fostered during her 2 years at Policy Analysis for California Education (PACE) at the University of California, Berkeley.

Robert C. Pianta, Ph.D., is Dean of the Curry School of Education, Novartis US Foundation Professor of Education, the director of the National Center for Research on Early Childhood Education, and the director of the Center for Advanced Study of Teaching and Learning at the University of Virginia in Charlottesville. A former special education teacher, Dr. Pianta is particularly interested in how relationships with teachers and parents, as well as classroom experiences, can help improve outcomes for at-risk children and youth. Dr. Pianta is a principal investigator on several major grants, including MyTeachingPartner, the Institute of Education Sciences Interdisciplinary Doctoral Training Program in Risk and Prevention, and the National Institute of Child Health and Human Development Study of Early Child Care and Youth Development. He was also a senior investigator for the National Center for Early Development and Learning and served as editor of the *Journal of School Psychology*. He is the author of more than 300 journal articles, chapters, and books in the areas of early childhood development, transition to school, school readiness, and parent–child and teacher–child relationships, including *School Readiness and the Transition to Kindergarten in the Era of Accountability* (with Martha J. Cox & Kyle L. Snow, Paul H. Brookes Publishing Co., 2007) and *Classroom Assessment Scoring System*™ (*CLASS*™; with Karen M. La Paro & Bridget K. Hamre, Paul H. Brookes Publishing Co., 2008), and he is the coeditor of *The Promise of Pre-K* (Paul H. Brookes Publishing Co., 2009); *Foundations for Teaching Excellence: Connecting Early Childhood Quality Rating, Professional Development, and Competency Systems in States* (Paul H. Brookes Publishing Co., 2011); and *Dual Language Learners in the Early Childhood Classroom* (Paul H. Brookes Publishing Co., 2011). Dr. Pianta consults regularly with federal agencies, foundations, and universities.

About the Contributors

Karen L. Bierman, Ph.D., Distinguished Professor, Department of Psychology, The Pennsylvania State University, 140 Moore Building, University Park, PA 16802

Karen Bierman is Distinguished Professor of Psychology and Director of the Child Study Center at The Pennsylvania State University. Her research focuses on social-emotional development and children at risk, with an emphasis on the design and evaluation of school-based programs that promote social competence, school readiness, and positive intergroup relations and that reduce aggression and violence.

Clancy Blair, Ph.D., M.P.H., Professor of Applied Psychology, New York University, 627 Broadway, New York, NY 10012

Clancy Blair is Professor in Applied Psychology at New York University. His research is concerned with self-regulation in young children. Furthermore, he is interested in executive function and what this means for low-income children's school readiness and academic achievement in early childhood.

Margaret Burchinal, Ph.D., Senior Scientist, Director of Data Management and Analysis Core, FPG Child Development Institute, The University of North Carolina at Chapel Hill, CB # 8185, Chapel Hill, NC 27599

Margaret Burchinal is Senior Scientist at the FPG Child Development Institute. She serves as Associate Editor for *Child Development* and *Early Childhood Research Quarterly* and has served as the primary statistician for many child care studies including the *Eunice Kennedy Shriver* National Institute of Child Health & Human Development Study of Early Child Care and Youth Development; the Abecedarian Project; the National Center for Early Development and Learning 11-state prekindergarten evaluation; and the Cost, Quality, & Outcomes Study.

April D. Crawford, Ph.D., Manager, Community Outreach Program, Children's Learning Institute, Department of Pediatrics, The University of Texas Health Science Center at Houston, 7000 Fannin, Suite 1910B, Houston, TX 77030

April Crawford's research interests include understanding how institutional settings shape children's early learning experiences and the extent to which programs aimed at quality improvement are differentially effective in a mixed-delivery early care system. She is coauthor of the *Teacher Behavior Rating Scale (TBRS)*—an observational rating scale that assesses the quantity and quality of teaching behaviors in early childhood–second grade classrooms.

Karen E. Diamond, Ph.D., Professor, Purdue University, Department of Human Development and Family Studies, 1200 W. State Street, West Lafayette, IN 47907-2055

Karen E. Diamond is a professor in Purdue University's Department of Human Development and Family Studies. Her research focuses on classroom interventions to improve outcomes for preschool children from low-income families and for children with disabilities. She is Past Editor of *Early Childhood Research Quarterly*.

Celene E. Domitrovich, Ph.D., Assistant Director, Prevention Research Center, The Pennsylvania State University, 108 South Henderson Building, University Park, PA, 16802

Dr. Domitrovich is Assistant Director of the Prevention Research Center at The Pennsylvania State University. She is interested in the development of social and emotional competence in children, the role of teachers in the acquisition of these skills, and how social-emotional learning is related to success in school. Dr. Domitrovich has conducted several randomized trials of preventive interventions for children in preschool through middle school and is particularly interested in type II translational research regarding the implementation and dissemination of evidence-based interventions in communities.

Jason T. Downer, Ph.D., Research Associate Professor, University of Virginia, Assistant Director, Center for Advanced Study of Teaching and Learning, University of Virginia, 350 Old Ivy Way, Suite 100, Charlottesville, VA 22903

Jason T. Downer, Ph.D., is Research Associate Professor at the University of Virginia, Assistant Director at the Center for Advanced Study of Teaching and Learning, and a licensed clinical psychologist in the Commonwealth of Virginia. His research interests emphasize the identification and understanding of relevant contextual and relational contributors to young children's early achievement and social competence. Dr. Downer also has a keen interest in translating research to practice through school-based, classroom-focused interventions.

Scott D. Gest, Ph.D., Associate Professor of Human Development and Family Studies, The Pennsylvania State University, 110 Henderson South Building, University Park, PA 16802

Scott D. Gest completed doctoral studies in developmental-clinical psychology and conducts research on peer relationships and academic adjustment in school settings. He is particularly interested in how classroom teachers and school-based prevention programs may influence peer social dynamics.

Sukhdeep Gill, Ph.D., Associate Professor of Human Development and Family Studies, The Pennsylvania State University, 14 RAB, 1031 Edgecomb Avenue, York, PA 17403

Sukhdeep Gill's research interests include program evaluation, home visitation, staff development, parenting interventions, and the needs of women and young children from diverse backgrounds. She has conducted several program evaluations of home visitation programs including Early Head Start (EHS), Nurse Family Partnerships, Healthy Families America, and the New Parent Support Program. She is currently involved in two studies of professional development issues and concerns of home visitation staff and an outcome study of EHS. She is a part of the REDI (Research-based and Developmentally Informed) research team, an NICHD-funded multisite randomized trial of curricular infusions targeting social-emotional competencies and language-literacy skills into Head Start programs.

D. Sarah Hadden, Ph.D., Assistant Director of Quality Assurance, Teachstone Training, L.L.C., 105 Monticello Avenue, Suite 101, Charlottesville, VA 22902

D. Sarah Hadden is Assistant Director of Quality Assurance at Teachstone Training, L.L.C., an educational company with a mission to support teaching and learning through the dissemination of proven, evidence-based education programs. Prior to joining Teachstone, she was on the research faculty at the University of Virginia's Center for Advanced Study of Teaching and Learning. As a former teacher and teacher educator, Dr. Hadden is particularly interested in translating research into practice.

Bridget E. Hatfield, Ph.D., Postdoctoral Fellow, Institute of Education Science, Center for Advanced Study of Teaching and Learning, University of Virginia, 350 Old Ivy Way, Suite 100, Charlottesville, VA 22903

Dr. Bridget E. Hatfield is an Institute for Education Science Postdoctoral Fellow at the Center of Advanced Study of Teaching and Learning at the University of Virginia. Her research is focused on understanding child and classroom influences on social and emotional development in young children. She was recently awarded the American Psychological Association Educational Psychology Early Career Research Award to investigate changes in salivary cortisol for preschool children with disruptive behavior problems following a teacher-child relationship intervention. She earned a Ph.D. in human development and family studies from The University of North Carolina at Greensboro.

Faiza Jamil, M.Ed., Doctoral Student, Center for Advanced Study of Teaching and Learning, University of Virginia, 350 Old Ivy Way, Suite 100, Charlottesville, VA 22903

Faiza Jamil is an Institute of Education Sciences Predoctoral Fellow at the Curry School of Education. She is an experienced teacher, and her research interests include the measurement of teacher effectiveness and psychosocial functioning.

Laura M. Justice, Ph.D., Professor, School of Teaching and Learning, Director, Children's Learning Research Collaborative, Ohio State University, 1945 North High Street, 356 Arps Hall, Columbus, OH 43210

Laura Justice is Professor in the School of Teaching and Learning at Ohio State University. She is also the Director of the Children's Learning Research Collaborative. Dr. Justice's research interests include early language impairment, reading disabilities, instructional quality, and efficacy trials.

Carolyn R. Kilday, Ph.D., Postdoctoral Research Fellow, The State University of New York–University at Buffalo, 212 Baldy Hall, Buffalo, NY, 14051

Carolyn R. Kilday received her Ph.D. from the University of Virginia in education research with a focus on preschool math teaching and learning. She is currently Postdoctoral Research Fellow at The State University of New York–University at Buffalo working on a project examining the effectiveness of preschool math and self-regulation curricula.

Mable B. Kinzie, Ph.D., Associate Professor, Instructional Science and Technology, Center for Advanced Study of Teaching and Learning, Curry School of Education, University of Virginia, Post Office Box 400273, Charlottesville, VA 22904

Mable B. Kinzie focuses on applications of instructional design and new technology to support learning and development across disciplines and learner groups; her current work emphasizes development of teaching quality to support early child development. With more than 50 interactive/instructional products and 50 publications, she has been recognized as a Harrison Outstanding Faculty Member at the University of Virginia and received national awards for scholarship and instructional development.

Susan H. Landry, Ph.D., Professor of Pediatrics, Children's Learning Institute, The University of Texas Health Science Center at Houston, 7000 Fannin, Suite 2318, Houston, TX 77030

Dr. Susan H. Landry is a developmental psychologist, the Albert and Margaret Alkek Chair in Early Childhood, and the Michael Matthew Knight Professor in the Department of Pediatrics at The University of Texas Health Science Center at Houston. She is Director and Founder of the Children's Learning Institute at The University of Texas. Her research includes examinations of biological and environmental influences on children's development from infancy through adolescence as well as numerous federally funded parent–child and early childhood classroom intervention studies.

Christine Li-Grining, Ph.D., Assistant Professor, Department of Psychology, 1050 Damen Hall, Loyola University Chicago, Chicago, IL 60660

Christine Li-Grining is Assistant Professor in the Department of Psychology at Loyola University Chicago and a co-investigator on Chicago School Readiness Project, a federally-funded randomized controlled trial intervention. Her research interests include self-regulation, school readiness, and academic achievement, as well as poverty-related risks in early and middle childhood development.

Michelle F. Maier, Ph.D., Research Associate, Center for Advanced Study of Teaching and Learning, University of Virginia, 350 Old Ivy Way, Suite 100, Charlottesville, VA 22903

Michelle F. Maier earned her doctoral degree in applied developmental psychology from the University of Miami. She is currently Postdoctoral Research Associate at the Center for Advanced Study of Teaching and Learning at the University of Virginia. Her research interests include child- and classroom-level risk and protective factors that influence the school readiness and classroom engagement of preschool children.

Anita S. McGinty, Ph.D., CCC-SLP, Research Scientist, Center for the Advanced Study of Teaching and Learning, the University of Virginia, 350 Old Ivy Way, Charlottesville, VA 22903

Anita S. McGinty, is a clinical speech-language pathologist and research scientist in the Center for Advanced Study of Teaching and Learning at the University of Virginia, Charlottesville. Dr. McGinty's research focuses on identifying and establishing practices within classrooms and homes that support young children's language and literacy development. Dr. McGinty has published numerous peer-reviewed articles and book chapters concerning early language and literacy development and co-authored a curricular supplement called *Read It Again! Pre-K* (Justice & McGinty, 2008), which is currently being evaluated in a multistate effort through a federally funded grant.

Robert L. Nix, Ph.D., Research Associate, Prevention Research Center, 109 South Henderson Building, The Pennsylvania State University, University Park, PA 16802

Robert Nix is a Research Associate in the Prevention Research Center at The Pennsylvania State University. He works on multiple preventive interventions that seek to improve the social-emotional skills and reduce the behavior problems of young children living in high-risk environments.

Douglas R. Powell, Ph.D., Distinguished Professor, Department of Human Development and Family Studies, Purdue University, 1200 West State Street, West Lafayette, IN 47907-2055

Douglas R. Powell is Distinguished Professor in the Department of Human Development and Family Studies at Purdue University. His research focuses on professional development interventions with prekindergarten teachers aimed at improving at-risk children's literacy and language skills. He also conducts research on parent educational involvement in the early years.

C. Cybele Raver, Ph.D., Developmental Psychology Professor in the Department of Applied Psychology, Steinhardt School of Culture, Education, and Human Development, New York University; Director of the Institute for Education Sciences Wagner School of Public Service, New York University; Director of the Institute of Human Development and Social Change, Steinhardt School of Culture, Education, and Human Development, Wagner School of Public Service, New York University, Kimball Hall, 246 Greene Street, Room 403W, New York, NY 10003

C. Cybele Raver directs New York University's Institute of Human Development and Social Change. She examines the mechanisms that support children's self-regulation in the contexts of poverty and social policy. Dr. Raver and her research team currently conduct Chicago School Readiness Project, a federally funded randomized controlled trial intervention.

Emily Solari, Ph.D., Assistant Professor, School of Education, University of California, One Shields Avenue, Davis, CA 95616

Emily Solari is Assistant Professor at the University of California, Davis. Her research concentrates on early identification and intervention in literacy and language development of English language learners and at-risk populations.

Catherine Tsao, M.A., Doctoral Candidate, Graduate School of Education and Information Studies, University of California, Los Angeles, Moore Hall, Post Office Box 951521, Los Angeles, CA 90095

Catherine Tsao's research interests include social-emotional development of children from birth to 5 years of age within early education settings. Her previous experience includes administration of a university-based infant/toddler laboratory program, instruction at the undergraduate level, training and technical assistance, and educational policy.

Jessica Vick Whittaker, Ph.D., Human Development Research Scientist, Center for Advanced Study of Teaching and Learning, University of Virginia, 350 Old Ivy Way, Suite 100, Charlottesville, VA 22903

Jessica Vick Whittaker is a developmental psychologist whose research is focused on examining how teacher–child relationships can support young children's academic and social-emotional development. She has helped develop and implement several interventions designed to improve the quality of teacher–child interactions in early care and education settings. She received her B.A. in psychology from Duke University and her Ph.D. in human development from the University of Maryland.

Jeffrey M. Williams, Ph.D., Assistant Professor of Psychology, The University of Texas Health Science Center at Houston, 7000 Fannin Street, Suite 2373M, Houston, TX 77030

Jeffrey William is an Assistant Professor at the Children's Learning Institute at The University of Texas Health Science Center at Houston. He specializes in the application of multivariate statistical models to complex research questions, primarily in early childhood education. Specifically, he is interested in factor analysis and item response theory; structural equation modeling; and mediation and moderation, including their multilevel applications.

Amanda P. Williford, Ph.D., Assistant Research Professor, Center for Advanced Study of Teaching and Learning, Curry School of Education, University of Virginia, 350 Old Ivy Way, Suite 100, Charlottesville, VA 22903

Amanda Williford is Assistant Research Professor at the University of Virginia's Center for Advanced Study of Teaching and Learning. Her research focuses on developmental trajectories of externalizing behavior problems, factors that predict stability of externalizing behavior, transition to kindergarten in at-risk populations, and community-based early intervention. Dr. Williford has authored a number of peer-reviewed articles examining aspects of children's development of self-regulation, children's display of disruptive behavior, and effects of early intervention programs.

Tricia A. Zucker, Ph.D., Assistant Professor, The University of Texas Health Science Center at Houston, 7000 Fannin Street, Suite 2300, Houston, TX 77030

Dr. Tricia Zucker is Assistant Professor in the Children's Learning Institute at The University of Texas Health Science Center at Houston. Dr. Zucker's research interests include early identification and prevention of reading disabilities, early childhood curriculum and instruction, literacy and technology, family- and school-based interventions, and early childhood assessment. Dr. Zucker currently serves on research projects examining language and literacy development of English language learners, the role of coaches in early childhood professional development, and implementing preschool response to intervention (P-RTI) frameworks in classrooms across Texas.

Foreword

It is particularly apt to begin a book about moving forward—with a foreword (even if these are spelled differently). This book is about moving forward in strengthening early childhood professional development by identifying, with greater specificity, the approaches that are effective, helping early educators to be receptive to such approaches, and extending effective approaches throughout systems of early care and education.

The chapters in the book focus especially on professional development that is individualized and that aims at improving early educators' work with children in their everyday settings through coaching, mentoring, and consultation (see definitions providing distinctions among these by the National Association for the Education of Young Children and the National Association of Child Care Resource & Referral Agencies). This broad approach differs markedly from the traditional approach of aiming to deepen early educators' knowledge about young children's development. While the traditional approach works under the assumption that increasing such knowledge will inevitably lead to improvements in practice, there is now growing acknowledgment that to improve practice, it is necessary to start with a direct focus on practice: to provide positive models of sensitive and stimulating interactions, observe and provide feedback on interactions in the classroom or home-based group, and provide opportunities for reflection and consolidation as new practices take hold.

Although we have many indications in the research that "practice-focused" professional development holds promise for improving quality in early care and education and thereby strengthening child outcomes, we need to be extremely careful not to become overly enthusiastic, assuming that all such approaches are effective. Having identified a promising general direction for early childhood professional development, we now need to take a careful look at which practice-focused approaches are effective and why. This book takes important steps in this direction by asking three sets of questions.

A first set of questions addresses the specific features of practice-focused professional development, asking which parameters underlie effects for teachers and children and whether these can be modified to boost effects. Each chapter with this focus builds on initial evidence regarding effective approaches. Here the authors ask whether existing approaches can be further strengthened by modifying either the content or mode of delivery. More specifically, the chapters in this book ask the following:

- Can coaching to strengthen language and literacy practices in early childhood classrooms be delivered through a combination of on site and web-based work? What duration and balance of each of these components can strengthen modest effects in this important area?

- We run the risk of overburdening teachers with goals for improving practices in multiple, separate domains of children's development. Can approaches be developed to effectively address teacher practices in math and science simultaneously? In cognitive as well as social-emotional development?

- Is increased dosage of coaching interventions always better? Does this depend on the overall quality of the program? On different facets of dosage, such as duration of delivery and frequency and length of contacts?

Although the first set of questions addressed in this book focus on content and mode of delivery of practice-focused professional development, a second set of questions focuses on the recipients. Not all early educators may be equally receptive to professional development. Barriers include stress levels that make it much more difficult to absorb new information and make changes and cognitive overload, because too many decisions are being required in the moment-to-moment life of the classroom or home-based group. The chapters in this book ask the following:

- How can professional development be structured to deliberately address the stress levels of early educators so that they can be more receptive to new approaches? What is the potential for approaches aimed at reducing stress especially in settings where the home lives of both the children and the early educators involve substantial hardship?

- Can professional development be structured to help early educators prepare for and rehearse some decisions in the classroom so that they become automatic? If so, will early educators be able to focus on a smaller number of more complex decisions that warrant greater attention?

A third critical set of issues focused on in this book concerns how to maintain the core elements of effective practice-focused approaches to professional development while extending their implementation throughout systems of early care and education. This book asks what can be learned from initial attempts to implement practice-focused professional development at scale. More specifically, authors involved in system-wide implementation reflect on their experiences, asking the following:

- Which features of the professional development approach need to be documented in manuals so that they could be implemented in new sites?

- What systems-level components are necessary to assure appropriate selection, training, and ongoing supervision of staff providing the on-site professional development?

- What steps can be taken throughout a system to monitor fidelity of implementation? When are adaptations of a program appropriate, and when do they constitute problems with fidelity?

These questions help us move to a more complex conceptualization of effectiveness, considering both effective program components (the elements of a professional development approach that underlie impacts) and effective implementation of a program model (the steps that are needed to preserve fidelity when an approach is widely implemented).

By looking in greater depth at the program features that drive the positive outcomes of practice-focused professional development, at the recipients of professional development and their characteristics and circumstances that can inhibit or promote responsiveness, and at how professional development approaches can be brought to scale without diluting their impacts, the chapters in this book not only look forward but help us move forward.

Martha Zaslow, Ph.D.
Director, Office for Policy and Communications
Society for Research in Child Development
Senior Scholar, Child Trends

Acknowledgments

We recognize that this book would not be possible without the dedication and hard work of the very wide and diverse range of people working in the field of early childhood education to support the development of young children. Scholars, child care professionals, teachers, parents, and administrators have all contributed to the "promise of pre-K" and should be remembered and appreciated daily for their work. We also acknowledge the support of the Institute of Education Sciences, U.S. Department of Education, through Grant R305A060021 to the University of Virginia. We have been fortunate to have received support for the work involved in putting this volume together, and we especially recognize our program officer, Caroline Ebanks, for her help and advice.

INTRODUCTION

Introducing a Conceptual Framework of Professional Development in Early Childhood Education

Carollee Howes and Catherine Tsao

Effective teachers in early childhood are able to both engage children in meaningful activities that promote their conceptual understanding of academic material and construct positive teacher–child relationships with all the children in their classroom (Howes et al., 2008; Pianta, Belsky, Houts, Morrison, & Early Childhood Care Research Network, ECCRN, 2007). These positive relationships provide children with a secure and safe base for exploring the interpersonal as well as the academic dimensions of the program. Positive relationships combined with meaningful activities enable effective teachers to integrate explicit instruction with sensitive and warm interaction. These effective teachers are able to provide individualized responsive feedback and intentional engagement while maintaining a classroom climate that is orderly and predictable but not overly structured or regimented. This highly complex level of teaching would be difficult with any age group, but it is particularly challenging with preschool-age children, who are wildly heterogeneous in their knowledge of school subjects, school-appropriate behaviors, and developmental trajectories.

1

The knowledge and skills required by teachers of young children are far removed from the common-sense ideas that any mother can teach young children or that play is simply the work of children and the role of the preschool teacher is to supervise children's experiences with materials.

Unfortunately, large-scale studies of teacher practices within preschool programs find too few children have effective teachers, especially teachers who are able to provide optimal instructional as well as emotional support for young children's academic learning (Howes et al., 2008), particularly in the areas of math and science. Paradoxically, meaningful instruction in math and science in early childhood is one of the best predictors of future academic success (Duncan et al., 2007).

A major issue for the early childhood education (ECE) field is how to produce these effective teachers. There is not an established pathway for early childhood teacher preparation, and teachers' preservice training varies from a few workshops or units of postsecondary formal education to masters degrees. Moreover, if teachers have had formal education or a degree in ECE, the content area of this work may be in child development, education, or some other child-related field (Early et al., 2007). Even when the name of the degree program is the same or similar, there is little standardization of content within and across programs. Thus there is a need to examine intervention research in ECE professional development (PD) that goes beyond a content analysis of teacher education programs. Indeed such an analysis found that teacher preparation programs most commonly offer separate courses to address language/literacy and teacher–child interactions (Scott-Little et al., 2011).

Since the 1980s, states and professional organizations have emphasized the need for increased teacher formal education and training in ECE, but these moves toward PD have, unfortunately, been accompanied by parallel shifts in lowered compensation and poorer working conditions (Whitebook & Ryan, 2011). Not surprisingly, given these conditions and the diffuse and diverse nature of teacher training, formal education and degrees are poor predictors of effective teaching (Early et al., 2007).

An additional reason for the lack of correspondence between formal education and effective teaching had been a similar lack of correspondence between teaching practices and children's preacademic outcomes. Large-scale studies of ECE programs have found not only low levels of effective teaching at the classroom level (Howes et al., 2008; Pianta, La Paro, & Hamre, 2008), but also that children spend relatively small portions of their days engaged in preacademic learning activities and an even smaller proportion of this time working with a teacher (Chien et al., 2010; Gormley, Gayler, Phillips, & Dawson, 2005; Phillips, Gormley, & Lowenstein, 2009). Therefore it was difficult from these large-scale studies with low frequencies of teacher–child interaction to identify evidence-based best practice. That is, for example, when children were seldom read to, talked with individually, or engaged in letter–sound group activities, it was difficult to ascertain whether, all, or any, of these specific practices were linked to gains in literacy or language development. Furthermore, serious policy questions were raised about effective teaching practices and culturally appropriate practices (Howes, 2010).

Fortunately, there is now rich evidence-based literature identifying literacy and language teaching practices and, to a lesser extent, math and science teaching practices associated with gains in children's learning. For examples of these practices see the chapters in this volume, as all of the intervention research programs discussed have used this literature as the basis for the content of the intervention. These evidence-based practices have by and large been identified within controlled research programs conceptually based in developmental science programs that examine children's development within classroom contexts (Toth, Pianta, & Erickson, 2011).

However, the process of instilling evidence-based practices and effective teacher–child interaction into ECE teachers is not a simple task. Changing teacher practices and patterns of interaction requires more than identifying and providing a curriculum that includes evidence-based practices and asking (or requiring) teachers to use it (Preschool Curriculum Evaluation Research Consortium, 2008). Teaching practices take on different meanings in different cultural communities, and introducing new practices needs to take these meanings into consideration (Howes, 2010). Teachers, particularly those with experience, often have well-established belief systems about how to teach (Powell & Stremmel, 1989). Changing practices requires changing teacher beliefs and knowledge bases, as well as teacher behaviors. Most important, isolating practices without considering the emotional and instructional climate of the classroom, classroom management, and the very nature of teacher–child interaction is not sufficient to promote improvements in teaching quality (Justice, Mashburn, Hamre, & Pianta, 2008).

Many teachers have never participated—as teachers or as children in families and classrooms—in the kinds of adult–child interactions that are expected of effective teachers (Raver et al., 2008). Therefore, successful intervention programs for teacher PD have moved to include relationship-building components, attending to the relationship that is built between the teacher and interveners, modeling and providing exemplars of sensitive and responsive interactions, and providing support for changing behaviors (Erickson & Kurz-Riemer 1999; Toth et al., 2011). Random-assignment studies that compare relationship-building components of intervention versus written or web-based exemplars of evidence-based practices found that the relationship-based group of teachers increased both teacher–child positive interaction and children's gains in literacy, language, and social behaviors (Downer, LoCasale-Couch, Hamre, & Pianta 2009; Mashburn, Downer, Hamre, Justice, & Pianta 2010; Pianta, Mashburn, Downer, Hamre, & Justice, 2008).

In this volume we include reports from research programs that intend to intervene into teacher's professional development that 1) randomized control studies, 2) targeted a set of fairly narrow evidence-based teaching practices as content and evidence-based strategies for implementation, and 3) measured success by change in teacher practices and child outcomes. The volume is divided into three sections. The first section, Effective Models of Professional Development Interventions in Promoting Teacher and Child Outcomes, describes the elements and outcomes of four PD interventions. The second section, Factors Facilitating and/or Moderating Implementation, examines teacher attributes that facilitate or moderate teachers' responses to and success in making changing toward more effective practices. The third section, Scaling Up Professional Development, examines the issues of scaling up professional development interventions. The final chapter in that section discusses implications for policy.

EFFECTIVE MODELS OF PROFESSIONAL DEVELOPMENT INTERVENTIONS IN PROMOTING TEACHER AND CHILD OUTCOMES

Evidence-Based Instructional Practices

All intervention programs incorporate systematic instruction in targeted domains of development. Common elements include direct instruction in evidence-based practices; exemplars of teaching practices, usually video or web based; and a level of accountability for the teacher's own use of these practices. The interventions focus on increasing teachers' frequency of use of very specific practices—that is, providing responsive feedback, because as described by Justice and McGinty (see Chapter 4) this is considered to be the locus of learning. Several of the interventions focused on multiple domains of preacademic learning, often combining social and emotional development with an academic content area.

Language and literacy are the domains of instructional practice that have the largest literature base to draw upon and are used in most of the intervention programs described in this volume (Powell, Diamond, & Burchinal, Chapter 1; Domitrovich, Bierman, Nix, Gill, & Gest, Chapter 3; Justice & McGinty, Chapter 4; Landry, Zucker, Solaris, Crawford, & Williams, Chapter 7; Pianta, Hamre, & Hadden, Chapter 8). The focused practices include encouraging oral language development by having teachers ask children to label illustrations of target words when reading books, ask open-ended questions, and encourage conversation (Powell et al., Chapter 1); having teachers incorporate sound games, alphabet centers, and interactive reading in their lessons (Domitrovich et al., Chapter 3); having teachers use MyTeachingPartner–scripted lesson plans to address phonological awareness, alphabet knowledge, print awareness, vocabulary knowledge, narrative skill, and social communication (Justice & McGinty, Chapter 4; Pianta et al., Chapter 8); and more generally encouraging teacher responsiveness, language enrichment and scaffolding techniques, shared-book reading, vocabulary and comprehension building, print and book awareness, reading motivation, phonological awareness, alphabet knowledge, and written expression (Landry et al., Chapter 7).

Math and science teaching practices have received less empirical examination and were used by only one intervention described in this volume. Kinzie, Whittaker, Kilday, and Williford (Chapter 2) used the MyTeaching-Partner format with a math–science curriculum. The scripted lesson plans included math and science activities that teachers were asked to implement along with activity centers.

Teacher practices in the domain of social and emotional skills focus on individual child skills, particularly in the area of emotional and self-regulation and teacher classroom-management practices to create harmonious classrooms. Raver, Blair, and Li-Grining (Chapter 5) have focused intervention on the teacher's own emotional regulation skills in developing classroom-management practices. In Domitrovich et al. (Chapter 3) intervention included a curriculum "Paths" that teachers used at circle time. This curriculum targeted four domains: 1) prosocial friendship skills, 2) emotional understanding and expression skills, 3) self-control, and 4) problem-solving skills focused on interpersonal negotiation and conflict resolution. The National Center for Research on Early Childhood Education intervention (Pianta et al., Chapter 7) uses direct instruction to teach teacher–child interaction practices.

Engaging Teachers in Intervention via Relationship Building

Direct instruction in teacher–child interaction allows teachers to "see" via video or the web what a sensitive and responsive interaction and relationship with a child looks like, and engaging teachers in consultation, coaching, and other forms of emotional support with the interveners allows teachers to experience what a positive and respectful relationship feels like. As already discussed, due to poverty and other stressful life circumstances (Raver et al., Chapter 5) and/or lack of mentors or models for responsive teaching of young children in groups, being engaged in a responsive and sensitive social interaction and positive relationship is not within the experience of some teachers. All the intervention programs described in this volume have included relationship building between the teacher enrollees and the interveners as a component of their program. Interventions have more of an effect on children's gains if the changes in teachers include increases in positive interactions within classrooms as well as an explicit curriculum for domain specific skills (Domitrovich et al., Chapter 3; Downer, Jamil, Maier, & Pianta, Chapter 6; Pianta et al., Chapter 8; Raver et al., Chapter 5).

Several of the interventions had an intervener in the classroom of the teacher engaged in the intervention through coaching (Domitrovich et al., Chapter 3; Powell et al., Chapter 1) or consulting (Downer et al., Chapter 6; Pianta et al., Chapter 8; Raver et al., Chapter 5). These intervention practices provide opportunities for specific feedback on teacher's observed practice and recommendations for improvements and they model desired practices in the teacher's classroom, thus allowing for the teacher's development in context.

Perhaps more controversial in this array of relationship-based practices is the practice of holding teachers engaged in the intervention accountable to behaving in the interaction patterns introduced in the intervention. Landry et al. (Chapter 7) describes the need to change teachers' beliefs and knowledge, as well as behaviors, in a supportive manner in order to reduce resistance to change. This may be particularly important for ECE teachers who have a long-established belief system around the need for instruction for young children to be based in play rather than in rote and drill. Downer et al. (Chapter 6) point out the need for interaction practices to become automatic, especially during times of conflict within the classroom. Thus the interventions described in this volume required teachers to supply video or real-time interaction episodes to be evaluated by the interveners. These episodes became the content of reflective supervision between the coach or consultant and the teacher involved in the intervention.

Evaluating the Success of the Intervention

The effectiveness of the PD intervention in each of the described intervention programs was measured by looking at changes in teacher behavior and in children's preacademic skills. These measures mirror the conceptual framework that assumes that changing teachers' practices of engagement with children is the necessary mediating step between a curriculum and children's gains. Evaluating the success of the intervention in terms of teachers as well as child change is consistent with the practice of holding teachers accountable for changes in children's behaviors. Simply put, the intervention programs described in this volume tested teachers as well as children.

Facilitating and/or Moderating
Implementation: Classrooms and Intrateacher Variability

The PD programs described in this volume ask a lot of the teachers. They ask them to learn and apply new and different teaching practices applicable to children's learning and to monitor with intention and to possibly change their own emotional regulation and patterns of engagement with others. Therefore one would expect individual variation in teachers' responses to the intervention and success with the intervention. Teachers with greater personal stress levels and less correspondence between personal belief systems and the content of the intervention might be expected to be less successful in changing their patterns of behavior. Likewise, teachers in classrooms with differing proportions of children with challenging life circumstances or cognitive styles and classrooms embedded in institutions with more or less supportive work environments would be expected to be associated with intervention success. One would also expect teachers' previous experiences with PD to influence intervention success. Two chapters in this volume provide conceptual frameworks for examining classroom and intrateacher variation associated with fit between intervention and teacher. Raver and colleagues (Chapter 5) focus on teachers' self-regulation as a moderator of successful change in teacher practice and children's school skills. They begin by asking this question: What contributes to some teachers' skill in maintaining a positive emotional climate, whereas other teachers resort to harsh, angry, and hostile emotional tones or to emotionally detached, withdrawn styles of interaction? To address this question, they review advances in affective neuroscience research, as well as research on the emotional processes between caregivers and children in the context of poverty, to explore important predictors of teachers' styles of emotional self-regulation. This literature forms the basis for a theoretically driven framework that helps us better understand the emotional and cognitive processes that lead to conflict and difficulties that a small proportion of teachers may face.

Downer and colleagues (Chapter 6) address a second moderator of successful PD intervention, cognitive overload. A teacher's cognitive overload occurs when the external demands of a situation and need for active, internal processing of incoming information overburden the capacity of the teacher's working-memory system. To counteract the effects of cognitive overload, PD interventions need to help teachers enhance automaticity in their responses. In this chapter, the authors summarize information-processing theory as it relates to teaching in ECE classrooms and discuss the implications of this theory for pre- and in-service training of early educators. In particular, the authors provide examples of applying these cognitive principles to video-based coursework and coaching and report on some randomized controlled-trial findings in support of integrating cognitive theory into early educator training. The chapter draws a broad set of conclusions about the need to take into account a larger set of basic psychological processes, which can be directly objectively measured, studied, and altered through PD offerings as precursors to changes in practice.

SCALING UP PROFESSIONAL DEVELOPMENT

This field has a long history of interventions that are never brought to scale. This volume makes an important contribution by including two chapters on bringing PD interventions to scale. Landry and colleagues (Chapter 7) describe the development, efficacy studies, and scale up of a comprehensive inclusive pre-K PD program for the entire state of Texas. The authors outline the development process behind the PD intervention program with attention to innovations within the conceptual framework designed to bring novel practices, technologies, and knowledge to pre-K teachers. They summarize experimental studies conducted to evaluate the usefulness of the PD program for both teacher and child behaviors. Finally, they elaborate on how the intervention has extended and sustained teacher networks to assist teachers and school communities in implementing the program more systematically.

Pianta et al. (Chapter 8) describe the NCRECE project, a double random assignment intervention program bringing the MyTeachingPartner to multiple locations while including a set of comparisons around coursework and consultation. The authors describe how effective PD can be scaled up through existing infrastructure (e.g., institutions of higher education) and investments in teacher quality. The volume concludes with a chapter by Hamre and Hatfield that examines the policy implication of the PD interventions described in this volume.

REFERENCES

Chien, N., Howes, C., Burchinal, M., Pianta , R.C., Ritchie , S., Bryant , D., … Barbarin, O. (2010). Children's classroom engagement and gains in academic and social-emotional outcomes across pre-kindergarten. *Child Development, 81*, 1534–1549.

Consortium Preschool Curriculum Evaluation Research. (2008). *Effects of preschool curriculum programs on school readiness* (NCER 2008–2009) (National Center for Education Research, Institute of Education Sciences). Washington, DC: U.S. Government Printing Office.

Downer, J., LoCasale-Couch, J., Hamre, B., & Pianta , R.C. (2009). Teacher characteristics associated with responsiveness and exposure to consultation and online professional development resources. *Early Education and Development, 20*, 431–455. doi:10.1080/10409280802688626

Duncan, G.J., Dowsett, C.J., Classens, A., Magnuson, K., Huston, A., Klebanov, P., … Japel, C. (2007). School readiness and academic achievement. *Developmental Psychology, 43*, 1428–1446.

Early, D., Maxwell, K.L, Burchinal, M., Alva, S., Bender, R.H., Bryant, D., … Zill, N. (2007). Teachers' education, classroom quality, and young children's academic skills: Results from seven studies of preschool programs. *Child Development*, (78), 558–580. doi:10.1111/j.1467-8624.2007.01014

Erickson, M.F., & Kurz-Riemer, K. (1999). *Infants, toddlers, and families: A framework for support and intervention.* New York, NY: Guilford Press.

Gormley, W.T., Gayler, T., Phillips, D., & Dawson, B. (2005). The effects of universal pre-K on cognitive development. *Developmental Psychology, 41*, 872–884. doi:10.1037/0012-1649.41.6.872

Howes, C. (2010). *Culture and child development in early childhood education: Practices for quality education and care.* New York, NY: Teachers College Press.

Howes, C., Burchinal, M., Pianta, R.C., Bryant, D., Early, D., Clifford, R., & Babarin, O. (2008). Ready to learn? Children's pre-academic achievement in prekindergarten. *Early Childhood Research Quarterly, 23*, 27–50.

Justice, L.M., Mashburn, A.J., Hamre, B.K., & Pianta, R.C. (2008). Quality of language and literacy instruction in preschool classrooms serving at-risk pupils. *Early Childhood Research Quarterly, 23*, 51–68. doi:10.1016/j.ecresq.2007.09.004

Mashburn, A., Downer, J., Hamre, B., Justice, L., & Pianta , R.C. (2010). Consultation for teachers and children's language and literacy development during pre-kindergarten. *Applied Developmental Science, 14*, 179–196. doi:10.1080/10888691.2010.516187

Phillips, D.A., Gormley, W.T., & Lowenstein, A. (2009). Inside the pre-kindergarten door: Classroom climate and instructional time allocation in Tulsa's pre-K programs. *Early Childhood Research Quarterly, 24*, 213–228. doi:10.1016/j.ecresq.2009.05.002

Pianta, R.C., Belsky, J., Houts, R., Morrison, F., & Early Childhood Care Research Network, National Institute of Child Health and Human Development. (2007). Opportunities to learn in America's elementary classrooms. *Science, 315,* 1795–1796.

Pianta, R.C., La Paro, K.M., & Hamre, B.K. (2008). *Classroom Assessment Scoring System^TM (CLASS^TM) Pre-K Manual.* Baltimore, MD: Paul H. Brookes Publishing Co.

Pianta, R.C., Mashburn, A., Downer, J., Hamre, B., & Justice, L. (2008). Effects of web-mediated professional development resources on teacher–child interactions in pre-kindergarten classrooms. *Early Childhood Research Quarterly, 23,* 431–451. doi:10.1016/j.ecresq.2008.02.001

Powell, D.R., & Stremmel, A.J. (1989). The relation of early childhood training and experience to the professional development of child care workers. *Early Childhood Research Quarterly, 4,* 339–355. doi:10.1016/0885-2006(89)90019-7

Raver, C., Jones, S.M., Li-Grining, C.P., Metzger, M., Champion, K.M., & Sardin, L. (2008). Improving classroom practices: Preliminary findings from a randomized trial implemented in head start settings. *Early Childhood Research Quarterly, 23,* 10–26.

Scott-Little, M.C., La Paro, K., Pianta, R.C., Hamre, B., Downer, J., Burchinal, M., & Howes, C. (in press). Implementation of a course focused on language and literacy within teacher-child interactions: Instructor and student perspectives across three institutions of higher education. *Journal of Early Childhood Teacher Education.*

Toth, S., Pianta, R.C., & Erickson, M.F. (2011). From research to practice: Developmental contributions to the field of prevention science. In D. Cicchetti & G.I. Roisman (Eds.), *Minnesota symposium on child psychology: The origins and organization of adaptation and maladaption* (Vol. 36, pp. 323–377). New York, NY: Wiley.

Whitebook, M., & Ryan, S. (2011). *Degrees in context: Asking the right questions about preparing skilled and effective teachers of young children Preschool policy brief* (Vol. 22, pp. 1–16). New Brunswick, NJ: National Institute for Early Education Research.

I

Effective Models of Professional Development Interventions in Promoting Teacher and Child Outcomes

1

Using Coaching-Based Professional Development to Improve Head Start Teachers' Support of Children's Oral Language Skills

Douglas R. Powell,
Karen E. Diamond, and Margaret Burchinal

Coaching and other individualized methods of professional development (PD) are increasingly viewed as a promising strategy for improving the quality of instruction in classrooms serving at-risk children (Powell & Diamond, 2011). One-to-one work with a teacher affords the opportunity to offer specific feedback on a teacher's observed practices, provide recommendations for improvements, and model desired practices in the teacher's classroom. Situating PD activities in a specific classroom presumably improves the translation of research to practice and facilitates the accommodation of variations in teachers' knowledge and skills through tailored PD supports.

Coaching may be particularly well suited for facilitating positive change in teachers' established patterns of practice related to children's oral language development. As described in this chapter, language skills

This research was supported by grant R305B070605 from the Institute of Education to Purdue University. We gratefully acknowledge the participation of Head Start teachers and the contributions of the intervention staff and research assistants.

are key predictors of later school success yet evidence indicates that classrooms serving at-risk children generally provide inadequate oral language experiences. Nearly two decades ago, Hart and Risley (1995) framed the magnitude of the task with a striking set of extrapolations based on their influential study of preschool language gaps between children from low-income, working-class, and middle-income families. They argued that to keep the language experience of poor children equal to the language experience of working-class children, children from poor families would need to receive 63,000 words per week of *additional* language experience.

This chapter examines the potential of coaching teachers serving at-risk prekindergarten children to improve teaching practices that promote children's oral language skills. We summarize research on teaching behaviors associated with target language skills and review studies on the implementation and effects of curriculum and PD strategies for helping teachers implement evidence-based oral language practices. We also describe a PD intervention aimed at improving Head Start teachers' oral language practices and report outcomes of a random assignment study of the preliminary implementation of the intervention.

DIMENSIONS AND PREVALANCE OF ORAL LANGUAGE INSTRUCTION

Oral language includes the interdependent skills of vocabulary knowledge, syntax, and listening comprehension. Both research and early childhood classroom practices give far more attention to vocabulary knowledge than to syntax and listening comprehension skills (Powell & Diamond, in press). Young children's understanding of word meanings is a strong predictor of reading comprehension in middle school (Scarborough, 2001) and first grade vocabulary knowledge predicts reading comprehension 10 years later (Cunningham & Stanovich, 1997).

Shared book-reading practices are a common focus of oral language instruction, partly because a book's narrative provides an immediate context for defining words, linking novel words to shared referents, and engaging children in conversations. Meta-analyses have found significant moderate effects of book reading interventions on children's oral language outcomes (Mol, Bus, & de Jong, 2009; National Early Literacy Panel, 2008). Research indicates that children's word knowledge is improved when teachers provide explicit instruction regarding a word's meaning (e.g., Justice, Meier, & Walpole, 2005; Marulis & Neuman, 2010) and repeated readings of the same book as a strategy for increasing the frequency of children's exposure to different word meanings (e.g., Biemiller & Boote, 2006; Sénéchal, 1997). Evidence suggests that, among children at the beginning stages of learning to read, the combination of repeated readings and teacher explanation of novel words is more effective than repeated readings without teacher explanation of novel words (Penno, Wilkinson, & Moore, 2002).

Several lines of research indicate that asking children questions to facilitate their active involvement in shared book reading can improve language skills. Specifically, the practice of asking children to label illustrations of target words versus passively listen to a reading of the same book is linked to children's listening comprehension and production of more words (e.g., Sénéchal, Thomas, & Monker, 1995). Another set of studies points to improvements in children's expressive vocabulary skills when they participate in dialogic reading, an approach in which the teacher (or parent) asks questions, adds information, and prompts the child to increase the sophistication of language used to describe events or pictures in a book (Lonigan, Anthony, Bloomfield, Dyer, & Samwel, 1999; Whitehurst et al., 1994). Perhaps a main benefit of children's active participation in shared book reading sessions is engagement in conversations with the teacher and peers about the book and experiences related to the book (Justice et al., 2005). These conversations are also an opportunity for teachers to model appropriate language use.

There is not a rigorous research literature on some oral language practices that long have been recommended on theoretical grounds. The presumed superiority of open-ended questions is a case in point. Constructivist perspectives on children's intellectual development submit that higher level questioning strategies (e.g., asking children to predict what will happen in the story, draw inferences about story events) are consistently beneficial for young children's language competence in particular and cognitive growth in general (e.g., Sigel & Saunders, 1979). Although correlational studies link the use of higher level questions to a number of language outcomes (e.g., comprehension skills; Dickinson & Smith, 1994), results of experimental studies that compare effects of lower and higher demand questions on children's vocabulary growth are less compelling (e.g., Justice, 2002) and suggest, for example, that an arrangement wherein children are asked low demand questions (recall story elements or describe pictures) when novel words first appear and high demand questions later in the book facilitates a deeper understanding of word meanings (Blewitt, Rump, Shealy, & Cook, 2009).

With regard to the prevalence of evidence-based practices, a growing research literature suggests that prekindergarten programs serving at-risk children typically provide limited supports for children's oral language development. Observational studies of teachers have found generally low levels of language modeling (Justice, Mashburn, Hamre, & Pianta, 2008), a limited range (0–4 minutes) of vocabulary instruction (Connor, Morrison, & Slominski, 2006), infrequent use of an explicit label for an object or action when communicating with children (Wasik & Bond, 2001), and limited engagement of children in meaningful conversations (Dickinson & Tabors, 2001). Moreover, teachers' views of appropriate instructional strategies may run contrary to evidence-based practices. For instance, some teachers may not be comfortable with children talking and may view a quiet classroom as a "good" classroom (Wasik, 2010). Teachers may also believe that vocabulary is best taught spontaneously, when children ask questions about an unfamiliar word, and see limited value in intentionally introducing new words in an explicit manner as part of book reading or another instructional context (O'Leary, Cockburn, Powell, & Diamond, 2010).

STRATEGIES TO IMPROVE TEACHERS' ORAL LANGUAGE INSTRUCTION

Curriculum and PD are the chief policy levers for improving teachers' oral language instruction. There is a longer history of research on effects of early childhood curricula (Powell, 1987; Preschool Curriculum Evaluation Consortium, 2008) than PD programs for early childhood educators (Powell, Diamond, Cockburn, in press). Recent studies have examined effects of curriculum and PD, separately and combined, on early literacy and language outcomes. The PD supports typically include coaching with teachers.

The available evidence suggests that providing teachers with a language-focused curriculum, paired with an introductory workshop on goals and implementation of the curriculum, may not be sufficient for improving oral language instruction in classrooms serving at-risk children. Three recent studies of curriculum implementation illustrate this emerging lesson in intervention research. First, a study of the Language-Focused Curriculum (Bunce, 1995), which provides daily lesson plans, classroom materials, and explicit instructions for eight language stimulation techniques such as repeating a child's utterance using varied syntax, found relatively low levels of teacher use of the language stimulation techniques. Prior to implementing the curriculum at the beginning of the academic year, teachers participated in a 3-day workshop on language development and uses of the curriculum to improve at-risk children's language skills and, in the middle of the academic year, teachers participated in a 2.5-hour refresher training focused on the curriculum's language stimulation techniques (Justice, Mashburn, Pence, & Wiggins, 2008; Pence, Justice, & Wiggins, 2008). A random assignment outcome study revealed that impact of the curriculum on children's language skills was moderated by children's classroom attendance (Justice, Mashburn, Pence, et al., 2008). Second, a descriptive study of implementation of the MyTeachingPartner–Language and Literacy Curriculum (Justice, Pullen, Hall, & Pianta, 2003) found that teachers implemented the language lessons with an overall good level of procedural fidelity (e.g., teacher has all lesson materials available and easily accessible), but with a generally low level of quality. More than half of 135 language lessons received low quality ratings (e.g., teacher rarely asked open-ended questions or repeated or extended children's utterances). Teachers participated in a 2-day workshop prior to implementing the curriculum, which included a 3–6 week scope and sequence of six instructional targets, weekly lesson plans and sample lesson scripts, supplementary materials and manipulatives for delivering lessons, and access to a web site that included exemplars of high-quality implementation (Justice, Mashburn, Hamre, et al., 2008). Hamre et al. (2010) found that higher levels of implementation of the curriculum were associated with growth in children's language and literacy skills. Lastly, research on Opening the World of Learning (OWL; Schickedanz & Dickinson, 2005), a language-focused curriculum that emphasizes vocabulary knowledge, found an overall implementation fidelity of 54%, with the lowest ratings for prescribed teaching practices (e.g., defining specific words) during book reading (Dickinson, Freiberg, & Barnes, 2011). It is interesting to note that investigators of each of the three studies speculated that ongoing PD may improve teachers' language instruction, including the fidelity of curriculum implementation.

Some investigators have found significant improvements in teachers' language instruction and children's language outcomes by providing teachers with intensive PD supports plus language-focused curriculum activities. Wasik and colleagues report particularly strong findings from several studies. Wasik and Bond (2001) trained preschool teachers to use shared book reading strategies that emphasized open-ended questions and other dialogic reading techniques (Whitehurst et al., 1994) to help children learn new vocabulary. Teachers received books and theme-focused prop boxes for vocabulary extension activities. The training included an expert modeling vocabulary instruction and interactive reading strategies during the first four weeks of a 15-week intervention. Positive intervention effects were found on teachers' use of target words and children's language skills. In a follow-up study, Wasik, Bond, and Hindman (2006) provided teachers with monthly group training (2 hours each) and in-classroom coaching (a minimum of 2 hours per month) across a 9-month period regarding book reading and conversational practices aimed at improving children's language and vocabulary knowledge. Teachers also were given children's trade books, 22 prop boxes, and concrete objects that represented target words in the books, and lesson plans. Observations of teachers' book reading and conversation behaviors indicated that intervention teachers used more practices that promoted language development than control group teachers. Children in intervention classrooms performed significantly better than children in control classrooms on standardized tests of language skills. More recently, Wasik and Hindman (2011) reported that an intervention comprised of coaching and group training sessions, lesson plans and classroom materials, and feedback to teachers on children's performance had positive effects on teachers' oral language instruction and knowledge. Vocabulary and syntax skills were among the school readiness outcomes targeted by an intervention designed to improve Head Start children's academic and social-emotional development. The Head Start Research-based, Developmentally Informed (REDI) intervention employed methods used by Wasik and Bond (2001) and Wasik et al. (2006) to strengthen teachers' support of children's vocabulary and syntax skills. Teachers received children's books scripted with interactive questions to support children's language development plus 4 days of workshop training and weekly in-class coaching that addressed the range of instructional practices targeted by the intervention. REDI outcome research found positive effects on teachers' discourse strategies such as the number of questions asked of children (Domitrovich, Gest, Gill, Bierman, Welsh, & Jones, 2009) and on children's vocabulary knowledge but not on sentence imitation and grammatical understanding (Bierman et al., 2008).

The studies described previously were not designed to assess the relative contribution of new curriculum resources and PD activities to teachers' instructional practices. Accordingly, it is impossible to determine from these investigations whether the PD supports facilitated fidelity of curriculum implementation. Moreover, it appears the content of curriculum resources and PD activities did not fully overlap in the Wasik et al. (2006), Wasik and Hindman (2011), and Domitrovich et al. (2009) investigations. That is, it seems that some of the training was not in service of teachers' appropriate use of curriculum materials (e.g., training for conversations with children did not necessarily entail lesson plans, props, or books).

A randomized controlled trial conducted by Assel and colleagues systematically varied teachers' receipt of in-classroom coaching (referenced as mentoring in the study) and two literacy and language curricula. They found that coaching was associated with positive child effects for a curriculum that emphasized letter knowledge and phonological awareness (Let's Begin with the Letter People; Abrams & Company, 2000) but not a curriculum that emphasized language skills (Doors to Discovery; Wright Group, 2001). Further, coaching was beneficial for the literacy, curriculum in Title I and universal prekindergarten classrooms, but not Head Start classrooms. Coaches worked with teachers twice per month in their classrooms to provide assistance with lesson planning and the classroom schedule, demonstrate specific curriculum components, and offer side-by-side coaching. Teachers assigned to one of the intervention conditions also participated in a 4-day workshop conducted by the publishing companies of each curriculum prior to implementing the curriculum (Assel, Landry, Swank, & Gunnewig, 2007).

The strategy of providing teachers with PD supports for improving language-focused practices within the context of their classroom's existing curriculum and materials has received less research attention than interventions involving teachers' use of a new curriculum with or without PD supports. The appeal of this strategy is based on pragmatic grounds pertaining to scalability. A PD program that does not mandate use of a particular curriculum may be more widely used than an intervention requiring teachers to abandon an existing curriculum or coordinate a supplemental curriculum with the existing curriculum (Landry, Anthony, Swank, & Monseque-Bailey, 2009). It is important to note that the centrality of a highly specified curriculum to facilitating improvements in oral language competence is not clear, as noted previously. Teaching practices that improve children's language use and word knowledge cannot be easily scripted in a curriculum because children benefit from teacher responsiveness that is well tuned to their language attempts in natural and often unplanned conversations (Justice, Mashburn, Hamre, et al., 2008; Wasik, 2010).

Studies of PD interventions that provided a major coaching component aimed at grafting evidence-based literacy and language instruction onto existing practices have found positive intervention effects on some teaching practices, particularly code-related instruction, but not on oral language instruction (Landry et al., 2009; Powell, Diamond, Burchinal, & Koehler, 2010). Each intervention provided teachers with detailed information, including video exemplars, for improving children's literacy and language skills. The Landry et al. (2009) intervention also included children's progress monitoring feedback to teachers. Landry and colleagues found that weekly in-classroom coaching increased teachers' quality of literacy (phonological awareness and writing) instruction but not book reading practices. Each intervention study assessed a range of literacy and language instructional practices, including vocabulary instruction but not the amount of teacher talk and related indicators of discourse. In contrast to the clear focus on oral language skills addressed in the interventions led by the Wasik (2010), Landry et al. (2009), and Powell et al. (2010), interventions covered a considerably broader scope of language and literacy content. This approach may have given insufficient attention to teaching behaviors that support children's language development. Implementing practices that effectively promote oral language skills is likely to require teachers to change the ways they talk with children (Dickinson et al., 2011) and thus may be more challenging for teachers to master than literacy instruction that is conducive to scripting in a curriculum.

In sum, a small but growing empirical literature on curriculum and PD strategies for improving children's oral language skills point to the following themes: 1) providing teachers with a language-focused curriculum and introductory training on its use is unlikely to yield significant change in the quality of language instruction; 2) overall there is mixed evidence for the strategy of providing ongoing individualized support to teachers for implementing a new language-focused curriculum; 3) the strategy of providing teachers with PD supports for improving language-focused practices within the context of their classroom's existing curriculum and materials has received little research attention.

RESEARCH ON A COACHING-BASED PROFESSIONAL DEVELOPMENT INTERVENTION

We conducted a randomized controlled trial to determine the preliminary effectiveness of a coaching-based PD intervention on Head Start teachers' oral language instruction, particularly practices aimed at increasing children's 1) vocabulary knowledge and 2) exposure to and use of language, compared with a business-as-usual control condition. The intervention incorporated technological innovations for providing exemplars of evidence-based instruction and facilitating coaching with teachers at a distance. The outcome study described below is based on the first wave of implementing the PD intervention.

Intervention Design

The one-semester intervention content emphasizes vocabulary knowledge instruction and strategies for promoting children's language use during large group instruction sessions and other parts of the day. Attention is given to children's understanding and use of useful words (Tier Two; Beck, McKeown, & Kucan, 2002). The protocol calls for four to six target words to be explicitly introduced each day as part of book reading during large group sessions (Penno et al., 2002), using child-friendly definitions that initially explain the word in the context of the book being read (Biemiller & Boote, 2006). Teachers are given five children's trade books to read during the first 5 weeks of the intervention. Target words and definitions are provided for each book. Teachers receive training on the identification of useful words and coaching support for selecting target words to introduce in books of their own choosing. The protocol also calls for repeated reading of a book in order to increase the frequency of children's exposure to target words. Teachers are encouraged to review previously taught words during large group time and to promote children's use of target words during center (free play) time. The intervention emphasizes teachers' modeling of language use as well as their use of both closed- and open-ended questions to facilitate children's talk during large group time. The oral language content is the sole content focus of the first 8 weeks of the one-semester intervention and a continuing focus during the second 8 weeks when instruction related to children's code-related skills is emphasized.

The intervention begins with a 1-day introductory workshop followed by 12 individualized coaching sessions with teachers (4 on site, 8 technologically mediated) across the semester. Teachers also have access to a case-based hypermedia resource comprised of more than 90 video exemplars of evidence-based practice across 10 cases. The video exemplars were filmed by project staff in preschool classrooms not involved in the current study. The hypermedia resource also includes pdf files of published articles prepared for professional audiences plus references to research articles.

Individualized coaching followed an observe-assess-recommend sequence wherein the coach observes a targeted teaching practice and provides two types of written feedback: statements about appropriately implemented dimensions of targeted practice and recommendations for improving the practice. Repeated practice of targeted instruction at regular intervals is aimed at offering an opportunity for the teacher to implement the coach's feedback on a prior implementation of the targeted practice.

In an on site coaching session, the coach observes for about 90 minutes and consults with the teacher about the observation for an additional 30 minutes. The coach records key aspects of feedback on a no-carbon-required form that is signed by both coach and teacher. The teacher keeps a copy. As part of the feedback, the coach may show the teacher a video exemplar(s) from the case-based hypermedia resource described previously. In the technologically mediated method of coaching, the teacher submits to the coach a video of targeted teaching practice. The coach selects video segments for critique, using computer software that provides a split screen arrangement, with the coach-selected segment on the left side of the computer screen and the coach's corresponding feedback on the right. Coach recommendations for improvements include direct links to video exemplars or other items in the hypermedia resource.

The current intervention was a significant revision of a predecessor PD intervention that had positive effects on teacher practices (ds = 0.62–0.99) and children's code-focused outcomes (ds = 0.17–0.29), but not oral language instruction and child outcomes. The predecessor intervention systematically compared on site and remote (technologically mediated) methods of coaching with teachers, and found both methods to be effective (Powell et al., 2010). Compared with its predecessor intervention, the PD program examined in the current study provided more coaching sessions and greater in-depth attention to teaching practices that promote oral language, including coaching feedback on repeated and sequential (versus one-time) implementation of targeted instruction.

The current intervention was developed through an iterative process of testing and revision that entailed four small-scale studies with prekindergarten teachers (not involved in the current study) to inform the design of specific intervention components (Diamond & Powell, 2011). The studies examined the following in different samples of teachers: 1) teachers' approaches to, and challenges in, supporting children's oral language development (O'Leary et al., 2010); 2) teachers' responses to sequential videotaping of repeated instruction; 3) teachers' navigation of the hypermedia resource; and 4) teachers' engagement of all intervention components implemented as planned.

Research Method

The original sample for the current study was 36 Head Start lead teachers/ classrooms (21 urban, 15 in rural and small-town communities) in a Midwestern state. Most teachers had a bachelor's (50%) or graduate degree (9%). Others had an associate's degree (35%) or some college (6%). Teachers had on average 10.88 (SD = 7.1) years of preschool teaching experience. Nearly all of the participating classrooms used the Creative Curriculum (Dodge, Colker, & Heroman, 2002), a resource used widely in Head Start nationally. Language development is one of four areas of development emphasized in the Creative Curriculum.

In late spring of 2009, teachers were randomly assigned to the intervention condition or to the control condition for fall semester 2009, stratified by urban and nonurban location. Margaret Burchinal conducted the random assignment. She had no role in recruiting the sample, designing and implementing the intervention, or collecting the data. Two of the 36 teachers resigned from their Head Start position prior to the beginning of fall semester 2009, leaving a sample of 18 intervention group and 16 control group teachers. There were no significant differences between intervention and control teachers in education level (p = .68) or years of teaching experience (p = .46).

Two literacy coaches worked with a caseload of 8 intervention teachers each during the semester. Each coach had a minimum of 5 years of preschool teaching experience and a master's degree in early childhood/child development.

Trained research assistants conducted structured observations in each of the 34 classrooms at the beginning (preintervention) and end (postintervention) of the semester. The observation spanned about 2 hours and included a large group session in which the teacher read a book of the teacher's choice. Measures included multiple-item ratings of vocabulary instruction (α = .87), with most items drawn from the revised version of the Early Literacy Classroom Observation Tool, Pre-K (ELLCO Pre-K; Smith, Brady, & Anastasopoulos, 2008). Each observed large group session was audiotaped and subsequently transcribed using Systematic Analysis of Language Transcripts (SALT; Miller, 2007), a tool for transcribing and analyzing language samples. SALT software generates standard measures of language, including number of utterances. Book text read by the teacher was not coded. In addition, research assistants coded from transcripts of the audiotaped group session the number of objects or actions labeled by the teacher and the number of words defined or reviewed by the teacher. Coders achieved a good level of agreement (κ = >.90) on use of the SALT conventions during reliability training, and independent coding by two research assistants per transcript yielded inter-coder agreement of κ = >.95.

Data on the fidelity of intervention implementation indicated that all but one teacher participated in each of the 12 coaching sessions, with an average of 8.6 calendar days (SD = 7.17) between coaching contacts. Teachers viewed an average of 32.73 exemplars of evidence-based practices across the intervention semester, including an average of 21.50 video clips viewed independently with the case-based hypermedia resource. Each of the 18 intervention teachers independently used the case-based hypermedia resource. Across the 71 on site coaching sessions conducted during the semester, literacy coaches observed a teacher's implementation of a specific instructional practice(s) for an average of 93.24 minutes and subsequently consulted with the teacher for an average of 31.20 minutes. In the technologically mediated delivery of coaching, coaches selected and provided feedback on an average of 2.78 segments (SD = .76) of the teacher-submitted video of instructional practice. Coach feedback on teacher-submitted videos was sent to teachers within an average of 5 calendar days (SD = 3.2) from date of coach receipt of the video. The content focus was implemented as set forth in the coaching protocol in on site and technologically mediate coaching contacts.

Results and Discussion

Outcome analyses employed analysis of covariance to examine the teaching practices of intervention and control group teachers at postintervention (end of fall semester), with scores on the same measure at preintervention (beginning of the semester) used as a covariate. Effect sizes were computed using the intervention regression coefficient divided by the root mean squared error from that model (i.e., best estimate of pooled SD given covariate).

Results of outcome analyses indicate that intervention teachers provided significantly more vocabulary instruction, including defining more novel words, than control group teachers at the end of the semester. Specifically, on average, intervention group teachers defined 8.82 words whereas control group teachers defined 4.58 words at postintervention. Intervention teachers also provided more labeling statements and/or questions about an object or action than control group teachers at the end of the semester. Results are reported in Table 1.1. Note there was a large, statistically significant effect size for vocabulary instruction practices and medium, nonsignificant effect sizes for the number of novel words defined by teachers and the number of labels provided by teachers.

At postintervention, teachers in the intervention group asked more questions of children during large group instruction than teachers in the control group. The number of teacher utterances and number of children's utterances also were higher at postintervention in intervention group classrooms than in control group classrooms. The effect sizes are in the moderate range, with children's utterances reaching statistical significance (see Table 1.1).

Results of this preliminary study, then, suggest that teachers' participation in a one-semester, coaching-based PD program led to significant improvements in vocabulary instruction, including the frequency with which teachers labeled objects and actions. Results also suggest that, at postintervention, children in intervention classrooms experienced significantly more language than children in control group classrooms during large group instruction. In

Table 1.1. Intervention effects on teaching practices

Variable	Control group		Intervention group		Effect size
	Pre	Post	Pre	Post	
Vocabulary					
Word inst. practices[a]	3.21 (0.73)	3.31 (0.68)	3.22 (0.78)	3.71 (0.82)	1.26*
No. words defined[b]	5.85 (5.03)	4.58 (3.01)	5.17 (3.76)	8.82 (5.58)	.69
No. labels[b]	7.15 (4.91)	5.04 (3.60)	7.17 (3.71)	8.19 (6.92)	.52
Promoting word use[b]					
No. child utterances	111.56 (50.79)	119.50 (47.13)	115.33 (68.85)	163.82 (79.82)	.73*
No. tchr. utterances	148.94 (67.34)	137.50 (46.70)	156.11 (84.12)	185.12 (85.04)	.70+
No. tchr. questions	58.81 (34.88)	54.31 (26.61)	55.89 (36.49)	66.29 (34.88)	.55

N = 18 intervention, 16 control teachers (randomized)
[a] Multiple-item ratings (1 = low, 5 = high);
[b] Systematic Analysis of Language Transcripts (SALT) transcription of audiotaped large group sessions.
+ .10 < p < .05.
*p < .05.
Key: No., number; Inst., instructor; Tchr., teacher

intervention classrooms, children and their teachers offered more utterances, and teachers asked more questions than in control classrooms at the conclusion of the intervention. Finer grained analyses are needed to determine the extent to which teachers' questions preceded children's talk, thereby perhaps serving as a prompt for children's utterances. Further analyses also are needed regarding the types of questions posed by teachers. Still, results of current analyses suggest that the intervention led to improvements in the amount of language produced and heard by children during large group sessions.

What elements of the intervention may have contributed to improvements in teachers' oral language instruction? Although the design of our outcome study does not yield answers to this question, speculative suggestions about active ingredients of the intervention may be offered by comparing results of the current study to outcomes of its predecessor intervention and related PD programs.

A content focus on explicit instructional practices in the context of specific guidance from an early literacy coach may be a salient ingredient of the current intervention. Teachers viewed on average nearly 33 exemplars of evidence-based instruction across the intervention semester. About 21 of these exemplars were viewed independently by teachers via video clips on the intervention's hypermedia resource. The intervention gave minimal attention to the availability and placement of literacy artifacts. In contrast, Neuman and Wright (2010) suggest that their coaching intervention with child care providers may not have influenced providers' instructional practices because coaches focused on environmental improvements (e.g., placement of materials in writing and reading centers) to a greater extent than teaching strategies.

It seems unlikely that access to illustrations of evidence-based instruction would lead to positive change in teaching practices without the concurrent provision of feedback and recommendations of a supportive coach. Pianta and colleagues found that teachers assigned to receive online consultation plus access to web-based PD resources that included video exemplars of evidence-based instructional practices showed greater increases in quality of interactions with children than teachers who received access to the web-based video clips only (Pianta, Mashburn, Downer, Hamre, & Justice, 2008). In the current intervention, illustrations of evidence-based instruction were closely aligned with content emphasized by coaches. For example, coach feedback on teacher-submitted video included an average of 2.61 embedded links to hypermedia resource content (mostly video clips).

The increased intensity of the current intervention, relative to its predecessor intervention, may have contributed to positive effects on teachers' oral language instruction. Forms of greater intensity in the current intervention include a larger number of coaching sessions, in-depth attention to a narrower set of teaching practices, and repeated practice of targeted instruction. It is impossible to determine from the current study which, if any, of these dimensions of intervention intensity may have accounted for positive effects on teaching practices. We speculate that, for teachers, the repeated practice provision of the current intervention may have entailed higher levels of supportive accountability coupled with nuanced feedback from coaches regarding a specific instructional practice than in the predecessor intervention, which focused on a different instructional practice in each coaching contact.

It is useful to consider the possibility that the curriculum employed in participating classrooms provided an enabling structure for our PD intervention to achieve positive outcomes. As noted earlier, both the current and predecessor interventions aimed to strengthen instruction within the context of a classroom's existing curriculum rather than introduce a new curriculum. Our PD intervention may be less effective in classrooms employing curricula that do not supply core classroom features (e.g., at least daily shared book reading) that our PD intervention assumes are in place. In the Landry et al. (2009) PD intervention study, teachers in classrooms using curricula that lacked a strong focus on emergent literacy appeared to have difficulty engaging the PD program because a scope and sequence of specific teaching practices were not readily available.

In sum, our random assignment study lends support to the use of coaching-based PD as a strategy for improving teachers' implementation of evidence-based practices that facilitate the oral language development of at-risk children. Research on subsequent waves of implementation of the intervention will increase our understanding of implementation and effects. In addition to pursuing the more refined analyses of teaching practices noted above, it would be beneficial for future research on the intervention to examine teachers' language-promoting behaviors outside of the large group book reading context. Another essential next step is to determine whether positive intervention effects on teaching practices (proximal outcomes) extend to children's oral language skills (distal outcomes).

REFERENCES

Abrams & Company. (2000). *Let's begin with the letter people.* Waterbury, CT: Author.

Assel, M.A., Landry, S.H., Swank, P.R., & Gunnewig, S. (2007). An evaluation of curriculum, setting, and mentoring on the performance of children enrolled in pre-kindergarten. *Reading and Writing, 20,* 463–494. doi:10.1007/s11145-006-9039-5

Beck, I.L., McKeown, M.G., & Kucan, L. (2002). *Bringing words to life: Robust vocabulary instruction.* New York, NY: Guilford Press.

Biemiller, A., & Boote, C. (2006). An effective method for building meaning vocabulary in primary grades. *Journal of Educational Psychology, 98,* 44–62. doi:10.1037/0022-0663.98.1.44

Bierman, K.L., Domitrovich, C.E., Nix, R.L., Gest, S.D., Welsh, J. A., ... Gill, S. (2008). Promoting academic and social-emotional school readiness: The Head Start REDI program. *Child Development, 79,* 1802–1817. doi:10.1111/j.1467-8624.2008.01227.x

Blewitt, P., Rump, K.M., Shealy, S.E., & Cook, S.A. (2009). Shared book reading: When and how questions affect young children's word learning. *Journal of Educational Psychology, 101,* 294–304. doi:10.1037/a0013844

Bunce, B.H. (1995). *Building a language-focused curriculum for the preschool classroom: Volume II.* Baltimore, MD: Paul H. Brookes Publishing Co.

Connor, C.M., Morrison, F.J., & Slominski, L. (2006). Preschool instruction and children's emergent literacy growth. *Journal of Educational Psychology, 98,* 665–689. doi:10.1037/0022-0663.98.4.665

Cunningham, A.E., & Stanovich, K.E. (1997). Early reading acquisition and its relation to reading experience and ability 10 years later. *Developmental Psychology, 33,* 934–945. doi:10.1037//0012-1649.33.6.934

Diamond, K.E., & Powell, D.R. (2011). An iterative approach to the development of a PD intervention for Head Start teachers. *Journal of Early Intervention, 33,* 75–93.

Dickinson, D.K., Freiberg, J.B., & Barnes, E.M. (2011). Why are so few interventions really effective?: A call for fine-grained research methodology. In S.B. Neuman & D.K. Dickinson (Eds.), *Handbook of early literacy research* (Vol. 3, pp. 337–357). New York, NY: Guilford Press.

Dickinson, D., & Smith, M. (1994). Long-term effects of preschool teachers' book readings on low-income children's vocabulary and story comprehension. *Reading Research Quarterly, 29,* 104–122. doi:10.2307/747807

Dickinson, D.K., & Tabors, P.O. (Eds.) (2001). *Beginning literacy with language: Young children learning at home and school.* Baltimore, MD: Paul H. Brookes Publishing Co.

Dodge, D.T., Colker, L.J., & Heroman, C. (2002). *The creative curriculum for preschool* (4th ed.). Washington, DC: Teaching Strategies.

Domitrovich, C.E., Gest, S.D. Gill, S., Bierman, K.L., Welsh, J.A., & Jones, D. (2009). Fostering high-quality teaching with an enriched curriculum and PD support: The Head Start REDI program. *American Educational Research Journal, 46,* 567–597.

Hamre, B.K., Justice, L.M., Pianta, R.C., Kilday, C., Sweeney, B., … Leach, A. (2010). Implementation fidelity of MyTeachingPartner literacy and language activities: Association with preschoolers' language and literacy growth. *Early Childhood Research Quarterly, 25,* 329–347. doi:10.1016/j.ecresq.2009.07.002

Hart, B., & Risley, T.R. (1995). *Meaningful differences in the everyday experience of young American children.* Baltimore, MD: Paul H. Brookes Publishing Co.

Justice, L.M. (2002). Word exposure conditions and preschoolers' novel word learning during shared storybook reading. *Reading Psychology, 23,* 87–106. doi:10.1080/027027102760351016

Justice, L.M., Mashburn, A.J., Hamre, B.K., & Pianta, R.C. (2008). Quality of language and literacy instruction in preschool classrooms serving at-risk pupils. *Early Childhood Research Quarterly, 23,* 51–68. doi:10.1016/j.ecresq.2007.09.004

Justice, L.M., Mashburn, A.J., Pence, K.L., & Wiggins, A. (2008). Experimental evaluation of a preschool language curriculum: Influence on children's expressive language skills. *Journal of Speech, language, and Hearing Research, 51,* 983–1001. doi:10.1044/1092-4388(2008/072)

Justice, L.M., Meier, J., & Walpole, S. (2005). Learning new words from storybooks: An efficacy study with at-risk kindergarteners. *Language, Speech, and Hearing Services in Schools, 36,* 17–32. doi:10.1044/0161-1461(2005/003)

Landry, S.H., Anthony, J.L., Swank, P.R., & Monseque-Bailey, P. (2009). Effectiveness of comprehensive professional development for teachers of at-risk preschoolers. *Journal of Educational Psychology, 101,* 448–465. doi:10.1037/a0013842

Lonigan, C.J., Anthony, J.L., Bloomfield, B.G., Dyer, S.M., & Samwel, C.S. (1999). Effects of two shared-reading interventions on emergent literacy skills of at-risk preschoolers. *Journal of Early Intervention, 22*, 306–322. doi:10.1177/105381519 902200406

Marulis, L.M., & Neuman, S.B. (2010). The effects of vocabulary intervention on young children's word learning: A meta-analysis. *Review of Educational Research, 80*, 300-335.

Miller, J. (2007). Documenting progress in language production: The evolution of a computerized language analysis system. In R. Paul (Ed.), *Language disorders from a developmental perspective: Essays in honor of Robin S. Chapman* (pp. 315–329). Mahwah, NJ: Erlbaum.

Mol, S., Bus, A., & de Jong, M. (2009). Interactive book reading in early education: A tool to stimulate print knowledge as well as oral language. *Review of Educational Research, 79*, 979–1007. doi:10.3102/0034654309332561

National Early Literacy Panel. (2008). *Developing early literacy: Report of the National Early Literacy Panel*. Washington, DC: National Institute for Literacy.

Neuman, S.B., & Wright, T.S. (2010). Promoting language and literacy development for early childhood educators: A mixed-methods study of coursework and coaching. *Elementary School Journal, 111*(1), 63–86. doi:10.1086/653470

O'Leary, P.M., Cockburn, M.K., Powell, D.R., & Diamond, K.E. (2010). Head Start teachers' views of phonological awareness and vocabulary knowledge instruction. *Early Childhood Education Journal, 38*, 187–195. doi:10.1007/s10643-010-0394-0

Pence, K., Justice, L.M., & Wiggins, A.K. (2008). Preschool teachers' fidelity in implementing a comprehensive language-rich curriculum. *Language, Speech, and Hearing Services in Schools, 39*, 329–341. doi:10.1044/0161-1461(2008/031)

Penno, J.R., Wilkinson, I.A.G., & Moore, D.W. (2002). Vocabulary acquisition from teacher explanation and repeated listening to stories: Do they overcome the Matthew effect? *Journal of Educational Psychology, 94*, 23–33. doi:10.1037//0022-0663.94.1.23

Pianta, R.C., Mashburn, A.J., Downer, J.T., Hamre, B.K., & Justice, L. (2008). Effects of web-mediated PD resources on teacher-child interactions in pre-kindergarten classrooms. *Early Childhood Research Quarterly, 23*, 431–451.

Powell, D.R. (1987). Comparing preschool curricula and practices: The state of research. In S.L. Kagan & E.F. Zigler (Eds.), *Early schooling: The national debate* (pp. 190–211). New Haven, CT: Yale University Press.

Powell, D.R., & Diamond, K.E. (2011). Improving the outcomes of coaching-based professional development interventions. In S.B. Neuman & D.K. Dickinson (Eds.), *Handbook of early literacy research* (Vol. 3, pp. 295–307). New York, NY: Guilford Press.

Powell, D.R., & Diamond, K.E. (in press). Promoting early literacy and language development. In R.C. Pianta, L.M., Justice, W.S. Barnett, & S. Sheridan (Eds.), *Handbook of early education*. New York, NY: Guilford Press.

Powell, D.R., Diamond, K.E., Burchinal, M.R., & Koehler, M.J. (2010). Effects of an early literacy professional development intervention on Head Start teachers and children. *Journal of Educational Psychology, 102*, 299–312. doi:10.1037/a0017763

Powell, D.R., Diamond, K.E., & Cockburn, M.K. (in press). Promising approaches to professional development for early childhood educators. In O. Saracho & B. Spodek (Eds.), *Handbook of research on the education of young children* (3rd ed.). New York, NY: Routledge.

Preschool Curriculum Evaluation Research Consortium. (2008). *Effects of preschool curriculum programs on school readiness (NCER 2008-2009)*. Washington, DC: National Center for Education Research, Institute of Education Sciences, U.S. Department of Education. Washington, DC: U.S. Government Printing Office.

Scarborough, H.S. (2001). Connecting early language and literacy to later reading (dis)abilities: Evidence, theory, and practice. In S.B. Neuman & D. Dickinson

(Eds.), *Handbook of early literacy research* (pp. 97–110). New York, NY: Guilford Press.

Schickedanz, J., & Dickinson, D.K. (2005). *Opening the World of Learning: A comprehensive literacy program*. Parsippany, NJ: Pearson Early Learning.

Sénéchal, M. (1997). The differential effect of storybook reading on preschoolers' acquisition of expressive and receptive vocabulary. *Journal of Child Language, 24*, 123–138. doi:10.1017/S0305000996003005

Sénéchal, M., Thomas, E., & Monker, J. (1995). Individual differences in 4-year-old children's acquisition of vocabulary during storybook reading. *Journal of Educational Psychology, 87*, 218–229. doi:10.1037//0022-0663.87.2.218

Sigel, I.E., & Saunders, R. (1979). An inquiry into inquiry: Question asking as an instructional model. In L. Katz (Ed.), *Current topics in early childhood education* (Vol. 2, pp. 169–193). Norwood, NJ: Ablex.

Smith, M.W., Brady, J.P., & Anastasopoulos, L.(2008). *Early Language and Literacy Classroom Observation Pre-K Tool (ELLCO Pre-K)*. Baltimore, MD: Paul H. Brookes Publishing Co.

Wasik, B.A. (2010). What teachers can do to promote preschoolers' vocabulary development: Strategies from an effective language and literacy PD coaching model. *The Reading Teacher, 63*, 621–633.

Wasik, B.A., & Bond, M.A. (2001). Beyond the pages of a book: Interactive book reading and language development in preschool classrooms. *Journal of Educational Psychology, 93*, 243–250. doi:10.1037//0022-0663.93.2.243

Wasik, B.A., Bond, M.A., & Hindman, A.H. (2006). The effects of a language and literacy intervention on Head Start children and teachers. *Journal of Educational Psychology, 98*, 63–74. doi:10.1037/0022-0663.98.1.63

Wasik, B.A., & Hindman, A.H. (2011). Identifying critical components of an effective preschool language and literacy coaching intervention. In S.B. Neuman & D.K. Dickinson (Eds.), *Handbook of early literacy research* (Vol. 3, pp. 322–336). New York, NY: Guilford Press.

Whitehurst, G.J., Arnold, D., Epstein, J., Angell, A., Smith, M., & Fischel, J. (1994). A picture-book reading intervention in day care and home for children from low-income families. *Developmental Psychology, 30*, 679–689. doi:10.1037//0012-1649.30.5.679

Wright Group. (2001). *Doors to Discovery: A new pre-kindergarten program*. Bothell, WA: Author.

2

Designing Effective Curricula and Teacher Professional Development for Early Childhood Mathematics and Science

Mable B. Kinzie, Jessica Vick Whittaker,
Carolyn R. Kilday, and Amanda Williford

Despite increased attention to the importance of math and science instruction, children in the United States continue to lag behind their peers in other countries on tests of math and science achievement (National Center for Education Statistics [NCES], 2011). The Program for International Assessment measures reading, math, and science literacy of 15-year-old children in 60 countries. In 2009, U.S. teens had average scores on math literacy that were lower than 17 countries and science scores that were lower than 12 countries (NCES, 2011). Clearly there is work to be done in improving our children's math and science knowledge and skills, and this work needs to begin in early childhood.

Teachers can nurture young children's skills and concept knowledge in mathematics and science by drawing on children's informal early understandings in order to develop children's own formal knowledge (Ginsburg, 1997; Stipek, 2008). High-quality curricula exist in these disciplines that can optimally perform in these ways (e.g., Brown, Greenfield, Juarez, & Dominguez, 2010; Clements & Sarama, 2008; Epstein, 2006; French, 2004; Greenes, Ginsburg, & Balfanz, 2004; Starkey, Klein, & Wakeley, 2004). However, the results of large-scale national studies indicate that there are challenges with early childhood curricular implementation quality and fidelity (Pianta et al., 2005), suggesting the importance of efforts to support teachers' implementation of math and science curricula in early care and education settings.

In this chapter, we provide an overview of early childhood math and science education and curricula and describe some of the challenges found in teaching practice in these domains. We offer an overview of teacher professional development (PD) intended to improve teachers' conceptual and pedagogical knowledge in mathematics and science and to support the fidelity of their curricular implementation. We then turn our attention to our own work on the design of the MyTeachingPartner-Mathematics/Science (MTP-M/S) curricula and PD intended to support curricular implementation and fidelity. Drawing from a small study on the association between the MTP-M/S intervention and teachers' classroom practices, we report the effects of the curricula and teaching supports on two forms of fidelity: adherence and dosage. In this study we addressed the following research questions: 1) Does receipt of PD supports directly linked to and supporting math and science curricula encourage fidelity of implementation, compared with receipt of the curricula alone? 2) What classroom characteristics (i.e., number of students) and teacher characteristics (e.g., level of education, teaching experience) are associated with teachers' implementation fidelity and use of PD supports? and 3) Is the use of the PD supports (web site access) associated with fidelity of implementation? To begin we consider the importance of the early childhood period for fostering children's knowledge and skills in mathematics and science.

IMPORTANCE OF DEVELOPING CHILDREN'S MATH AND SCIENCE SKILLS IN EARLY CHILDHOOD

The mathematical and scientific literacies that make it possible for children to fully engage in creative problem solving, collaboration, and everyday learning opportunities all have their seeds in early childhood experiences (National Association for the Education of Young Children [NAEYC] and National Council of Teachers of Mathematics [NCTM], 2002; National Research Council [NRC], 2006). During children's early years, informal mathematical and scientific understandings are readily developed through play and engaging with the world (Clements, 2004; Duschl, Schweingruber, & Shouse, 2007), with children demonstrating the capacity for complex and abstract thought (Bowman, Donovan, & Burns, 2001). These early skills form the foundation for later skill development and learning across curricular domains, but particularly in math and science (Bowman et al., 2001). Further, young children's early math skills and knowledge have been found to be predictive of later school success (National Mathematics Advisory Panel [NMAP], 2008; little early assessment has been done in science). In fact, children's mathematical knowledge of number and ordinality at school entry have been found to be a more significant predictor of academic success in the fifth grade than early reading skills (Duncan et al., 2007).

Despite the apparent importance of a strong early start in mathematics and science, there continues to be little related instruction in early education, in part due to an emphasis on early literacy but also on assumptions that young children may not be developmentally ready for mathematics and science. These assumptions are not supported by the research (NMAP, 2008), which instead indicates that "what is developmentally appropriate is largely contingent on prior opportunities to learn" (Duschl et al., 2007, p. 2).

Opportunities for learning are often missed across early childhood education. Math and science are covered in cursory or random ways (for instance, classroom science centers with materials that are seldom used or which are employed primarily for science-themed craft projects), or in discrete units lacking broader connections between themes (NAEYC & NCTM, 2002; NRC, 2005). The prevalence of the belief that children's early learning is best accomplished through self-discovery, with the teacher's primary role to support the process, is sometimes in conflict with direct instruction approaches. Further, little instructional time is spent on math and science. Results from the National Center for Early Development and Learning's (NCEDL) Multi-State Study of Pre-Kindergarten and the Study of State-Wide Early Education Programs (SWEEP; Early et al., 2010) indicate that, across the entire classroom day, children were observed engaging in math-related activities for only 8% of the time, and science for 11%, compared with 17% of the time for language and literacy-related activities and "no coded learning activity" for a substantial 44%. Similar results have been reported from other research inquiries (Graham, Nash, & Paul, 1997; Stipek, 2008; Tu, 2006).

At-risk children seem to be at even greater risk for inadequate math instruction, as research suggests that they are "served in child care programs of such low quality that learning and development are not enhanced and may even be jeopardized" (Bowman et al., 2001, p. 8). Further, at-risk children, compared with their peers who are not at risk, have fewer key mathematical skills at school entry, with the gap widening as children start school and move into the primary grades (NCES, 2004, 2009). As a result, high-quality curricula that scaffold knowledge and skill development for young children are important, particularly for those at risk, as is research on effective instructional practices and ways to enhance teacher effectiveness (NMAP, 2008).

EARLY CHILDHOOD MATH AND SCIENCE CURRICULA

There is emerging research demonstrating that high-quality math and science curricula can support children's learning (e.g., Clements & Sarama, 2008; French, 2004; Starkey et al., 2004), but these curricular packages are not yet in wide circulation and use, and there are few packages that address both mathematics and science. In the mathematics domain, some of the best known early childhood curricula include *Building Blocks* (Clements & Sarama, 2007), *Big Math for Little Kids* (Ginsburg, Greenes, & Balfanz, 2003), *Numbers Plus* (Epstein, 2006), and *Pre-K Mathematics* (Klein, Starkey, & Ramirez, 2002). Similar mathematical concepts and skills are addressed by these packages, targeting the learning standards ("Focal Points") advanced by the National Council of Teachers of Mathematics (NCTM, 2006) for grades pre-K through second, including number sense, number operations, geometry, and measurement. Effectiveness for encouraging student learning has been established via randomized trials involving several of these curricular packages (Clements & Sarama, 2008; Ginsburg, Lewis, & Clements, 2008; Starkey et al., 2004).

When curricula for pre-K science are considered, four major packages have been produced to date: *Preschool Pathways to Science (PrePS™)* (Gelman & Brenneman, 2004; Gelman et al., 2010), Young Scientist Series (Clark-Chiarelli, Gropen, & Hatfield-Davis, 2008), *Early Childhood Hands-On Science (ECHOS;* Greenfield et al., 2009), and *Science Start!* (French, 2004). All focus on science process skills, such as prediction, observation, and recording and analysis of observations, as well as development of science vocabulary. Evaluation results show improvements in science concept knowledge and processing skills for ECHOS (Greenfield et al., 2009) and the Young Scientist Series (Clark-Chiarelli et al., 2008) and in receptive and expressive language abilities for Science Start (French & Peterson, 2009).

We designed MTP-M/S to encourage school readiness in both mathematics and science for an at-risk pre-K population across 33 weeks of activities (more than many other curricula) and with embedded supports to help ensure success for teachers with little experience in math and science education. In addition, within mathematics we chose to emphasize children's development of understandings foundational to place value and within science to develop children's conceptual understandings across the year, in consort with seasonal change (see descriptions that follow); both are departures from most curricula. Finally, developing our own curricula also enabled us to design a related teacher PD program focusing on high-quality teaching with these curricula, as research suggests that access to a high-quality curriculum in and of itself is not sufficient to improve teacher practices and child outcomes (Pianta et al., 2005).

HIGH-QUALITY CURRICULA ALONE ARE INSUFFICIENT

Large-scale national studies suggest that, even when offered validated curricula, pre-K teachers often struggle to implement them with high quality and fidelity, largely as a function of their lack of content knowledge and confidence (Pianta et al., 2005). This lack of content knowledge and confidence is not limited to pre-K teachers. The Third International Mathematics and Science Study (TIMSS; Hiebert et al., 2003) found eighth-grade mathematics instruction in the United States focused predominantly on procedures rather than on making connections between ideas or eliciting math concepts. Santagata (2009) offered these possible explanatory hypotheses: "U.S. teachers do not possess a deep understanding of the mathematics they are asked to teach" and "Teaching mathematics with attention to conceptual underpinnings is not consistent with the tradition of school mathematics in the United States" (p. 40). Clearly, teachers' practice matters.

Teachers can directly influence student learning, and between-teacher variation has been shown to account for between 12% and 14% of student math achievement across a year in first, second, and third grades (in the Tennessee statewide Project STAR; Nye, Konstantopoulos, & Hedges, 2004). For 3 years Gordon, Kane, and Staiger (2006) followed the performance of students in classrooms served by new teachers in the city of Los Angeles. Students who had been taught for 2 years by teachers ranked in the bottom quartile for estimated impact on student learning lost an average of 5 percentile points, while students taught by teachers ranked in the top quartile gained 5 percentile points (relative to similarly performing students of similar demographics). The authors note the enormity of this 10-point difference and speculate on the effects were these levels of teacher performance experienced by students across additional years:

> For some perspective, the black-white achievement gap nationally is roughly 34 percentile points. Therefore, if the effects were to accumulate, having a top-quartile teacher rather than a bottom-quartile teacher four years in a row would be enough to close the black-white test score gap. (p. 8)

For children at risk of school failure, this pattern of teacher effects may be exacerbated: In the study by Nye and colleagues (2004), the teacher effect variance was much larger for schools of lower socioeconomic status—the quality of children's teachers mattered more in these schools in determining children's achievement. And there is research that suggests that the teachers in those poorer schools are of lower quality: LoCasale-Crouch and colleagues (2007) examined the teaching quality in 692 pre-K classrooms across 11 states and found that the teachers serving the highest proportions of at-risk children were also the teachers found to be of lowest quality.

Teachers and students in lower performing schools are at a particular disadvantage, as teachers in these schools receive less preparation, reportedly do not feel capable of influencing student learning, and have lower expectations for student achievement (see Santagata, 2009, for a summary). In general, the preschool teaching force lacks experience due to high turnover rates and is often not provided with adequate preservice preparation and ongoing PD (NRC, 2005, 2006). Even teachers educated through 4-year early childhood college programs and receiving state licensure are thought to lack adequate preparation in mathematics (NAEYC & NCTM, 2002).

Providing pre-K teachers with PD in math and science—conceptual areas in which they report less confidence and experience—is critical, as is examining how best to provide it (Ginsburg et al., 2008; NMAP, 2008; Zaslow, Tout, Halle, Whittaker, & Lavelle, 2010). This, combined with a better understanding of how the classroom context and teacher character-istics are associated with curricular implementation, will help us to provide adequate supports to teachers so that they can feel confident in their teach-ing of early math and science skills and thus may be more likely to provide regular and comprehensive math and science instruction to their students.

PROFESSIONAL DEVELOPMENT IN MATH AND SCIENCE

Although a small number of well-designed studies show the value of sus-tained, high-quality teacher PD (a review by Yoon and colleagues, 2007, noted that across nine such studies, an average of 49 hours of PD resulted in student achievement gains of 21 percentile points), research indicates that early childhood preservice teacher preparation programs do not always appropriately prepare teachers in the area of mathematics (Copple, 2004; Ginsburg, Cannon, Eisenband, & Pappas, 2006). Experts suggest that in order to successfully implement math and science curricula, teachers need support with regard to: 1) mathematics and science concept knowledge; 2) an understanding of developmentally appropriate mathematics and sci-ence in early childhood education; and 3) an understanding of how to foster children's mathematical and scientific development with a research-based curriculum (NRC, 2006, 2009). Some teachers feel uncomfortable teaching mathematics (Copley, 1999) or are unfamiliar with techniques for develop-ing children's conceptual understandings or scientific thinking (NRC, 2005). PD in the area of mathematics and science should be sustained, focus on high-quality instructional implementation that is coherent with instruction-al goals, and provide an opportunity for active learning, including discussion of strategies with teachers (Garet, Porter, Desimone, Birman, & Yoon, 2001; Ginsburg et al., 2006; NRC, 2006). Perhaps the most important purpose of PD related to math is to help teachers develop an understanding of the developmental trajectories of children's math learning and the correspond-ing teaching strategies to support children at each stage. Likewise, PD can assist teachers with the specific skills and knowledge needed to facilitate children's scientific inquiry (NRC, 2006). Cohen and Hill (2000) examined elementary teachers' self-reports of PD experiences and use of specific mathematics teaching strategies and found that teachers who attended a 2-day workshop about a specific math curriculum showed higher use of the recommended teaching strategies, and those who attended a longer work-shop (5 days) showed higher use of the recommended teaching strategies than teachers who only attended a 2-day workshop. Teachers who attended the workshops also reported reducing their use of less effective strategies (Cohen & Hill, 2000).

Another PD training program, TRIAD (Technology-enhanced, re-search-based, instruction, assessment, and PD; Sarama, Clements, Starkey, Klein, & Wakeley, 2008), which corresponds with the pre-K math curricu-lum SRA Real Math Building Blocks (Clements & Sarama, 2008), is aimed at providing ongoing PD focused on specific curricular goals and activi-ties throughout the school year. Workshop sessions provide teachers with hands-on practice in teaching math activities specific to the curriculum with feedback on teachers' practice provided through monthly visits from a coach. Teachers' participation in TRIAD has been linked to the quality of their mathematics teaching and their students' scores on a test of early mathematics skills (Clements & Sarama, 2008). This emerging research indicates that providing teachers with a high-quality curriculum in addi-tion to PD that supports its use can be effective in influencing teaching practices and child outcomes.

Less research has been conducted on PD related to preschool science, but research with elementary school teachers demonstrates that ongoing teacher training regarding science inquiry, through a series of three work-shops with follow-up mentoring and half-day networking sessions, was asso-ciated with teachers' more frequent use of recommended teaching strategies (Borman, Cotner, Lee, Boydston, & Lanehart, 2009). In addition, research with secondary chemistry teachers indicates that intensive teacher training that is focused on very specific topics can help teachers achieve mastery of the content knowledge in that topical area (Powell, Pamplin, Blake, & Ma-son, 2010). Although these methods have not been examined at the pre-school level, it does suggest that PD can lead to a greater understanding of science concepts and higher quality science instruction. In addition, this re-search highlights the effectiveness of PD in encouraging teachers to adhere to specific practices and curricula with high-fidelity.

PROFESSIONAL DEVELOPMENT AIMED AT SUPPORTING FIDELITY OF IMPLEMENTATION

Because of the challenges with implementation fidelity found in pre-K teaching practice (Pianta et al., 2005), it is especially important that PD aim to improve this fidelity, or the potential inherent in high-quality cur-ricula will not be realized (Zaslow et al., 2010). Here we describe the con-structs subsumed in fidelity and how PD can be developed to support it.

Forms of Fidelity

Fidelity of implementation is commonly defined as "the extent to which a person adheres to a prescribed program, in both adhering to the rules of the program and in capturing the spirit of it." Fidelity can be specifically exam-ined by evaluating the components of adherence, dosage, quality of delivery, participant responsiveness, and program differentiation (Carroll et al., 2007;

Dusenbury, Brannigan, Falco, & Hansen, 2003; Mihalic, 2004). Adherence refers to the extent to which the teacher implements the given intervention or curriculum in a manner aligned with the intentions of the developer. *Dosage* refers to the extent to which a person is exposed to the intervention, in any form. The *quality of delivery* refers to the extent to which the intervention is implemented in a way that aligns with effective, high-quality teaching practices. *Participant responsiveness* refers to the extent to which participants in the intervention perceived that it was relevant and useful in their practice. *Program differentiation* is the process of identifying the essential elements of the intervention, without which it would not remain effective.

Professional Development to Enhance Fidelity

Ensuring fidelity can help teachers reach specific academic goals through faithful implementation of well-designed curricula, which can lead to improved child outcomes (e.g., Hamre et al., 2010). For example, an evaluation of a preschool math curriculum found that quality of delivery was significantly positively associated with children's gain scores across the year in mathematics (Clements & Sarama, 2008; Clements, Sarama, Spitler, Lange, & Wolfe, in press). The researchers implemented the TRIAD PD model (Sarama et al., 2008) to encourage high-quality mathematics teaching. The reverse has also been observed, specifically in curricular research: Low fidelity of implementation of the intended treatment corresponds with low program effectiveness (O'Donnell, 2008).

PD is more effective when it is focused on specific, well-articulated objectives and emphasizes teaching practice (Zaslow et al., 2010); therefore, PD that targets strategies or practices specific to an intervention can more effectively support teachers' fidelity to that intervention. For example, a 3-year longitudinal study of self-reported PD activities of elementary-, middle-, and high-school teachers indicated that PD that focused on specific math teaching strategies increased teachers' use of those strategies in the classroom (Desimone, Porter, Garet, Yoon, & Birman, 2002; U.S. Department of Education, 2000). Results from this study also suggest that PD is more effective when a network of linked teachers (i.e., from the same school or district) are able to work collaboratively and actively participate in the PD sessions, a conclusion echoed by an extensive review of the early childhood PD literature (Zaslow et al., 2010). Ways to encourage fidelity in implementation of an intervention has become a topic of increasing discussion. For example, in his Curriculum Research Framework (CRF), Clements (2007) recommends that proposed curricula be examined via a series of small-scale research studies, to help identify and improve modes of delivery that encourage and support teachers' fidelity to the curricula. This, in turn, can be associated with student learning outcomes, where teachers who exhibit higher fidelity to a successful curriculum help to produce greater student gains.

A review of research on mathematics in early childhood (NRC, 2009) indicates that PD for in-service teachers focused specifically on teaching and learning math in early childhood is a critical component in the effective implementation of mathematics teaching. However, not all types of PD are equally effective at supporting high-quality implementation. It is recommended that PD be sustained over time and that it focus on helping teachers understand children's learning trajectories and how to effectively implement a given curriculum (NRC, 2009).

In the section that follows, we describe the development of the MTP-M/S early childhood curricula and a teacher support package designed to support the fidelity of its implementation.

DEVELOPMENT OF MYTEACHINGPARTNER-MATH AND SCIENCE CURRICULA AND PROFESSIONAL DEVELOPMENT SUPPORTS

MyTeachingPartner-Math and Science Curricula

The MTP-M/S curricula were designed in response to the need for high-quality pre-K math and science curricula and were aligned to national and state standards. For math, we built on the National Council of Teachers of Mathematics (NCTM) focal points for pre-K (2006) and Clements's (2004) development trajectories for grades pre-K through second. The math domains covered include number sense, operations, geometry, and measurement. In science, the benchmarks from the American Association for the Advancement of Science (AAAS) (1993) and National Science Education Standards (National Research Council, 2006) articulate trajectories for grades kindergarten through second and kindergarten through fourth respectively; we used a review of state pre-K standards to refine our curricular focus for pre-K. The MTP-Science curriculum addresses three domains of science: life science, earth science, and physical science and provides inquiry-based activities to meet instructional objectives that are aligned with state and national standards.

The MTP-M/S curricula include two math and two science activities (15–20 minutes long) every week for 33 weeks across the school year. Weekly "center time" options enable the teacher to revisit specific math and science activities with small numbers of purposefully selected students. We also provide teachers with monthly knowledge and skills checklists, to enable their tracking of students' performance.

The curricular design was guided by specific consideration of relevant learning theory; structured inquiry, along with situated cognition, authentic instruction, and cognitive development, formed the theoretical basis for our activity designs.

Structured Inquiry   "When engaging in inquiry, students describe objects and events, ask questions, construct explanations, test those explanations against current scientific knowledge, and communicate their ideas to others" (National Research Council [NRC], 2006, p. 2). Although this may seem too cognitively advanced for most 4-year-olds, inquiry can be tailored to the capabilities of the student, on a continuum from completely teacher directed (*confirmation* inquiry) to totally student driven (*open* inquiry; Rezba, Auldridge, & Rhea [1999], cited in Bell, Smetana, & Binns, 2005). For MTP-M/S, we articulated inquiry as an intermediate, *structured* inquiry, in which teachers pose questions and suggest procedures, but children actively observe, predict, collect, analyze, and communicate their processes and results, activities most young children can perform and enjoy. Every activity offers the opportunity to engage, investigate, discuss, and extend, a modification of the 5E Model (Bybee et al., 2006) that is developmentally appropriate but still cognitively demanding.

Situated Cognition, Authentic Instruction, and Cognitive Development   Authentic events provide context for collaborative knowledge construction and skill acquisition. Instead of a static month-long "unit" on plants, for instance, students' explorations are linked as much as possible to the seasons and what is happening outside *right now*. In fall, students explore the environment near their schools and collect seeds as they ripen. In winter, students sort and describe seeds and consider their use as a food source. In early spring, students sprout and examine seeds (and the "baby plants" that emerge) before planting the sprouts. In later spring, students experiment to study the effects of light and water on the growth of these plants, just as plants begin to flourish outside.

Children's cognition is expressly cultivated within these situations. Building on the work of Ginsburg and Golbeck (2004), the activity designs emphasize thinking (reflective, as a function of inquiry, and also problem solving) and the modeling and eliciting of mathematical and scientific language to express and give form to that thinking. Students are given individual roles within many of the MTP-M/S activities, and every activity provides "Make It Work" recommendations for adaptation for students who may need more scaffolding or more challenge.

Because understandings develop over time, MTP-M/S offers opportunities to develop deep understandings within and across activities. Year-long trajectories were articulated for math and science, offering a frame for development of a range of related functional understandings and skills for our students, both within and across domains, an approach recommended by Clements (Clements, 2004; NRC, 2005). Consideration of the evolution of knowledge and skills is particularly important for the design of early childhood learning experiences—research indicates that what is optimal at any point in time (e.g., both developmentally appropriate and offering suitable cognitive demand) is largely dependent on students' prior opportunities to learn (NRC, 2007).

Multiple Modalities and Focus on Interdisciplinary Skills   As recommended by Willingham (2005), different learning modalities were selected for MTP-M/S activities, based on what is optimal for the desired knowledge and skill, while still offering multiple ways of coming to know something (NAEYC & NCTM, 2002). This is facilitated through varied activity design, a variety of visual representations, the multiple extensions suggested for every activity, and the related activities sent home for students and families to pursue together.

As recommended by the National Research Council (NRC, 2006), we used book reading to introduce new or complex concepts and to guide the inquiry process. More than 45 math and science texts suitable for pre-K provide appealing entry points for teacher and student inquiry and support the development of students' preliteracy and language skills. A range of visual representations is employed, such as the number chart that teachers and children construct together, for a few numbers at a time. The chart displays numbers both graphically (via filled 10 frames) and numerically and is arranged in such a way as to support place value conceptions (numbers arrayed in rows from 0 to 9 in the "one's place," an adaption of that used in Big Math for Little Kids; Ginsburg et al., 2003). Common manipulatives are employed, and teachers are explicitly guided in ways to help students develop related concepts as these are used (attribute blocks, for example, serve as a jumping-off point for a discussion of the characteristics of shapes).

Because successful learners employ math across their lives and not just during "math" activities (Clements, 2004), we embed rich suggestions for extensions of every activity, offering simple ways to employ relevant skills in interesting ways to solve problems. This practice is continued at home via monthly "parent letters" that describe what students are learning and illustrate everyday activities that can reinforce exploration and application. Besides offering opportunities for repeated practice and deepening understandings, these in-school and at-home extensions promote math and science as being "positive, self-motivated, self-directed, problem solving activity" (Clements, 2004)—important conceptions as children develop their attitudes toward these disciplines. For more detail on our design-based approach to curriculum design and pilot testing for MTP-M/S, see Kinzie, Whittaker, McGuire, Lee, and Kilday (in submission).

Professional Development Supports

Our teaching supports were intended to promote high-fidelity implementation of the MTP-M/S curricula. In addition, given that large-scale observational studies show clear linkages between the quality of teacher–student interactions and student learning outcomes (NCEDL and SWEEP, see Early et al., 2005), we applied a well-validated framework for encouraging classroom quality, the Classroom Assessment Scoring System™ (CLASS™; Pianta, La Paro, & Hamre, 2008), selecting video clips that demonstrated the characteristics of this quality, particularly emphasizing the constructs of concept development, quality of feedback, and language modeling in this process.

The theoretical basis for the MTP-M/S teacher support design is informed by the tenets of social learning theory, situated cognition, and authentic instruction. For instance, application of principles associated with situated cognition led us to embed teacher supports in the physical and social contexts of practice—teachers' classrooms and their teaching (Putnam & Borko, 2000).

An extension and refinement of situated PD supports are achieved when supports are embedded directly in the context of practice, as in the context of curricula that teachers implement. In acknowledging the inadequate preparation of the preschool teaching force, the National Research Council (2005) recommends curricula that are comprehensive enough to enable success for teachers without strong preparation or experience. This can be done by embedding PD supports directly into the curricula and so encourage transfer of recommended teaching techniques to teachers' practice. We offered teachers a collection of teaching supports that are embedded within the curricula and are quick and easy to use while preparing for an activity.

Within-Activity Curricular Supports   Within the activity instructions, there are several key forms of support for every activity, including recommendations for language to model and elicit and suggestions for both multiple extensions of the activity across the school day and for adaptations teachers can make to enable differentiated instruction (to best fit the needs of their students). As a function of our iterative curricular design/ development process, we gathered observational evidence of the need to strengthen certain attributes of the instructional design, and as a result we included the scaffolding of an explicit visual layout of the four-step inquiry model embodied in every activity and a greater emphasis on recommendations for teacher questioning, with more question options suggested and displayed in a prominent fashion. Although we conceived of these as part of the teacher support package, we did not withhold these components from any group of teachers using our curricula. See Figure 2.1 for a depiction of the activity design, including within-activity supports.

Online-Only Embedded Supports   As across our broader society, teacher PD is moving to the web, taking advantage of distributed thinking and teamwork capacities offered by this medium (Dede, in National Research Council, 2007). Delivering PD support via the Internet can help make teacher PD more *scale-able* and accessible, and therefore more likely to make a difference in the practice of many teachers. The Internet affords the use of visual exemplars (either videos or animations) of classroom practice, which have been found to

October-Science-W3-A1	Worms 1	Small Group

GET READY

Objectives
- Create an ecosystem in a bottle
- Conduct scientific experiment

Use the Lingo
- Worm
- Soil
- Experiment
- Control

Materials (Provided; Not provided):
- Coarse gravel/small rocks
- Hand lens (one per student)
- Paper lunch bags (two per small group)
- Gallon Ziploc bags (one per small group)
- **Two-liter plastic soda bottles (two per small group)**
- **Clean egg shells (two per small group)**
- **Water**
- **Worms (10 per small group)**
- **Lettuce (two or three leaves per small group)**
- **Garden soil (not potting soil)**
- **Hobby knife or box cutter**

Additional Preparation Required:
You will make **one** Experimental and **one** Control bottle for **EACH** small group.
- Remove the labels from the two-liter bottles.
- Cut off the top ⅓ of the bottles (best done using a hobby knife or box cutter braced against a table top, laying the bottle on its side and rolling against the blade). Save the bottle caps.
- Fill two Ziplocs with garden soil (not potting soil).
- Divide gravel (so all four bottles will have same amount)
- Acquire red worms (a.k.a. "red wigglers;" 20–30 worms total) from a fishing bait store or online supplier (estimated cost $3).

ENGAGE

1. Science chant
2. Say: *Today we are going to do an experiment! It will help us learn about ways worms affect their environment. An experiment lets us make a prediction or a guess about something, then test whether or not our guess is correct.*

INVESTIGATE

3. Examine worms (encourage students to treat living things with care):
- Give each student a hand lens to examine worms.
- Do not expose the worms to direct sunlight.
4. Encouraging students to participate, make one Experimental (with worms) and one Control (without worms) Eco-bottle:
- Place about 2 inches of gravel/rocks in each bottle.
- Place about 3 inches of soil in each bottle.
- Crush one eggshell into each bottle.
- Pour water into each bottle until it just begins to appear in the gravel.

INVESTIGATE (continued)

- Add 10 worms to the Experimental Eco-bottle **only.**
- Tear lettuce leaves into small (½") pieces; put into bottles in a loose layer:
- Place one bottle cap into each bottle
5. Cover the bottles with the brown paper bags and place in a cool, dark area.
6. Discuss the differences between the two bottles. Explain that you have created an experiment. Say: *Over the next couple of weeks we are going to find out how worms affect their environment by comparing the soil in the bottle with the worms to the soil in the bottle without the worms. We'll be able to see whether the worms affect the lettuce and whether they affect the bottle caps.*

DISCUSS

7. Ask for predictions. Connect to student knowledge of worms.
- Tell students: *We will check the bottles each day to see what happened.* (Optional: Keep a record of observations by photos, sketches or written records of student observations)
- *What do you think is going to happen to the lettuce? Do you think that anything will happen to the bottle cap?* (Discuss how the bottle cap is made of plastic and will not decompose)
- *What does the soil look like? What do the worms look like? Were you able to notice anything new about the worms, dirt, or rocks with the hand lens?*
- *What do you think the worms will do in the bottle? Will plants grow better in the soil with or without worms? Why?*

EXTEND

8. Engage students in conversation about worms and connect to immediate environment as opportunities arise.
- During outside time, ask students where worms might be, what they are doing, how they are helping, etc.
- To transition students, ask each student to tell you one fact about worms.
- Book Area: *Wonderful Worms,* by Linda Glaser and other books on worms, gardening, or composting.

MAKE IT WORK

For Students with More Advanced Skills
- Ask students to record observations by making daily drawings of the changes in the bottles, and compare to the drawing from the previous day(s).

For Students Requiring More Support
- Some students may have difficulty being close to the worms. Provide pictures from the book, *Wonderful Worms,* so that students who are afraid to be near the worms can still participate.

Figure 2.1. MyTeachingPartner-Mathematics/Science Activity Design including within-activity teaching supports. (From Kinzie, M., Pianta, R.C., Whittaker, J., Foss, M.J., Pan, E., Lee, Y., Williford, A.P., & Thomas, J.B. [2010]. *MyTeachingPartner-Math/Science.* Charlottesville: The Center for Advanced Study of Teaching and Learning, Curry School of Education, University of Virginia; reprinted by permission.)

be more effective than textual descriptions in encouraging preservice teachers' ability to describe specific applications of targeted teaching skills (Moreno & Ortegano-Layne, 2008). We drew upon this capacity and developed more than 130, 2- to 3-minute Demonstration Videos of high-fidelity curricular implementations that also embody the qualities of high-quality teacher–child interactions. All were recorded in at-risk pre-K classrooms and are embedded within the curricula in order to be quickly reviewed during teachers' preparation.

Brief Teaching Tips (we aimed for 25 words or less for each, to make them more readily reviewed by busy teachers) are embedded in every activity, addressing best pedagogical practices, common ways students construct understandings (including misconceptions), or key math or science concepts. Figure 2.2 depicts the provision of Demonstration Videos and a Teaching Tip for a science activity. Other online-only supports include weekly video-based 5-Minute Quality Teaching Challenges, featuring one of the activities teachers will implement that week. Every month we highlight a different dimension of quality teaching on the main menu, including a 1- to 2-minute video, a brief description of the dimension and why it's important, and links to a Quality Teaching Library offering 150 video examples across many instructional settings, formats, and content areas. Eight PD workshops guide teacher processing of these supports and offer opportunities for peer and self-reflection, and these are described next.

Figure 2.2. Online-only supports: Video demonstrations and teaching tips. (From Kinzie, M., Pianta, R.C., Whittaker, J., Foss, M.J., Pan, E., Lee, Y., Williford, A.P., & Thomas, J.B. [2010]. *MyTeachingPartner-Math/Science.* Charlottesville: The Center for Advanced Study of Teaching and Learning, Curry School of Education, University of Virginia; reprinted by permission.)

Workshops   In recent years, blended-teacher PD programs have been crafted from experiences across multiple media, with online supports augmented by those in other formats (NRC, 2007). Putnam and Borko (2000) assert that participation in the physically and socially situated discourse of the teaching community aids in the construction of professional knowledge, an approach supported by sociocultural and *communities of practice* literatures (Adger, Hoyle, & Dickinson, 2004). To the extent that teachers' own classrooms serve as the context for such exploration, the learning experience becomes more powerful. For this reason, many forms of PD attempt to focus specifically on teachers' own practice, often via video observations. Such video observation and discussion allow for authentic experiential learning (Kolb, 1984) and reflection on action (Schön, 1987) without the pressures of being in "the teaching moment" (Borko, Jacobs, Eiteljorg, & Pittman, 2008).

Reflection on the practice of other teachers facing the same teaching challenges (with similar students and equivalent learning goals) is also possible in these settings. This was the approach taken by Santagata (2009), whose PD for teachers of sixth-grade mathematics employed analysis of carefully selected video clips to enable content exploration, lesson analysis, and making links to practice. The use of purposively chosen, preexisting video clips also enables embedding within the activity instructions for the curriculum teachers are preparing to implement.

In our blended support model, the online support components were complemented by a series of eight workshops (1 full-day and 7 part-day [2.5 hours]) specifically designed to enhance teachers' use of these supports and to encourage self-reflection and peer discussion of their own teaching practice. Each workshop featured explorations on a dimension of quality teaching, defined by the CLASS Pre-K (Pianta, La Paro, et al., 2008). In addition, there was exploration of relevant math and science concept knowledge, peer and self-review of teaching, error-analysis activities (in which common student behaviors are modeled and teachers practice identifying and responding to errors in student thinking), and group discussion, based in part on the recommendations of the NRC (2006). Between workshops, teachers completed reflective assignments including review of online supports, video analysis of their own teaching with a focus on strategies presented at the workshops, and peer-debrief sessions.

We turn our attention next to consideration of the association between the MTP-M/S curricula (containing the within-activity curricular supports described above) and MTP-M/S teacher PD (involving both online teacher supports and the companion teacher workshops) and teachers' fidelity of implementation.

THE ASSOCIATION BETWEEN MYTEACHINGPARTNER-MATH AND SCIENCE CURRICULA AND PROFESSIONAL DEVELOPMENT SUPPORTS AND TEACHERS' IMPLEMENTATION FIDELITY

Participants

Participants in the year-long trial included 35 pre-K teachers in state-funded classrooms from a single school district in a large mid-Atlantic city. Teachers were randomly assigned to one of three conditions representing variations in curricular access and PD support. Teachers in the Control group implemented the district's existing math and science curricula ($N = 9$; these teachers are not included in subsequent analyses). Teachers in the MTP-M/S Basic group ($N = 15$) received the MTP-M/S curricula, plus the teaching materials needed to implement the activities. Teachers in the MTP-M/S Plus group ($N = 11$) received the same MTP-M/S curricula and materials as the Basic group and also a blended form of teacher supports (online and workshop based).

All teachers in this study taught in classrooms that included students with one or more risk factors for later school failure (poverty, second language learners, or health or developmental problems). The teachers were mostly female (97%) and ranged in age from 24 years to 65 years ($M = 46$, $SD = 10.6$). Teachers reported their race/ethnicity as Caucasian (50%) or African American (50%). Teachers held an average of 19 years of experience working with children ($SD = 10.26$) and all held at least a bachelor's degree (52% had a degree in early childhood education) as was a requirement for teachers in state-funded classrooms.

Procedures

Teachers in both the MTP-M/S Basic and Plus groups implemented the math and science curricula over the course of the 36-week school year. The curricula included 66 math and 66 science activities (designed to last 20–30 minutes) along with weekly center-time activity options. Teachers were asked to implement two math and two science activities every week. Teachers in the MTP-M/S Plus group also had access to online-embedded teacher supports via the MTP-M/S web site (described previously). Teachers in the Plus group were also invited to participate in a series of 1 full-day workshops and 7 part-day workshops (2.5 hours of instructional time) held once a month from September through April and focusing on curricular implementation (see above for a further description of workshop content).

Coding of Videotapes

As part of their participation in the study, we asked teachers to videotape themselves implementing MTP-M/S curricular activities. Teachers were asked to include one activity per tape and to submit 15 videotapes per month by mail. Tapes were selected for coding based on an effort to obtain an adequate sample of teachers' practice across the year (September, October, November, February, March, and April), across domains (math and science), and across activity settings (whole versus small group). We selected two tapes per month for each teacher, for a possible total of 12 tapes. If for 1 month for a given teacher we selected a math whole-group tape and a science small-group tape, the next month for that same teacher we selected a math small-group and science whole-group activity. On average, 11 tapes were coded per teacher (range 4–12).

Coding focused on documentation of implementation fidelity including items about teachers' adherence to and quality of facilitation of MTP math and science lessons (described in the following section). Twenty percent of tapes were double coded by a "master" coder in order to calculate interrater reliability.

Measures

Classroom and Teacher Characteristics

Teachers reported on the number of students in their classrooms and completed a personal demographic survey after enrolling in the study. They reported on *level of education* (advanced degree = 1, bachelor's degree = 0), *field of study* (early childhood education, elementary education, or other), and *years of experience teaching pre-K*, among other variables.

Implementation Fidelity: Adherence

The MTP-M/S Fidelity measure was designed to assess teachers' adherence to the MyTeachingPartner-M/S curricular design. It was developed during a year of pilot testing and refined before implementing for the field trial. The design of the measure was informed by a review of the theoretical foundations for the instructional design of the curricula, to help us determine the extent to which the learning experiences children were offered were in alignment with what we intended. The final fidelity measure used for the field trial contained 12 items assessing the teacher's adherence to the specific lesson plan and facilitation of children's participation for each activity. Example items included "Teacher actively models the use of math and/or scientific language," and "Children perform the activity tasks specified in the lesson plan."

For the field trial, a master coder trained a set of three coders and together they coded a series of tapes (from the previous year's pilot test) until reliability was reached. Coders then watched and coded tapes independently with 20% of the tapes double coded by the master coder to check for drift.

Upon conclusion of coding, the items were weighted so that all items were on a 3-point scale. Dichotomous items were scored 0 for "no" and 2 for "yes." Ordinal items were scored 0 for "none" or "some" (combined due to lack of variability), 1 for "most," and 2 for "all." To determine interrater reliability we used weighted kappas for the dichotomous items and intraclass correlation coefficients (ICCs) for the ordinal items. We found that inter-rater reliability was adequate for most items (all coders reached or exceeded the benchmark of .6 on 75% of the items). The interrater reliability across items ranged from .61 to .88 with an average of .76. A total score was calculated by summing the 12 items for a total possible score of 24. The final measure was found to have excellent internal consistency (α = .95).

Implementation Fidelity: Dosage   Dosage was calculated using the overall number of activities/tapes that teachers submitted. We asked teachers to videotape all of the possible math and science activities that they conducted for a total possible of 168 activities across the year (66 math, 66 science, and 36 center time activities). Upon examination, there was a range across teachers in number of tapes submitted (M = 105.56, SD = 36.18).

This type of data has been used in previous studies as a measure of intervention implementation (e.g., Pianta, Mashburn, Downer, Hamre, & Justice, 2008). However, we acknowledge that it may also in part reflect teachers' adherence and/or quality of implementation. Teachers who were more adherent (e.g., had all the materials ready for a lesson, and/or always videotaped their lessons) or delivered the intervention with better quality may have felt more comfortable submitting tapes, but may not have actually implemented any more lessons than teachers who submitted fewer tapes. Thus, there may have been teachers who implemented more math and science lessons than their submitted tapes reflected.

Exposure to Teacher Supports   Teachers' use of web-based resources was tracked using a server that automatically recorded the information about which online supports teachers accessed and the length of time (total number of minutes) that the teacher spent on each page on the MTS-M/S web site. This allowed us to calculate the duration that each teacher spent on the various pages, as well as the number of pages accessed per web site visit. There were specific supports designed to increase fidelity in small- and whole-group activities that included Teaching Challenges and the CLASS video library (described previously). For this study we specifically examined usage of these pages. We examined the association between overall time spent on the web site, time spent on the individual types of pages outlined above, and pages per visit as they related to teachers' implementation fidelity. We also recorded attendance at the eight PD workshops.

Results

Teacher's Implementation Fidelity   Table 2.1 provides descriptive information about teachers' adherence to the curricula by group. Overall,

Table 2.1. Classroom and teacher characteristics and fidelity to intervention components by study condition

	Curricula only (basic; n = 15)					Curricula plus supports (plus; n = 11)				
	n	%	M	SD	Range	n	%	M	SD	Range
Classroom characteristics										
Number of students	14		16.07	1.64	12.00–18.00	10		16.60	1.43	14.00–18.00
Teacher characteristics										
Level of education	14					10				
Bachelor's degree	5	36%				7	70%			
Advanced degree	9	64%				3	30%			
Field of study										
Early childhood or elementary Education	11	79%				8	80%			
Other	3	21%				2	20%			
Years of teaching PK	14		10.00	8.67	2.00–32.00	10		4.45	2.87	2.00–10.00
Implementation fidelity										
Total adherence—observed	15		13.67	3.93	6.78–18.33	11		15.19	1.97	12.00–17.92
Math adherence	15		14.30	3.85	6.80–18.83	11		15.34	1.96	12.50–18.83
Science adherence	15		12.83	4.76	2.00–17.83	11		14.95	2.52	10.67–19.17
Dosage—total number of tapes	15		98.00	41.34	16.00–142.00	11		115.91	25.98	74.00–171.00
Number of math tapes	15		50.53*	20.08	10.00–72.00	11		63.55*	12.09	48.00–92.00
Number of science tapes	15		47.27	21.39	6.00–69.00	11		51.64	13.94	25.00–79.00
Web site usage (plus only)										
Overall web site (in minutes)						11		631.52	408.29	70.72–1263.27
Teaching challenge pages						11		46.18	51.07	0.00–163.02
CLASS Video library pages						11		101.28	98.44	0.00–343.17
Pages per visit						11		4.47	2.04	1.15–7.51

* Significant difference $p = .05$

Key: PK = prekindergarten; CLASS = Classroom Assessment Scoring System teachers in both groups showed fairly high adherence, as assessed by our fidelity measure. Across activities, out of a possible total of 24 points, Basic teachers scored an average of 13.67 (*SD* = 3.98) and Plus teachers scored an average of 15.19 (*SD* = 1.97). In examining the distribution on each fidelity item, the majority of teachers got scores of "yes" on the dichotomous items and scores of "most" or "all" on the ordinal items. The effect size for the mean difference in teachers' fidelity based on group was relatively large at *d* = .49. However, our analyses indicated that this apparent difference in overall adherence to the curricula was not significant, likely due to lack of power to detect significant effects based on our small sample size. These results suggest that with a larger sample size, we would find significant differences between groups in mean fidelity scores and variability in scores. Examining the standard deviations for each group, it appeared that there was more variability in teachers' scores in the Basic group than in the Plus group.

To descriptively explore this variability, we divided teachers into low (less than 1 *SD* below the mean), mid (between -1 and +1 *SD*s), and high (greater than 1 *SD* above the mean) fidelity teachers (see Figure 2.3). Twenty-seven percent of Basic teachers scored in the low group compared with none of the Plus teachers. Compared with the Basic teachers, a greater percentage of Plus teachers were in both the mid- (82% versus 67%) and high-fidelity (18% versus 7%) groups.

In terms of dosage, on average, teachers in the Plus group submitted more tapes overall (*M* = 115.91, *SD* = 25.98) than teachers in the Basic group (*M* = 98.00, *SD* = 41.34). This overall difference was not significant (t [24] = 3.64, *p* = .19). However, when number of tapes submitted was disaggregated by math and science, teachers in the Plus group (*M* = 63.55, *SD* = 12.09) submitted significantly more math tapes than teachers in the Basic group (*M* = 50.53, *SD* = 20.08) [t (24) = 4.22, *p* = .05]), and this difference

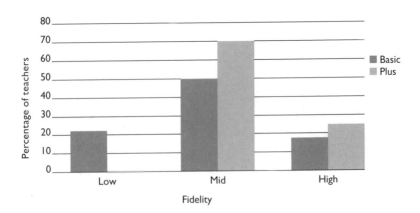

Figure 2.3. Teachers' implementation fidelity by group.

had a large effect size of *d* = .79. These results demonstrate that teachers in the Plus group were implementing more activities than teachers in the Basic group and that there was great variability in dosage for teachers in the Basic group.

Associations Among Classroom and Teacher Characteristics and Implementation Fidelity and Use of Professional Development Supports   With our second research question, we explored whether certain classroom and teacher characteristics were associated with implementation fidelity, and if so, whether these associations differed by group. We found no significant associations between classroom and teacher characteristics for teachers in the Basic group. For teachers in the Plus group, an interesting pattern of associations emerged. Having more education was negatively correlated with total adherence (r = -.64, p < .05) but positively correlated with dosage (r = .76, p < .05). Number of students in the classroom was also highly positively correlated with total adherence (r = .94, p < .01).

We were also interested in the association between teacher characteristics and teachers' use of the web-based PD supports. We found that age (r = -.64, p < .05) and experience working with pre-K children (r = -.66, p < .05) were negatively correlated with total time spent using web-based supports. In contrast, level of education was positively associated with web site time spent on Teaching Challenges (r = .74, p < .05) and the CLASS video library (r = .70, p < .05).

Relation Between Teacher Professional Development Supports and Implementation Fidelity   For our third research question, we examined whether teachers' use of PD resources was associated with fidelity of implementation. When examining workshop attendance, there was very little variability. Almost all teachers attended the majority of the workshops. Therefore we did not include this variable in further analysis. When examining web site access, we found that the number of tapes that teachers submitted was positively correlated with the number of different pages on the web site that teachers accessed in a session (r = .81, p < .01), and specifically with time spent on the CLASS video library (r = .79, p < .01) (see Table 2.1 for descriptive information on usage of web-based supports). Use of web-based supports was not associated with teachers' adherence to the curricula. Table 2.2 provides all intercorrelations among PD supports and implementation fidelity.

IMPLICATIONS AND RECOMMENDATIONS FOR EARLY MATH AND SCIENCE PROFESSIONAL DEVELOPMENT

Research to establish the characteristics of high-quality curricula that support young children's mathematics and science knowledge and skill

Table 2.2. Intercorrelations among teachers' website usage and implementation fidelity

	Total adherence	Math adherence	Science adherence	Total tapes	Number of math tapes	Number of science tapes	Overall web site	Teaching challenge	CLASS Video library pages	Pages per visit
Total adherence	-----	.92**	.94**	.09	.10	.07	.19	-.44	-.30	-.30
Math adherence		-----	.73**	-.02	-.02	-.02	.40	-.18	-.09	-.26
Science adherence			-----	.21	.23	.18	.03	-.53	-.34	-.20
Total tapes				-----	.98**	.98**	.26	.48	.79**	.81**
Number of math tapes					-----	.94**	.14	.41	.81**	.82**
Number of science tapes						-----	.37	.50	.77**	.74**
Overall website usage							-----	.46	.31	.21
Teaching challenge pages								-----	.54	.50
CLASS video library pages									-----	.40

*p < .05, **p < .01

Key: CLASS = Classroom Assessment Scoring System

development is especially important in laying the foundation for later educational success, particularly for children at risk for early school failure (Bowman et al., 2001; National Mathematics Advisory Panel, NMAP, 2008). Whereas some math and science curricula have shown promise for early childhood, research indicates that high-quality curricula alone are insufficient to improve teacher practices and child outcomes (Pianta et al., 2005). Teachers' practice is especially important in determining children's learning outcomes, especially for at-risk children and in schools of lower socioeconomic status (LoCasale-Crouch et al., 2007; Nye et al., 2004) where teachers have been found to receive less preparation, to report less confidence in influencing student learning, and to have lower expectations for students (see the research synthesis offered by Santagata, 2009).

In this study, we examined two forms of implementation fidelity for pre-K curricula in mathematics and science: adherence to the curricular design and dosage of activities. Our results indicate that teachers' overall adherence to the curricula was relatively high for both groups, suggesting the value of the within-activity curricular supports experienced by teachers in both Basic and Plus groups. Although the apparent difference in adherence in favor of the teachers in the Plus group ($M = 15.19$, $SD = 1.97$) compared with those in the Basic group ($M = 13.67$, $SD = 3.98$) was not statistically significant, the effect size of this difference was found to be relatively large ($d = .49$); it is probable that statistical significance would have been obtained with a larger sample. There was much greater variability in Basic group's adherence to the curricula when compared with the Plus group, who received additional PD support (online-only embedded supports together with workshops focused on reflective use of those supports). Taken together, these results suggest that the within-activity curricular supports aided in adherence to the curricula but that the combination of these supports with the addition of online supports may produce the greatest fidelity of implementation, as expressed by findings for adherence for math and science activities and dosage of math activities.

Our analyses indicate that teachers in the Plus group with higher levels of education submitted a greater number of tapes but showed lower levels of adherence to the curricula. Perhaps these teachers felt more inclined to deviate from the curricula and use their own adaptations, which could have improved on the curricular design. Our future analyses will include a measure of quality of curricular implementation that will help to determine the correlation between adherence and quality. In addition, older teachers and teachers with more experience were found to spend less total time using the web-based supports. It could be that these teachers felt more confident in their teaching practices and felt that they didn't need to use the web-based resources as frequently. Alternatively, more experienced, late-career teachers could be more resistant to trying new techniques and teaching practices, as suggested by the professional life cycle work of Huberman (1989) and Hargreaves (2005), or they may not have been as comfortable accessing and using technology-based resources. It is also possible that these teachers had less access (although all participating teachers had a computer and Internet connectivity to their classrooms, some may not have had computers at home, resulting in less access and perhaps less familiarity). If the latter is true, this finding has implications for making web-based supports accessible to all teachers and possibly providing individualized supports on web usage for teachers who may need a greater amount of scaffolding. Again, data on quality of instruction will help us to determine whether the use of web-based supports led to higher quality instruction and whether this finding might be moderated by experience such that web-based supports led to higher quality instruction for less experienced but not more experienced teachers.

STUDY LIMITATIONS

The results we report here are from a small study and should be interpreted with caution, particularly those results *within* teacher groups (e.g., the associations between the use of web-based supports and the Plus group's fidelity of implementation). In addition, our teacher sample is relatively homogeneous, as all teachers were drawn from one district's state-funded pre-K program, limiting the potential to generalize our findings.

CONCLUSION AND NEXT STEPS

The teaching supports associated with MTP-M/S were designed in response to recommendations for teacher support with regard to 1) mathematics and science concept knowledge, 2) an understanding of developmentally appropriate mathematics and science for inclusion in early childhood education, and 3) an understanding of how to foster children's mathematical and scientific development with a research-based curriculum (NRC, 2006, 2009). The results presented here for fidelity of adherence and dosage offer evidence of some success in this endeavor, and indicate that MTP-M/S is a promising curricular package: Teachers appeared willing to use it in their classrooms, to use it with relatively high-fidelity, and to make use of additional teaching supports when these were available to them (and to good effect relative to their curricular adherence and dosage).

Although research is beginning to emerge on the importance of high-quality and -fidelity curricular implementation (Clements & Sarama, 2008; Clements et al., in press), there remains very little research on the association between implementation and child outcomes, particularly in the areas of math and science. A next step for researchers, and specifically for our research program, is to examine the relationships between the fidelity of curricular implementation and possible gains in student learning. Our hope is to examine the use of our curricula and PD supports with a larger and more heterogeneous sample of pre-K teachers in order to better understand the effects of both on teacher practices and student outcomes. Ultimately, we hope that through efforts such as these, we will identify how to best support teachers in implementing high-quality math and science curricula and positively influence children's learning trajectories in these domains.

REFERENCES

Adger, C.T., Hoyle, S.M., & Dickinson, D.K. (2004). Locating learning in in-service education for preschool teachers. *American Educational Research Journal, 41*(4), 867–900. doi:10.3102/00028312041004867

American Association for the Advancement of Science. (1993). *Benchmarks for science literacy: A tool for curriculum reform.* New York, NY: Oxford University Press.

Bell, R.L., Smetana, L., & Binns, I. (2005). Simplifying inquiry instruction. *The Science Teacher, 72*(7), 30–33.

Borko, H., Jacobs, J., Eiteljorg, E., & Pittman, M.E. (2008). Video as a tool for fostering productive discussions in mathematics professional development. *Teachng and Teacher Education, 24,* 417–436. doi:10.1016/j.tate.2006.11.012

Borman, K.M., Cotner, B.A., Lee, R.S., Boydston, T.L., & Lanehart, R. (2009). *Improving elementary science instruction and student achievement: The impact of a professional development program.* Paper presented at the annual meeting of the Society for Research in Educational Effectiveness, Crystal City, VA.

Bowman, B.T., Donovan, M.S., & Burns, M.S. (2001). *Eager to learn: Educating our preschoolers.* Washington, DC: National Research Council.

Brown, J.A., Greenfield, D.B., Juarez, C.L., & Dominguez, X. (2010). *ECHOS: Early childhood hands-on science.* Paper presented at the Institute of Educational Sciences (IES), Washington, DC.

Bybee, R.W., Taylor, J.A., Gardner, A., Van Scotter, P., Powell, J.C., Westbrook, A., & Landes, N. (2006). *BSCS 5E instructional model: Origins, effectiveness, and applications.* Colorado Springs, CO: Biological Sciences Curriculum Study (BSCS).

Carroll, C., Patterson, M., Wood, S., Booth, A., Rick, J., & Balain, S. (2007). A conceptual framework for implementation fidelity. *Implementation Science, 2*(40). doi:10.1186/1748-5908-2-40

Clark-Chiarelli, N., Gropen, J., & Hatfield-Davis, J. (2008). *Foundations of science literacy: Uncovering children's thinking about physical science.* Paper presented at the Institute of Educational Sciences, Washington, DC.

Clements, D.H. (2004). Major themes and recommendations. In D.H. Clements & J. Sarama (Eds.), *Engaging young children in Mathematics: Standards for early childhood mathematics education* (pp. 7–72). Mahwah, NJ: Lawrence Erlbaum.

Clements, D.H. (2007). Curriculum research: Toward a framework for "research-based curricula". *Journal for Research in Mathematics Education, 38*(1), 35–70.

Clements, D.H., & Sarama, J. (2007). *Building Blocks-SRA real math teacher's edition, Grade PreK.* Columbus, OH: SRA/McGraw-Hill.

Clements, D.H., & Sarama, J. (2008). Experimental evaluation of the effects of a research-based preschool mathematics curriculum. *American Education Research Journal, 45*(2), 443–494. doi:10.3102/0002831207312908

Clements, D.H., Sarama, J., Spitler, M.E., Lange, A.A., & Wolfe, C.B. (in press). Mathematics learned by young children in an intervention based on learning trajectories: A large-scale cluster randomized trial. *Journal for Research in Mathematics Education.*

Cohen, D.K., & Hill, H.C. (2000). Instructional policy and classroom performance: The mathematics reform in California. *Teachers College Record, 102*(2), 294–343. doi:10.1111/0161-4681.00057

Copley, J.V. (Ed.). (1999). *Mathematics in the early years*. Reston, VA: National Council of Teachers of Mathematics.

Copple, J.V. (2004). Mathematics curriculum in the early childhood context. In D.H. Clements, J. Sarama & A.M. DiBiase (Eds.), *Engaging young children in mathematics: Standards for early childhood mathematics education* (pp. 83–87). Mahwah, NJ: Erlbaum.

Desimone, L.M., Porter, A.C., Garet, M.S., Yoon, K.S., & Birman, B.F. (2002). Effects of professional development on teachers' instruction: Results from a three year longitudinal study. *Educational Evaluation and Policy Analysis, 24*(2), 81–112. doi:10.3102/01623737024002081

Duncan, G.J., Dowsett, C.J., Claessens, A., Magnuson, K., Huston, A.C., Klevanov, P., ... Japel, C. (2007). School readiness and later achievement. *Developmental Psychology, 43*(6), 1428–1446. doi:10.1037/0012-1649.43.6.1428

Duschl, R.A., Schweingruber, H.A., & Shouse, A.W. (2007). *Taking science to school: Learning and teaching science in grades K–8*. Washington, DC: National Academies Press.

Dusenbury, L., Brannigan, B., Falco, M., & Hansen, W.B. (2003). A review of research on fidelity of implementation: Implications for drug abuse prevention in school settings. *Health Education Research, 18*(2), 237–256. doi:10.1093/her/18.2.237

Early, D., Barbarin, O., Bryant, D., Burchinal, M., Chang, F., Clifford, R., ... Barnett, W.S. (2005). *Pre-kindergarten in eleven states: NCEDL's multi-state Study of pre-kindergarten & study of State-Wide Early Education Programs (SWEEP)*. Chapel Hill, NC.: National Center for Early Development & Learning.

Early, D., Iruka, I.U., Ritchie, S., Barbarin, O.A., Winn, D.M.C., Crawford, G.M., ... Pianta, R.C. (2010). How do pre-kindergarteners spend their time? Gender, ethnicity, and income as predictors of experiences in pre-kindergarten classrooms. *Early Childhood Research Quarterly, 25*, 177–193. doi:10.1016/j.ecresq.2009.10.003

Epstein, A.S. (2006). *Numbers plus: A comprehensive approach to early mathematics education*. Washington, DC: Institute of Educational Sciences, U.S. Department of Education.

French, L.A. (2004). Science as the center of a coherent, integrated early childhood curriculum. *Early Childhood Research Quarterly, 19*(1), 138–149.

French, L.A., & Peterson, S.M. (2009). Learning language through preschool science. In C. Andersen, N. Scheuer, M. del Puy Leonor Perez Echeverria & E.V. Teubal (Eds.), *Representational systems and practices as learning tools: Learning language through preschool science* (pp. 77–92). Rotterdam, Netherlands: Sense Publishers.

Garet, M.S., Porter, A.C., Desimone, L., Birman, B.F., & Yoon, K.S. (2001). What makes professional development effective? Results from a national sample of teachers. *American Educational Research Journal, 38*(4), 915–945. doi:10.3102/00028312038004915

Gelman, R., & Brenneman, K. (2004). Science learning pathways for young children. *Early Childhood Research Quarterly, 19*(1), 150–158. doi:10.1016/j.ecresq.2004.01.009

Gelman, R., Brenneman, K., Macdonald, G., & Román, M. (2010). *Preschool Pathways to Science (PrePS™): Facilitating scientific ways of thinking, talking, doing, and understanding*. Baltimore, MD: Paul H. Brookes Publishing Co.

Ginsburg, H.P. (1997). Mathematics learning disabilities: A view from developmental psychology. *Journal of Learning Disabilities, 30* 20–33

Ginsburg, H.P., Cannon, J., Eisenband, J.G., & Pappas, S. (2006). Mathematical thinking and learning. In K. McCartney & D. Phillips (Eds.), *Handbook of early child development* (pp. 208–229). Oxford, England: Blackwell.

Ginsburg, H.P., & Golbeck, S.L. (2004). Thoughts on the future of research on mathematics and science learning and education. *Early Childhood Research Quarterly, 19*, 190–200. doi:10.1016/j.ecresq.2004.01.013

Ginsburg, H.P., Greenes, C., & Balfanz, R. (2003). *Big math for little kids: Classroom set.* Parsippany, NJ: Dale Seymour.

Ginsburg, H.P., Kaplan, R.G., Cannon, J., Cordero, M.I., Eisenband, J.G., Galanter, M., & Morgenlander, M. (2006). Helping early childhood educators to teach mathematics. In M. Zaslow & I. Martinez-Beck (Eds.), *Critical issues in early childhood professional development* (pp. 171–202). Baltimore, MD: Paul H. Brookes Publishing Co.

Ginsburg, H.P., Lewis, A., & Clements, M. (2008). *School readiness and early childhood education: What can we learn from federal investments in research on mathematics programs?* Paper presented at the working meeting on recent school readiness research: Guiding the synthesis of early childhood research, Washington, DC. Retrieved from http://aspe.hhs.gov/hsp/10/SchoolReadiness/apb3.pdf

Gordon, R., Kane, T.J., & Staiger, D.O. (2006). *Identifying effective teachers using performance on the job.* Washington, DC: The Brookings Institution.

Graham, T.A., Nash, C., & Paul, K. (1997). Young childrens exposure to mathematics: The child care context. *Early Childhood Education Journal, 25*(1), 31–38.

Greenes, C., Ginsburg, H.P., & Balfanz, R. (2004). Big math for little kids. *Early Childhood Research Quarterly, 19,* 159–166.

Greenfield, D.B., Jirout, J., Dominguez, X., Greenberg, A., Maier, M., & Fuccillo, J. (2009). Science in the preschool classroom: A programmatic research agenda to improve science. *Early Education and Development, 20*(2), 238–264. doi:10.1080/10409280802595441

Hamre, B.K., Justice, L.M., Pianta, R.C., Kilday, C., Sweeney, B., Downer, J.T., & Leach, A. (2010). Implementation fidelity of MyTeachingPartner literacy and language activities: Association with preschoolers' language and literacy growth. *Early Childhood Research Quarterly, 25,* 329–347. doi:10.1016/j.ecresq.2009.07.002

Hargreaves, A. (2005). Educational change takes ages: Life, career and generational factors in teachers' emotional responses to educational change. *Teaching and Teacher Education, 21,* 967–983. doi:10.1016/j.tate.2005.06.007

Hiebert, J., Gallimore, R., Garnier, H., Givvin, K.B., Hollingsworth, H., Jacobs, J., … Stigler, J. (2003). *Teaching mathematics in seven countries: Results from the TIMSS 1999 video study.* Washington, DC: Institute of Education Sciences, U.S. Department of Education.

Huberman, M. (1989). The professional life cycle of teachers. *Teachers College Record, 91*(1), 31–57.

Kinzie, M., Pianta, R.C., Whittaker, J., Foss, M.J., Pan, E., Lee, Y., Williford, A.P., & Thomas, J.B.. (2010). *MyTeachingPartner-Math/Science.* Charlottesville: The Center for Advanced Study of Teaching and Learning, Curry School of Education, University of Virginia.

Kinzie, M.B., Whittaker, J., McGuire, P., Lee, Y., & Kilday, C.R. (in submission). *Pre-kindergarten mathematics & science: Design-based research on curricular development.*

Klein, A., Starkey, P., & Ramirez, A. (2002). *Pre-K mathematics curriculum.* Glendale, IL: Scott Foresman.

Kolb, D.A. (1984). *Experiential learning: Experience as the source of learning and development.* Englewood Cliffs, NJ: Prentice-Hall.

LoCasale-Crouch, J., Konold, T., Pianta, R.C., Howes, C., Murchinal, M., Bryant, D., … Barbarin, O. (2007). Observed classroom quality profiles in state-funded prekindergarten programs and associations with teacher, program, and classroom characteristics. *Early Childhood Research Quarterly, 22,* 3–17. doi:10.1016/j.ecresq.2006.05.001

Mihalic, S. (2004). The importance of implementation fidelity. *Emotional and Behavioral Disorders in Youth, 4,* 83–86.

Moreno, R., & Ortegano-Layne, L. (2008). Do classroom exemplars promote the application of principles in teacher education? A comparison of videos, animations, and narratives. *Educational Technology Research & Development, 56,* 449–465. doi:10.1007/s11423-006-9027-0

National Association for the Education of Young Children & National Council of Teachers of Mathematics. (2002). *Early childhood mathematics: Promoting good beginnings.* Washington, DC: Authors.

National Center for Education Statistics. (2004). *The condition of education 2004.* Washington, DC: U.S. Department of Education.

National Center for Education Statistics. (2009). *The condition of education 2009.* Washington, DC: U.S. Department of Education.

National Center for Education Statistics. (2011). *Highlights from PISA 2009: Performance of U.S. 15-year-old students in reading, mathematics, and science literacy in an international context.* Washington, DC: U.S. Department of Education.

National Council of Teachers of Mathematics. (2006). *Curriculum focal points for prekindergarten through grade 8 mathematics: A quest for coherence.* Reston, VA: Authors.

National Mathematics Advisory Panel. (2008). *Final report of the National Mathematics Advisory Panel.* Washington, DC: U.S. Department of Education. Retrieved from http://www.ed.gov/about/bdscomm/list/mathpanel/report/final-report.pdf

National Research Council. (2005). *Mathematical and scientific development in early childhood.* Washington, DC: National Academies Press.

National Research Council. (2006). *National science education standards.* Washington, DC: National Academies Press.

National Research Council. (2007). *Enhancing professional development for teachers: Potential uses of information technology.* Washington, DC: The National Academies Press.

National Research Council. (2009). *Mathematics learning in early childhood: Paths toward excellence and equity.* Washington, DC: National Academies Press.

Nye, B., Konstantopoulos, S., & Hedges, L.V. (2004). How large are teacher effects? *Educational Evaluation and Policy Analysis, 26*(3), 237–257.

O'Donnell, C. (2008). Defining, conceptualizing, and measuring fidelity of implementation and its relationship to outcomes in K–12 curriculum intervention research. *Review of Educational Research, 78*(1), 33–84. doi:10.3102/0034654307313793

Pianta, R.C., Howes, C., Burchinal, M., Bryant, D., Clifford, R., Early, D., & Barbarin, O. (2005). Features of pre-kindergarten programs, classrooms, and teachers: Do they predict observed classroom quality and child-teacher interactions? *Applied Developmental Science, 9*(3), 144–159. doi:10.1207/s1532480xads0903_2

Pianta, R.C., La Paro, K.M., & Hamre, B.K. (2008). *Classroom Assessment Scoring System^{TM} (CLASS^{TM}).* Baltimore, MD: Paul H. Brookes Publishing Co.

Pianta, R.C., Mashburn, A.J., Downer, J.T., Hamre, B.K., & Justice, L. (2008). Effects of web-mediated professional development resources on teacher–child interactions in pre-kindergarten classrooms. *Early Childhood Research Quarterly, 23*(4), 431–598. doi:10.1016/j.ecresq.2008.02.001

Powell, C.B., Pamplin, K.L., Blake, R.E., & Mason, D.S. (2010). Summer professional development in chemistry for inservice teachers using OWL Quick Prep. *Journal of Science Education and Technology, 19*(2), 126–132. doi:10.1007/s10956-009-9186-y

Putnam, R.T., & Borko, H. (2000). What do new views of knowledge and thinking have to say about research on teacher learning? *Educational Researcher, 29*(4), 4–15. doi:10.2307/1176586

Santagata, R. (2009). Designing video-based professional development for mathematics teachers in low-performing schools. *Journal of Teacher Education, 60,* 38–51. doi:10.1177/0022487108328485

Sarama, J., Clements, D.H., Starkey, P., Klein, A., & Wakeley, A. (2008). Scaling up the implementation of a pre-kindergarten mathematics curriculum: Teaching for understanding with trajectories and technologies. *Journal of Research on Educational Effectiveness, 1,* 89–119. doi:10.1080/19345740801941332

Schön, D.A. (1987). *Educating the reflective practitioner: Toward a new design for teaching and learning in the professions.* San Francisco, CA: Jossey-Bass.

Starkey, P., Klein, A., & Wakeley, A. (2004). Enhancing young children's mathematical knowledge through a pre-kindergarten mathematics intervention. *Early Childhood Research Quarterly, 19,* 99–120. doi:10.1016/j.ecresq.2004.01.002

Stipek, D. (2008). The price of inattention to mathematics in early childhood education is too great. *Society for Research in Child Development Social Policy Report, 22,* 13.

Tu, T. (2006). Preschool science environment: What is available in a preschool classroom? *Early Childhood Education Journal, 33*(4), 245–251. doi:10.1007/s10643-005-0049-8

U.S. Department of Education. (2000). *Does professional development change teaching practice? Results from a three-year study; Executive Summary.* Washington, DC: Office of the Under Secretary, Planning and Evaluation Service, Elementary and Secondary Education Division.

Willingham, D.T. (2005). Do visual, auditory, and kinesthetic learners need visual, auditory, and kinesthetic instruction? *American Educator, 29*(2).

Yoon, K.S., Duncan, T., Lee, S. W.Y., Scarloss, B., & Shapley, K.L. (2007). *Reviewing the evidence on how teacher professional development affects student achievement.* Wasington, DC: National Center for Educational Evaluation and Regional Assistance, Institute of Education Sciences, U.S. Department of Education.

Zaslow, M., Tout, K., Halle, T., Whittaker, J.V., & Lavelle, B. (2010). *Toward the identification of features of effective professional development for early childhood educators: Literature review.* Washington, DC: Child Trends.

3

Improving Preschool Education with Curriculum Enhancements and Professional Development

The Head Start REDI Intervention Model

Celene E. Domitrovich, Karen L. Bierman,
Robert L. Nix, Sukhdeep Gill, and Scott D. Gest

Early education has become a primary strategy for improving the long term academic success of the nation's children. This approach is based on research documenting that a high-quality preschool experience improves children's school readiness and promotes benefits over time including higher scores on standardized achievement tests, lower levels of special education, and lower dropout rates (Burchinal, Peisner-Feinberg, Pianta, & Howes, 2002; Howes et al., 2008; National Institute of Child Health and Human Development [NICHD] Early Child Care Research Network, ECCRN, 2004). For high-risk children such as those growing up in poverty, preschool is especially important for providing the cognitive stimulation and emotional support that may be lacking in the child's social context but that are necessary for the development of school readiness skills (Bierman, Nix, & Makin-Byrd, 2008; Senechal & LeFevre, 2002). Although there are individual differences in children's social-emotional, self-regulation, and cognitive skills, all of these capacities are malleable through early educational experiences.

Not all preschool experiences are of equal value to children. The quality of the preschool experience is a critical factor determining its impact on child school readiness (Mashburn et al., 2008; NICHD EC-CRN, 2004). Accumulating research suggests that two distinct aspects of quality are important: the content and focus of the preschool curriculum (e.g., what is being taught) and the quality of the teaching process which is reflected in the nature of teacher–child interactions (e.g., how the classroom is organized and managed and how learning activities are structured and supported). Enhancing preschool curriculum has proven effective in building child skills in both cognitive and social-emotional domains (Bierman, Domitrovich, & Darling, 2009; Lonigan, Burgess, & Anthony, 2000; Sarama & Clements, 2009). However, providing enhanced curricula alone, without attending to the quality of teaching practices, may limit the impact on child outcomes (Wasik, Bond, & Hindman, 2006). Ideally, efforts to improve preschool quality include a dual emphasis on enriching the content of the curriculum to ensure that key school readiness skills receive attention, and providing teachers with the professional development (PD) needed to promote high-quality and developmentally appropriate teaching practices and supportive student–teacher relationships.

In this chapter we present findings from the Head Start REDI (Research-based developmentally informed) project, an intervention that integrated the provision of curriculum-based enhancements targeting emergent literacy and social-emotional skills with multifaceted and sustained PD support to teachers. First, we describe the theoretical and empirical rationale for the REDI intervention design, along with the content and structure of program delivery and PD support. Then, we review research evidence from the randomized controlled trial, describing the impact of the REDI intervention on teaching quality and child school readiness outcomes. Overall, the findings we present suggest that the extensive emphasis on PD included in the REDI program produced significant improvements in teaching quality, particularly among teachers who were open and responsive to the mentoring process. In a final set of analyses conducted for the purpose of this chapter, we explore how the observed quality of teaching in the classroom and the enriched curriculum both contributed to growth in children's school readiness skills. We conclude that, in the quest to improve preschool quality and child school readiness, it is valuable to include a focus on teacher PD and general teaching skills in the context of delivering a specific enriched curriculum. We then discuss the implications of the findings for future research on the PD of early childhood teachers and models of early childhood intervention.

BUILDING BLOCKS OF SCHOOL READINESS: THE VALUE OF ENHANCING PRESCHOOL CURRICULUM

Models of early childhood education encourage teachers to provide rich preschool environments that allow children to learn through active exploration and responsive discussion with sensitive adults (Bredekamp & Copple, 1997; National Association for the Education of Young Children, 2010; Roopnarine & Johnson, 2009). This places considerable burden on teachers to identify activities that are highly interactive, engaging, and sequenced to enhance child skill acquisition. Evidence-based preschool curricula facilitate effective preschool education by supplying teachers with learning objectives and instructional activities that are validated in developmental research and by helping them select and organize learning activities in a systematic and strategic way so that children are exposed sequentially to the developmental skills associated with school readiness. Prior research supports the use of curricula to guide instruction in both emergent literacy and social-emotional domains (Bierman & Erath, 2006; Justice & Pullen, 2003).

Preschool Curricula that Promote Emergent Literacy Skills

In the domain of emergent literacy skills, evidence-based curricula focus both on activities that build specific emergent literacy skills and those that strengthen language skills more generally, based upon developmental research documenting the importance of both types of skills for later reading (Dickinson & Neumann, 2006). Specifically, longitudinal research has established that one of the strongest predictors of early elementary reading success is the preschool acquisition of component skills that help children decode printed text, including phonological awareness (e.g., the ability to recognize and manipulate the smaller units of sound within spoken words, such as syllables and phonemes), letter-recognition, and knowledge of letter-sound correspondence (Scarborough, 2001). Even when intellectual ability and vocabulary skills are controlled, letter knowledge and phonological awareness predict enhanced levels of reading proficiency in first and second grade (Snow, Burns, & Griffin, 1998). In addition, as children move through the elementary grades, oral language skills play an increasingly important role in reading comprehension. Both vocabulary and the ability to understand and produce grammatically varied utterances and narratives are necessary for children to be able to extract meaning from printed text and to understand and follow teachers' oral instructions (Dickinson, McCabe, Anastasopoulos, Peisner-Feinberg, & Poe, 2003). Economically disadvantaged children are less likely than peers living in higher socioeconomic-status families to have reading materials available in the home, to experience interactive reading with parents and other adults, or to engage in complex conversations (Senechal & LeFevre, 2002). As a result, their exposure to the kind of rich, decontextualized talk that expands vocabulary and promotes narrative skill is often limited.

Research has demonstrated that it is possible to reduce the school readiness gap by providing teachers with systematic curricula and learning materials that promote these specific language and emergent literacy skills. These types of interventions are typically universal models that are delivered in the classroom. Learning games that explicitly target children's listening skills improve children's phonological awareness and thereby enhance reading ability (Adams, Foorman, Lundberg, & Beeler, 1998). Studies also have tested the impact of providing children with instruction in alphabetic principles, alone and in combination with intervention, to promote phonological awareness, and found that both curriculum components have added value in producing gains in reading achievement (Assel, Landry, Swank, & Gunnewig, 2007; Ball & Blachman, 1991; Lonigan et al., 2000). When book reading is more interactive and includes scripted questions within the text and the presentation of props to foster word knowledge, it promotes richer conversational exchanges in the classroom and gains in child vocabulary and oral comprehension skills (Wasik & Bond, 2001; Wasik et al., 2006; Whitehurst, Arnold, Epstein, & Angell, 1994; Whitehurst, Epstein, et al., 1994). These studies validate the approach of enhancing preschool programs with evidence-based curricula to promote emergent literacy skills; they provide teachers with developmentally sequenced learning activities, which assure that children are exposed systematically to the emergent literacy skills needed to support their readiness to read at school entry.

Preschool Curricula that Promote Social-Emotional Skills

Language and emergent literacy skills are essential for school readiness, but when asked what children need to be successful in kindergarten, most teachers place equal emphasis on behavioral and social-emotional aspects of school readiness, such as the ability to pay attention, follow directions, and get along with others (Rimm-Kaufman, Pianta, & Cox, 2000). Evidence-based preschool curricula have also proven effective in promoting these social-emotional skills.

Self-management is one skill domain that is essential for both academic and social success. Children who are able to maintain attention to tasks, manage their behavior, and work cooperatively with other children exhibit higher levels of achievement in school than children with delays or impairments in these skills (Hughes & Kwok, 2006; McClelland, Acock, & Morrison, 2006). In addition, emotion knowledge, perspective-taking, and social problem-solving skills enable children to manage the demands of the kindergarten classroom. Studies show concurrent associations among these social-emotional skills and cognitive abilities in early childhood (Garner & Waajid, 2008; Miller, Gouley, Seifer, Dickstein, & Shields, 2004), and longitudinal research suggests that social-emotional and self-regulation skills are uniquely related to children's academic achievement, primarily through their influence on classroom participation and social engagement (Ladd, Birch, & Buhs, 1999).

Several evidence-based curricula have been developed to promote social-emotional skills in young children. Similar to the interventions in the language and literacy domain, the majority of these are universal approaches delivered by teachers through explicit lessons and activities (Bierman et al., 2009; Joseph & Strain, 2003). In most cases, these curricula attempt to build skills in several key domains simultaneously, including prosocial behaviors (e.g., helping, sharing, taking turns), emotional understanding (e.g., recognizing and labeling the feelings of oneself and others), and self-control and social problem-solving skills for effective conflict management (Domitrovich, Cortes, & Greenberg, 2007; Lynch, Geller, & Schmidt, 2004; Webster-Stratton, Reid, & Hammond, 2004). In some cases, the emphasis is on one particular skill domain, such as social problem-solving skills (Shure & Spivack, 1982) or emotional understanding (Izard et al., 2008; Izard, Trentacosta, King, & Mostow, 2004). Research on the efficacy of these interventions confirms that systematic curricula and learning activities can be implemented by early childhood educators and promote significant growth in social-emotional competencies (Domitrovich et al., 2007; Izard et al., 2004, 2008; Lynch et al., 2004; Webster-Stratton et al., 2004).

TEACHING QUALITY AND ITS RELATION TO CHILD SCHOOL READINESS

Observational studies of preschool classrooms indicate that the quality of teacher-student interactions influence learning (Curby, Rimm-Kaufman, & Ponitz, 2009; Mashburn et al., 2008). Research on teaching quality suggests that there are specific types of interactions between students and teachers in preschool settings that foster school readiness (NICHD ECCRN, 2000) and contribute to higher levels of achievement in early elementary school (Howes et al., 2008; NICHD ECCRN, 2004; Peisner-Feinberg et al., 2001). Two particularly important areas of teaching quality involve 1) teachers' use of language in the classroom and the way they implement learning activities, and 2) teachers' positive behavior management strategies and sensitivity to children's emotional needs.

Language Use and Instructional Support

The linguistic development of young children is fostered in the context of conversational exchanges with others. Research shows that adults play an active role in shaping this process by expanding and recasting what children say and by using richer and more nuanced vocabulary, different verb tenses, and grammatically varied sentence structures (Nelson & Welsh, 1998). This type of language scaffolding has been studied primarily in the context of book reading (Dickinson, 2001) but can take place anywhere in the classroom and have an impact on student skill growth (Gest, Holland-Coviello, Welsh, Eicher-Catt, & Gill, 2006). When teachers provide a language-rich classroom environment, children benefit in areas of language development and reading readiness (Beals, DeTemple, & Dickinson, 1994; Dickinson & Tabors, 2001; NICHD ECCRN, 2000). Interventions that enhance the quality of language exchanges between teachers and young children significantly improve the number of children's utterances and multiword combinations (Girolametto, Weitzman, & Greenberg, 2003).

Research suggests that providing explicit curriculum components alone is typically not sufficient to promote improvements in teaching quality, unless there are concurrent changes in the nature of the interactions between teachers and students in the classroom setting (Justice, Mashburn, Hamre, & Pianta, 2008). For this reason, in recent years researchers have begun to combine evidence-based curriculum enrichments with extended PD activities for teachers, in order to strengthen the generalized impact of the curriculum on child skill acquisition.

Recognizing the importance of teacher language use for children's emergent literacy skill development, Wasik et al. (2006) developed an evidence-based curriculum in interactive reading (with sequenced and scripted books, lessons, and materials), and enriched it with additional PD for teachers. The extra training that teachers received focused on general strategies of language use in the classroom, designed to improve the quality of teacher–student language exchanges in the classrooms. The PD model involved a repeating sequence of short training sessions on specific strategies, modeling by the program developer, observation of the teacher using the new strategies in the classroom, and oral and written feedback. Teachers received an average of two hours of coaching per month. The study was not designed to disentangle the individual contributions of each of the intervention components, but rather to enrich the impact of the overall curriculum by providing teachers with the PD they needed to teach the curriculum effectively and generalize the language strategies that were part of the curriculum throughout the day. The intervention had positive effects on both teacher and student outcomes (Wasik et al., 2006). Observations confirmed that the intervention teachers engaged in more conversation that was of high-quality (i.e., open-ended questions) during book reading and throughout the day. Direct assessments of children's language skills also indicated that the program was a success. Children whose teachers received the intervention displayed better vocabulary on the Expressive One-Word Picture Vocabulary Test and greater receptive language on the Peabody Picture Vocabulary Test–III (Wasik et al., 2006).

Positive Classroom Management and Emotional Support

High quality teaching in early childhood promotes student social competence in addition to language and cognitive skills, and research has linked several specific teaching practices with the acquisition of social-emotional skills (Mashburn & Pianta, 2006). For example, positive discipline–which relies on classroom rules, specific praise to reinforce desired behaviors, minimal use of controlling directions, and the avoidance of punitive strategies, such as threats or rebukes–is associated with improvements in both language development and adaptive student behavior (Arnold, McWilliams, & Arnold, 1998; Whitebook, Howes, & Phillips, 1990). Child self-regulation skills are fostered when teachers provide clear expectations and predictable and appropriate routines, rather than relying on directives and negative consequences (Raver, Jones, Li-Grining, Zhai, Bub, & Pressler, in press). Similarly, the use of induction strategies, in which teachers provide reminders, cues, and feedback to help children monitor their own behavior and self-correct, is thought to encourage student self-control efforts (Berkowitz & Grych, 1998; Bierman, 2004).

In addition, teachers who develop warm and positive relationships with their students foster a sense of security that encourages exploration and active engagement in learning (Howes & Smith, 1995; Kontos & Wilcox-Herzog, 1997; NICHD ECCRN, 1998). Student–teacher relationships develop over time through repeated exchanges and are typically conceptualized in terms of the degree to which they are positive and supportive or characterized by conflict (Mashburn & Pianta, 2006). A positive student–teacher relationship has been shown to facilitate language learning (Dickinson & Smith, 1994) and to contribute independently to children's academic adjustment in elementary school and middle school (Burchinal et al., 2002).

Teachers who also create emotionally supportive classroom environments create a context for social-emotional learning. Specifically, those teachers who validate children's emotions and respond with empathy when children are upset facilitate a similar prosocial and empathic orientation in them that carries over into peer interactions, thus fostering social competence (Gottman, Katz, & Hooven, 1997). When conflicts arise between students, teachers who use social problem-solving dialogue can enhance children's skills for nonaggressive conflict management by helping them identify the problem, generate and select a solution that is acceptable to everyone, and implement their plan (Denham & Burton, 2003; Shure & Spivack, 1982).

Two intervention studies document the value of providing preschool teachers with PD support focused on promoting their positive classroom management skills. In a study designed to promote social-emotional competence and prevent conduct problems in young children (preschool through first grade), Webster-Stratton, Reid, and Stoolmiller (2008) tested the efficacy of the Incredible Years teacher management and child social-emotional curriculum (Dinosaur School) as a universal prevention program. This comprehensive program includes teacher training focused on promoting positive classroom management skills and a social-emotional curriculum that provides lessons in prosocial behavior, emotional understanding, and self-control. The PD training in this trial included four days of in-service training, delivered during monthly workshops. In addition, a trained program staff visited the classroom regularly and co-led all Dinosaur School lessons with the teacher. Similar to other early childhood interventions that involve the combination of curricular components and PD, the trial was not designed to examine to effects of the individual components but the power of the combination. Compared with teachers in the "usual practice" control classrooms, teachers in the intervention were rated as warmer, more affectionate, more consistent, and less punitive in their interactions with students (Webster-Stratton et al., 2008). Moreover, children whose teachers delivered the curriculum and participated in the training workshops displayed more social competence and emotion regulation and less aggression, with the effects greatest for children who exhibited elevated behavior problems at the start of the year.

A second, independent randomized controlled trial of an adapted version of the Incredible Years program validated the power of this intervention to improve teaching practices. In the Chicago School Readiness program, teachers received 30 hours of workshop training focused on supporting children's emotional and behavioral regulation through nonpunitive classroom management strategies. Teachers were also taught stress management strategies to counteract the negative effects of work-related stress in themselves. In-class mental health specialists supported teachers with individual "coaching." In addition, these mental health specialists developed targeted behavior management plans for children with the highest levels of emotional and behavioral problems. As a result of the intervention, teaching practices improved (Raver et al., 2008), and there was a reduction in children's internalizing and externalizing symptoms, assessed by teacher ratings and direct observations (Raver et al., 2009). Recent analyses suggest that children in the Chicago School Readiness Program also made gains in attention/impulse control and executive functioning, which accounted for further gains in vocabulary, letter naming, and early math skills (Raver et al., in press).

Summary

Overall, this accumulating research evidence suggests that two complementary approaches may produce optimal enhancements in preschool education quality and thereby help to close the gap in school readiness associated with early disadvantage. First, the content and focus of the preschool curriculum (e.g., what is being taught) needs to be enriched to ensure that it includes evidence-based approaches to promoting the emergent literacy, numeracy, and social-emotional skills that are core to school readiness. Second, the quality of the teaching practices and the nature of teacher–child interactions (e.g., how the classroom is organized and managed, how learning activities are structured and supported) need to be enhanced. In particular, teachers need to rely on evidence-based best practices to guide the way they interact with their students, especially in areas of language use, instructional support, behavior management, and emotion coaching (Domitrovich, Moore, & Greenberg, in press).

THE HEAD START RESEARCH-BASED DEVELOPMENTALLY INFORMED PROGRAM

In the next section, we describe the Head Start REDI program, which integrated curriculum-based enhancements targeting emergent literacy and social-emotional skills with the provision of multifaceted and sustained PD support focused on improving teaching quality. The broad goal of this dual emphasis was to improve the Head Start program impact on child school readiness. The theory underlying the REDI program is that improvements in children's language and literacy skills and social-emotional functioning would benefit from enrichment in areas of both the curriculum and the quality of teaching practices.

The REDI intervention targeted the promotion of specific school readiness competencies in the domain of cognitive development (i.e., language and emergent literacy skills) and the domain of social-emotional development (i.e., prosocial behavior, emotional understanding, self-regulation, and aggression control). The intervention was designed for delivery by classroom teachers and integrated into their ongoing classroom programs. It included curriculum-based lessons that followed a developmental sequence, center-based extension activities, and training in specific interaction strategies to be used by teachers throughout the day.

Language and Emergent Literacy Skills Enrichment

Four language and emergent literacy skills were targeted in REDI: 1) vocabulary, 2) syntax, 3) phonological awareness, and 4) print awareness. Three program components targeted these skills, including a set of sound games, alphabet center activities, and an interactive reading program. The sound games were designed to promote phonological awareness by focusing on listening skills, rhyming, alliteration, words and sentences, and syllables and phonemes (Adams et al., 1998). The games were organized developmentally, so that difficulty increased over the course of the year. Teachers were asked to use a 10–15 minute sound game activity at least three times per week.

To promote print knowledge, teachers were provided with a developmentally sequenced set of activities and materials to be used in their alphabet centers, including letter stickers, a letter bucket, materials to create a "Letter Wall," and craft materials for various letter-learning activities. Teachers were asked to make sure that each child visited the alphabet center several times per week, and they were given materials to track the children's acquisition of letter names.

The interactive reading curriculum was based on the program developed by Wasik and Bond (Wasik & Bond, 2001; Wasik et al., 2006), which was adapted from the program developed by Whitehurst and colleagues (Whitehurst et al., 1994). The REDI curriculum included two books per week, which were scripted with questions to help teachers encourage children's active engagement and lively discussion. Each book had a list of targeted vocabulary words that were presented with the aid of physical props and illustrations. Moreover, books were selected so that content coincided and reinforced lessons of the social-emotional skills curriculum.

In the REDI trial, teachers presented curriculum materials in a systematic way during the week, and also received mentoring in the use of "language coaching" strategies (such as expansions and grammatical recasts) to provide a general scaffold for language development in the classroom (Dickinson & Smith, 1994). The overall goal was to improve teachers' strategic use of language in ways that would increase children's oral language skills, including vocabulary, narrative, and syntax.

Social-Emotional Skills Enrichment

The preschool PATHS curriculum (Domitrovich, Greenberg, Kusche, & Cortes, 2005) was used in REDI to promote children's social-emotional skills. This curriculum targeted four domains: 1) prosocial friendship skills, 2) emotional understanding and expression skills, 3) self-control, such as the capacity to inhibit impulsive behavior and organize goal-directed activity, and 4) problem-solving skills focused on interpersonal negotiation and conflict resolution. The curriculum was divided into 33 lessons that are delivered by teachers during circle time. These lessons included modeling stories and discussions and utilized puppet characters, photographs, and teacher role-play demonstrations. Each lesson included extension activities, such as cooperative projects and games that provided children with opportunities to practice the target skills with teacher support at a later time. In REDI, teachers were asked to conduct one PATHS lesson and one extension activity each week.

Teachers were encouraged to help their children generalize the content of the PATHS lessons throughout the week. As previously stated, the books selected for interactive reading touched on the same topic as the PATHS lesson of the week and afforded an additional opportunity to discuss core concepts in a different context. In addition, teachers were encouraged to use positive classroom management and specific praise to model appropriate, respectful ways of interacting with others. They were also encouraged to use emotion coaching and induction strategies to promote appropriate self-control.

Professional Development

The REDI PD model included both formal workshops and coaching, which consisted of weekly classroom visits, modeling, technical assistance, and consultation. The training and support were designed not only to help teachers learn the mechanics of conducting the curriculum lessons in the context of Head Start, but also to help the teachers understand the theory and rationale for the enhancements.

Formal training workshops were delivered in a large-group format, with small-group breakout sessions used to facilitate discussion and reflection. Trainers utilized a variety of methods including didactic instruction, practice exercises, and videotape review and discussion. An initial 3-day workshop took place in the summer prior to the beginning of the school year. This workshop included approximately 1 half-day of general orientation, one day of language and literacy skill training, one day of social-emotional skill training, and 1 half-day of program-specific meetings about the logistics of implementing REDI. A second training workshop was held mid-year in January, and focused on more advanced teaching processes, such as the use of inductive strategies to promote self-regulation and the use of social problem-solving dialogue in the classroom. Both lead and assistant teachers attended these workshops and were encouraged to share responsibility for implementation.

Lead and assistant teachers also received weekly support provided by REDI trainers, local master teachers with several years of experience who were supervised by project-based educational consultants. The REDI trainers spent an average of 3 hours per week in each classroom observing, modeling intervention techniques, and team-teaching lessons.

In addition, REDI trainers spent an hour per week meeting with both the lead and assistant teachers to review progress. In these meetings, teachers first presented their weekly implementation form, describing what they had done, reflecting on the effectiveness of the various activities and lessons, and noting any teaching questions or challenges. This served as a platform for the REDI trainers to comment on specific positive teaching practices they had observed that week and to provide suggestions for improvements or solutions for challenges that were encountered.

In the second half of each meeting, REDI trainers reviewed specific teaching strategies that were a formal part of the intervention. These process strategies were organized hierarchically and introduced sequentially, according to frequency of use and the skill level required for implementation. During the first half of the year, REDI trainers focused on teaching strategies that were designed to promote a positive classroom environment, including the use of positive management strategies, such as specific praise and organizing transition routines, acknowledging and validating children's feelings, and preventing behavior problems. Trainers also introduced and emphasized language coaching strategies, especially the use of questions, expansions, and decontextualized talk, as well as the generalized use of target vocabulary. During the second half of the year, trainers emphasized strategies that could be used to respond to and refocus problem behaviors in positive ways, particularly the use of induction strategies and social problem-solving dialogue. The goal was to maximize the use of teaching strategies that supported child language and social-emotional skill development and minimize the use of strategies based on external controls, such as negative consequences and time-outs.

In presenting the various teaching strategies, REDI trainers used examples and videotaped models to introduce skill concepts, encouraged discussion about applying the specific strategy in the teachers' particular classrooms, and suggested practice activities. Teachers were encouraged to identify personal goals regarding their use of the focal teaching strategies in the coming week. Although REDI trainers presented the same sequence of strategies to all teachers, the pace was adjusted to accommodate individual teachers' mastery of the material.

OVERVIEW OF THE REDI INTERVENTION TRIAL

In the following sections, we review research evidence from the randomized controlled trial of REDI focused on the intervention impact on teaching quality and child outcomes. In new analyses conducted for this chapter we also examine how different patterns of enriched curriculum and high-quality teaching were associated with growth in child outcomes.

Design of the Evaluation Trial

Forty-four Head Start classrooms, including 88 head and assistant teachers and 356 4-year-old children, participated in the randomized controlled trial used to evaluate REDI. Approximately one-half of the participating classrooms were located in a larger, moderately densely populated urban county of Pennsylvania, and the other half were located in two smaller, rural counties of Pennsylvania. Head Start centers were stratified on county location, length of program day, the proportion of Spanish speaking children, and center size to assure even representation in the intervention and comparison conditions. Within each stratified group, centers were randomly assigned to intervention or the "as usual" comparison conditions. Teachers were studied as they implemented the REDI intervention for the first time.

To evaluate intervention effects, baseline and postintervention assessments were completed on all teachers and their students. Teacher assessments occurred at the end of the academic year prior to their implementation of REDI and at the end of the REDI implementation year and included self-reports and observations of teaching practices by the research team. Child assessments occurred at the beginning and end of the Head Start year and included direct testing of language, literacy, and social-emotional skills, observations of peer interactions, and teacher and parent ratings of behavior (for details, see Bierman, Domitrovich, et al., 2008, and Domitrovich, Gest, Gill, Bierman, et al., 2009).

Intervention Implementation

An important initial question was the degree to which teachers were able to effectively implement curriculum enrichments in both the language-literacy and social-emotional domains simultaneously. Although it was a scheduling challenge at first, particularly for teachers in half-day programs, most teachers were able to deliver the majority of the curriculum. Based upon teacher report, they conducted an average of 1.77 PATHS lessons and extension activities, 6.08 dialogic reading lessons, 2.57 sound games, and 3.56 alphabet center activities.

Several measures were collected to track the quality of the curriculum implementation. Each week, teachers rated the quality of their implementation of program components using 3-point scales (e.g., "Were you able to complete the lesson as written? How well did the children understand the major points of the lesson?") In addition, at the end of each month, REDI trainers rated the quality of the teachers' curriculum implementation, based on their observations in the classroom. The average teacher rating (across the year) was 2.78 (on a 3-point scale), reflecting the teachers' confidence in their implementation quality and their perceptions of positive child engagement. Similarly, across components, REDI trainers gave teachers average ratings of approximately "3" on the 4-point rating scale, reflecting good fidelity in the delivery of the curriculum components. REDI trainer ratings averaged between 3.0–3.5 on the 4-point scale for child engagement in the lessons, reflecting the ease with which teachers were able to engage students in the curriculum lessons. Hierarchical linear models were also applied to the REDI trainer ratings to examine growth patterns over the course of the school year. Trainer ratings of implementation quality increased significantly over the course of the year for interactive reading (teacher delivery and child engagement) and Alphabet center (child engagement) (see Domitrovich, Gest, Gill, Jones, & Sanford DeRousie, 2009). These findings suggest that the workshop and curriculum materials provided teachers with considerable support to implement the REDI program with fidelity from the very beginning; moreover, the ongoing support of REDI trainers helped teachers maintain those initial levels and improve their own skills and child engagement in some areas.

In addition to delivering curriculum components with fidelity, a key goal of the REDI program was to increase the quality of teaching practices. To assess the course of improvements in teaching quality, REDI trainers completed monthly ratings on teachers' generalized use of the teaching practices that were a focus of the intervention. Using a 5-point scale with multiple items for each domain, trainers rated language richness (e.g., recasts of children's statements to support grammatical understanding, decontextualized talk), social-emotional support (e.g., encourages the identification and labeling of feelings), behavior management (e.g., uses induction strategies to promote autonomy), and sensitivity-responsiveness (e.g., is available and warm). Hierarchical linear models were used to examine growth over time in teachers' use of these REDI teaching practices. Significant linear growth was documented in each of the four targeted teaching practices (see Domitrovich, Gest, Gill, Jones, et al., 2009, for more detail). Average ratings of language richness increased from 2.78 in September to 3.49 in April, indicating that teachers showed a steady increase in the quality of their language use in the classroom (on the 5-point rating scale, 3 = *sometimes*). Average ratings of social-emotional support increased from 2.80–3.63 over the course of the year. Average ratings of behavior management increased from 3.02–3.71, and average ratings of sensitivity responsiveness increased from 3.42–3.93. These findings suggest that the ongoing support from the REDI trainer was particularly important and useful in promoting changes in the use of the broader teaching practices advocated by the program. Put another way, teachers showed fairly high-quality and consistent implementation of the scripted lessons in the REDI curriculum from the very beginning of the year. The mastery of the high-quality teaching practices (which were not scripted and required more teacher skill and creativity) took longer, but teachers were able to use the ongoing support and mentorship of the REDI trainers to continually improve in the quality of these teaching practices over the course of the year.

In the Domitrovich et al. (2009b) study, we also explored the degree to which certain characteristics of teachers or their job situations might affect their implementation of the REDI curriculum and teaching practices. We examined several sets of preintervention factors, including teachers' PD (i.e., formal education, amount of on-the-job training, and years of teaching experience), teachers' stress level and overall emotional wellbeing (i.e., depression, feelings of efficacy regarding their teaching, and degree of emotional exhaustion experienced on the job), teachers' perceptions of their work environment (i.e., satisfaction, climate, values, and support), teachers' ratings of the acceptability of the intervention, and REDI trainers' perceptions of their working alliance with teachers. We found that education level uniquely predicted language richness and social-emotional support. We also found that teachers who reported being more emotionally exhausted at the end of the academic year prior to intervention were rated by REDI trainers as engaging in richer patterns of language interactions and more effective behavior management practices over the year. This likely reflects the fact that rich language use and effective behavior management are effortful, and good teachers are more tired by the end of the year than teachers who show lower levels of high-quality interactions with their students. Teachers' ratings of the acceptability of the intervention were related to improvements in social-emotional support. By far, however, REDI trainers' ratings of teachers' openness to consultation was the best predictor of implementation of the focal teaching practices, being related to growth in language richness, social-emotional support, behavior management, and sensitivity responsiveness. These findings highlight important relations between the PD process and growth in the use of high-quality, effective teaching practices.

REDI INTERVENTION OUTCOMES

Teaching Outcomes

The ratings provided by teachers and REDI trainers during the course of the year suggested a positive intervention impact on teaching quality. However, both teachers and trainers were involved in the intervention itself, which could produce biased viewpoints. Therefore, to provide an unbiased evaluation of the impact of intervention on teaching quality, end-of-year observations of teachers were conducted by research assistants. These assistants conducted observations in intervention and "usual practice" classrooms, and were blind to study condition. In their direct observations, they utilized three rating scales: the Teaching Style Rating Scale (TSRS; Domitrovich, Cortes, & Greenberg, 2000), the Classroom Assessment Scoring System (La Paro & Pianta, 2003), and the Classroom Language and Literacy Environment Observation (CLEO; Holland-Coviello, 2005). The TSRS assessed positive discipline (e.g., use of specific praise and redirection), classroom management (e.g., preparedness and use of consistent routines), and positive emotional climate (e.g., scaffolding to help students regulate emotions). The CLASS assessed emotional support (e.g., positive climate) and instructional support (e.g., concept development and quality of feedback). The CLEO included time samplings of language use (e.g., number of statements made, number of questions asked, and instances of decontextualized talk) and ratings of language richness-sensitivity (e.g., elaboration of children's utterances).

Compared with teachers in the Head Start "as usual" condition, teachers in Head Start REDI received significantly or marginally significantly higher scores on the TRSR positive emotional climate and classroom management scales, the CLASS instructional support scale, the CLEO counts of positive language use, and the CLEO ratings of language richness-sensitivity. A summary of these analyses is presented in Table 3.1 (see Domitrovich et al. (2009a), for details about the analyses and for results regarding specific subscales). These intervention effect sizes were moderate to large, ranging from .39–.89, and representing differences between teachers in the two conditions of more than one-third standard deviation to almost one full standard deviation.

These findings indicate that the REDI intervention successfully improved teaching quality. Compared with the control group, REDI teachers established a more positive classroom climate, used more preventive behav-

Table 3.1.   Impact of Head Start REDI on broad summary scales of teaching quality

	Control group mean (SD)	Intervention group mean (SD)	Effect size (p-value)
Emotional-behavioral Support			
Positive emotional climate (TSRS)	2.52 (1.05)	3.18 (1.24)	.69[a]*
Emotional support (CLASS)	5.65 (.81)	5.97 (.45)	.39
Classroom management (TSRS)	4.09 (.71)	4.32 (.67)	.60[a]**
Positive discipline (TSRS)	3.91 (.91)	4.39 (.72)	.65[a]
Cognitive-linguistic Support			
Instructional support (CLASS)	3.76 (.72)	4.14 (.68)	.45+
Statements (CLEO)	5.77 (1.78)	7.03 (1.58)	.82***
Questions (CLEO)	2.98 (1.15)	3.95 (1.20)	.89***
Decontextualized utterances (CLEO)	.61 (.64)	1.06 (.86)	.68**
Language richness-sensitivity (CLEO)	3.07 (.53)	3.41 (.44)	.67**

Domitrovich, C.E., Gest, S.D., Gill, S., Bierman, K.L., Welsh, J.A., & Jones, D., *American Educational Research Journal,* 46 pp. 567–597, copyright © 2009 by American Educational Research Association Reprinted by Permission of SAGE Publications.

+ $p < .10$ * $p < .05$ ** $p < .01$ *** $p < .001$

[a]Because modal values tended to be near scale extremes for outcomes from the TSRS, random-effects ordered probit models were used to analyze treatment differences and estimate p-values. For the same reason, for outcomes from the TSRS, we are presenting Vargha and Delaney's A, which is a nonparametric effect size estimate appropriate for any ordinal variable regardless of distribution, rather than Cohen's d, which is sensitive to deviations from normality. An A of .56, .64, and .71 corresponds to a small, medium, and large effect size, respectively (Vargha & Delaney, 2000).

Key: TSRS = Teaching Style Rating Scale, CLASS = Classroom Assessment Scoring System, CLEO = Classroom Language and Literacy Environment Observation, REDI = Research-based developmentally informed.

ior management strategies, and talked with children more frequently and in more cognitively complex ways. Additional analyses revealed this effect was not moderated by teacher status, suggesting that both lead and assistant teachers made similar significant changes in their behavior as a result of participating in REDI. Although unique contributions cannot be disentangled, the changes in multiple aspects of teaching quality were likely the result of providing enhanced curriculum materials in the language-literacy and social-emotional domains that facilitated the kinds of teacher–student interactions we wanted to see, and they were likely the result of intensive PD and ongoing mentorship provided throughout the intervention year.

Child Outcomes

In addition to showing positive effects on teaching quality, the Head Start REDI program successfully accelerated children's growth in the targeted domains of language and emergent literacy skills and social-emotional competence. Children's vocabulary and language skills were assessed with the Expressive One-Word Picture Vocabulary Test (Brownell, 2000). Emergent literacy skills were assessed with a composite of the Blending, Elision, and Print Awareness scales of the Test of Preschool Early Literacy (Lonigan, Wagner, Torgesen, & Rashotte, 2007). Children's emotional knowledge was assessed with the Emotion Recognition Questionnaire (Ribordy, Camras, Stafani, & Spacarelli, 1988). Their social problem-solving skills were assessed by counting the number of competent responses they freely generated on the Challenging Situations Task (Denham, Bouril, & Belouad, 1994). Children's behavior was also directly observed. In a procedure developed for this study, we assigned children to small time-limited play groups of classmates and collected ratings of their social competence (e.g., prosocial behavior, emotion regulation skill) and aggression as they negotiated the collective use of novel toys.

Hierarchical linear models, accounting for the nesting of children within classrooms, indicated that children in Head Start REDI exhibited significantly more growth during the prekindergaren year in vocabulary, emergent literacy, emotion recognition, and social problem-solving skills, compared with children in control group classrooms. Marginally significant findings suggested that they also displayed more social competence in the classroom at the end of the year. A summary of some of the results from these analyses is presented in Table 3.2 (see Bierman et al., 2008, for details of these analyses and results for other outcomes). These adjusted intervention effect sizes were small to moderate, ranging from .15–.45, and represented differences in growth between children in the intervention and control group classrooms of about one sixth to almost one-half of a standard deviation.

THE IMPORTANCE OF BOTH HIGH-QUALITY TEACHING AND AN ENRICHED CURRICULUM

An assumption of the REDI intervention design was that a dual focus on enriched curriculum and promoting high-quality teaching practices would maximize positive effects for children. One way to examine those relations was to examine the different patterns of enriched curriculum and high-quality teaching that existed in our sample. Thus, in additional analyses we categorized classrooms according to whether they were in the intervention or control condition—and hence included the enriched or standard Head Start curriculum—and whether teachers demonstrated above- or below-average levels of

Table 3.2. Impact of Head Start REDI on child skills and behaviors

	Control group mean (SD)	Intervention group mean (SD)	Effect size (p-value)
Vocabulary	41.03 (11.24)	42.79 (11.55)	.15*
Emergent literacy skills	-.24 (.94)	.21 (1.00)	.45***
Emotion recognition skills	1.52 (.26)	1.61 (.24)	.23*
Social problem-solving skills	2.29 (2.05)	3.16 (2.55)	.35**
Social competence (observer ratings)	2.21 (.53)	2.36 (.49)	.26+
Aggression (observer ratings)	.37 (.34)	.30 (.31)	-.19

From Bierman, K.L., Domitrovich, C.E., Nix, R.L., Gest, S.D., Welsh, J., Greenberg, M.T., ... Gill, S. (2008). Promoting academic and social-emotional school readiness: The Head Start REDI program. *Child Development, 79*(6), 1802–1817. Child development by SOCIETY FOR RESEARCH IN CHILD DEVELOPMENT Reproduced with permission of BLACKWELL PUBLISHING, INC. in the format Journal via Copyright Clearance Center.

+ p < .10 * p < .05 ** p < .01 *** p < .001

Key: REDI = Research-based developmentally informed.

teaching quality. We hypothesized that children in those classrooms with the enriched curriculum and high-quality teaching would show the most improvement over the course of the prekindergarten year, and that children in the classrooms with neither the enriched curriculum nor high-quality teaching would show the least improvement. Most important, these analyses could reveal when the enriched curriculum, even in the absence of high-quality teaching, had a positive effect, and when high-quality teaching, in the absence of an enriched curriculum, had a positive effect.

To create an overall indicator of teaching quality, we standardized the end-of-year TSRS total score, the CLASS total score, the CLEO time-sampling of language use, and the CLEO ratings of language richness-sensitivity. We then took an average of these four standardized scores ($\alpha = .80$) and divided classrooms according to whether they were above or below average on that global indicator of teaching quality. Overall, there were 17 classrooms in the intervention condition with above-average teaching quality by the end of the year, 5 classrooms in the intervention condition with below-average teaching quality, 10 classrooms in the control condition with above-average teaching quality, and 12 classrooms in the control condition with below-average teaching quality.

We created dichotomous indicators denoting which classrooms fell into each of the four categories. To examine how the combination of enriched curriculum and teaching quality affected children's outcomes, we reran the hierarchical linear models we initially used to assess the efficacy of the REDI intervention on children's growth in language-literacy and social-emotional skills. However, in these models we substituted three dichotomous indicators representing the combination of enriched curriculum and teaching quality for the single indicator of intervention condition. Using control condition classrooms with below-average teaching quality as the default category, these three dichotomous indicators revealed relative change for children in the other kinds of classrooms. Because all continuous variables were standardized, the parameter estimate for each dichotomous indicator is similar to an adjusted effect size. The results of these analyses are presented in Table 3.3.

The value in the first column of the first row reveals that children in the classrooms that included the enriched curriculum and high-quality teaching tended to score .13 of a standard deviation higher in vocabulary at the end of the Head Start year, compared with children in classrooms without the enriched curriculum and with lower-quality teaching ($p < .10$). Students in these classrooms also had significantly higher levels of vocabulary at the end of the year compared with students in the control group classrooms with above-average teaching quality, highlighting the importance of the interaction between the enriched curricula and high-quality teaching for growth in vocabulary and language skills.

The values in the second row suggest that children in classrooms with the enriched curriculum, regardless of whether they had high- or lower-quality teaching, received scores more than one third of a standard deviation higher

Table 3.3.   Combined effect of enriched curriculum and teaching quality on children's outcomes

	High-quality teaching in the intervention condition	High-quality teaching in the control conditon	Lower-quality teaching in the intervention condition
Vocabulary	.13+	-.07[b]	.03
Emergent literacy skills	.37***	.03[b]	.37**
Emotion recognition skills	.28*	.06	.17
Social problem-solving skills	.35*[a]	-.02[b]	.33
Social competence (observer ratings)	.39*	.32	.45+
Aggression (observer ratings)	-.36+	-.46*	-.49+

$+ p < .10$ * $p < .05$ ** $p < .01$ *** $p < .001$

Values represent children's growth in each kind of classroom, compared with children in classrooms with lower-quality teaching in the control condition. Superscript letters indicate additional significant differences ($p < .05$) between children in different kinds of classrooms. For example, children in intervention classrooms with high-quality teaching showed greater gains in vocabulary ($\beta = .21, p < .01$) than children in control condition classrooms with high-quality teaching. Although children showed less aggression if they were in any kind of classroom other than ones with lower-quality teaching in the control condition, there were no significant differences among children in the other three kinds of classrooms.

in emergent literacy skills, compared with children in classrooms without the enriched curriculum, regardless of teaching quality. This suggests that the enriched curriculum was more important than teaching quality in promoting growth in early literacy skills.

The values in the third row suggest that the combination of an enriched curriculum and high-quality teaching was especially important for growth in emotion recognition skills. When children were exposed to the enriched curriculum and high-quality teaching, they displayed the most growth.

This same finding held for growth in social problem-solving skills. However, the fact that the value for children in the small number of classrooms with the enriched curriculum but lower quality teaching was just slightly smaller than the value for children in classrooms with the enriched curriculum but high-quality teaching suggests that the enriched curriculum was probably more important than teaching quality for growth in social problem-solving skills.

The pattern of scores for observer ratings of social competence suggests that the presence of the enriched curriculum might be especially important for helping children learn how to play positively with peers. The pattern of scores for observer ratings of aggression suggests that either an enriched curriculum or high-quality teaching can be effective in reducing problems in this domain.

Although there are several factors, (selection effects and small numbers of classrooms in each cell) that qualify these results, the emerging pattern is provocative. These findings suggest that children did best in classrooms in which they received an enhanced language-literacy and social-emotional curriculum provided in the context of high-quality teaching. There was one instance in which the high-quality teaching that naturally occurred in the control group classrooms appeared sufficient to prevent a negative outcome (i.e., observed aggression), but more often the enhanced curriculum appeared to partially compensate for the lower quality of teaching children might experience (i.e., emergent literacy skills, social problem solving skills, social competence, and aggression). These exploratory analyses help elucidate the results from the randomized controlled trial and affirm the dual focus of the REDI intervention model on providing an enhanced curriculum and ongoing PD to improve teaching quality.

CONCLUSIONS

Historically, in the field of early childhood education there has been debate about the use of explicit instruction to promote cognitive development (Elkind & Whitehurst, 2001). Those educators against the approach are concerned that this method has the potential to undermine teaching quality and children's social-emotional wellbeing by reducing sensitive responding and limiting child-initiated activities. Those educators in favor of explicit instruction hold that some children—particularly those children who are economically disadvantaged and less likely to experience cognitively stimulating environments at home—are able to learn at faster rates with specialized instructional support than they could by relying on their own initiative (Landry, Swank, Smith, Assel, & Gunnewig, 2006). These educators advocate for a developmentally appropriate use of instruction which is a balance of teacher-directed and child-centered approaches. Given the development and rapid dissemination of evidence-based academic and preventive interventions, many of which include some form of direct instruction, understanding this issue is critical to advancing the field of early education.

As described in this chapter, findings from the REDI trial demonstrate that it is possible to incorporate the use of explicit instruction to promote language, emergent literacy, and social-emotional skills while maintaining and even enhancing teaching quality (Bierman et al., 2008; Domitrovich et al., 2009a). Implementation research has shown that for an intervention to be effective, it must be conducted with fidelity to the original model (Durlak, 2010). For a universal curriculum such as REDI, this involves more than just conducting an adequate number of lessons or activities (i.e., dosage) and includes delivering those components with quality. High quality delivery adheres to the content of the program, engages and supports students, and includes generalizing the core concepts of the intervention throughout the day (Dusenbury, Brannigan, Hansen, Walsh, & Falco, 2005). Data from the REDI trial indicate that high levels of implementation across all of these indicators was achieved and that variation in implementation was related to child outcomes (Domitrovich et al., 2009b; Domitrovich, Gest, Jones, Gill, & DeRousie, 2010).

The REDI PD model was intensive and included the combination of training workshops and weekly mentoring. The mentoring provided by the trainers included classroom visits, modeling, and support provided through a variety of methods including reflection, discussion, and goal setting. Our belief when designing the program was that this model was necessary in order to provide the implementation support that would be needed to integrate multiple curriculum enhancements into a Head Start program which already included a base curriculum necessary for achieving federal standards. Our results suggest that with REDI trainer support teachers were able to make significant gains in multiple aspects of high-quality teaching. Moreover, those teachers who were open to consultation and receptive to our program tended to make the largest gains.

The PD of teachers will be a critically important focus of future research on evidence-based interventions. There is general consensus that providing teachers with ongoing coaching when introducing new curricula and teaching practices is a promising approach that is more effective than the use of traditional in-service training alone (Haskins & Loeb, 2007), but very little is known about the ideal structure (e.g. frequency, intensity) that should be followed or the ways in which it might need to be adjusted to address the needs of individual participants. There is very little research on the mechanisms by which coaching has a positive impact on teacher behavior. In order to develop theoretical models of PD, large scale studies of interventions that utilize various coaching strategies and that measure potential mechanisms of change are needed. The findings from these studies could then be used to develop standardized models to be tested in randomized trials. Including measures of individual and setting factors as moderators in these studies would enable further refinement of the models.

Recent studies have investigated the more general impact that preschool teaching quality has on child school readiness outcomes (Justice et al., 2008), and they suggest that curriculum interventions may be even more effective if they attend to and support teaching quality in more comprehensive ways, rather than simply focusing narrowly on the way that teachers are implementing specific lessons. When patterns of teaching quality were examined within the REDI control and interventions classrooms, it was the combination of the enriched curriculum with high-quality teaching that resulted in the greatest gains in children's school readiness skills. However, it was encouraging to see that the enriched curriculum could help children, even in the absence of high-quality teaching. Given that the promotion of high-quality teaching can occur in the context of implementing an empirically based, structured, and enriched curriculum, it likely limits impact to focus on high-quality teaching outside of such context. Ideally, attention to the curriculum and teaching quality can be considered simultaneously in the planning of professional development for practitioners in early education settings. Training does not have to be provided in the same way for every individual and more targeted intervention may be needed for teachers whose basic skills are lacking. It may be that for certain teachers who exhibit lower teaching quality, an explicit curriculum provides the structure that they need to develop deeper knowledge about a content area and refine the practices that are needed to execute it effectively. The structure and scaffolding provided by the curriculum—and facilitated by coaching support—might be more effective for these teachers than trying to inculcate principles of good teaching more abstractly.

Given the higher cost of more intensive coaching, it is important to develop empirically based decisions about the content of trainings, who they are delivered to, and when they are provided, so that training can be more cost effective to programs. For teachers who already display high-quality teaching, providing an enriched curriculum with relatively little professional support might be sufficient.

The collection of findings from Head Start REDI that are presented in this chapter suggest that enhancing the curriculum with evidence-based components and improving overall teaching quality should be considered as a comprehensive strategy to maximize the impact of the Head Start experience on children's school readiness. The REDI findings add to the results from other studies (Dickinson & Sprague, 2001; Girolametto, Weitzman, Lefebvre, & Greenberg, 2007; Wasik et al., 2006; Webster-Stratton, Reid, & Hammond, 2001) that suggest curriculum enhancements facilitate school readiness outcomes in settings that range in teaching quality, but that their effectiveness is optimized when they are implemented by teachers who also have good teaching skills.

REFERENCES

Adams, M.J., Foorman, B.R., Lundberg, I., & Beeler, T. (1998). *Phonemic awareness in young children: A classroom curriculum.* Baltimore, MD: Paul H. Brookes Publishing Co.

Arnold, D.H., McWilliams, L., & Arnold E.H. (1998). Teacher discipline and child misbehaviour in day care: Untangling causality with correlational data. *Developmental Psychology, 34,* 276–287. doi:10.1037//0012-1649.34.2.276

Assel, M.A., Landry, S.H., Swank, P.R., & Gunnewig, S. (2007). An evaluation of curriculum, setting, and mentoring on the performance of children enrolled in prekindergarten. *Reading and Writing, 20,* 463–494. doi:10.1007/s11145-006-9039-5

Ball, W.W., & Blachman, B.A. (1991). Does phoneme segmentation training in kindergarten make a difference in early word recognition and developmental spelling? *Reading Research Quarterly, 26,* 49–66.

Beals, D.E., DeTemple, J.M., & Dickinson, D.K. (1994). Talking and listening that support early literacy development of children from low-income families. In D.K. Dickinson (Ed.), *Bridges to literacy* (pp. 19–40). Oxford, England: Blackwell.

Berkowitz, M.W., & Grych, J.H. (1998). Fostering goodness: Teaching parents to facilitate children's moral development. *Journal of Moral Education, 27,* 371–391. doi:10.1080/0305724980270307

Bierman, K.L. (2004). *Peer rejection: Developmental processes and intervention strategies.* New York, NY: Guilford Press.

Bierman, K.L., Domitrovich, C.E., & Darling, H. (2009). Early Prevention Initiatives. In J. Roopnarine & J. Johnson (Eds.), *Approaches to early childhood education, 5th ed.* (pp. 147–164). Columbus, OH: Pearson Merrill Prentice Hall.

Bierman, K.L., Domitrovich, C.E., Nix, R.L., Gest, S.D., Welsh, J., Greenberg, M.T., ... Gill, S. (2008). Promoting academic and social-emotional school readiness: The Head Start REDI program. *Child Development, 79*(6), 1802–1817. doi:10.1111/j.1467-8624.2008.01227.x

Bierman, K.L., & Erath, S.A. (2006). Promoting social competence in early childhood: Classroom curricula and social skills coaching programs. In K. McCartney & D. Phillips (Eds.), *Blackwell handbook on early childhood development.* Malden, MA: Blackwell.

Bierman, K.L., Nix, R.L., & Makin-Byrd, K.N. (2008). Using family-focused interventions to promote child behavioral readiness for school. In A.Crouter & A. Booth (Eds.), *Early disparities in school readiness: How do families contribute to successful and unsuccessful transitions to school?* (pp. 283–297). Mahwah, NJ: Lawrence Erlbaum.

Bredekamp, S., & Copple, C. (Eds.). (1997). *Developmentally appropriate practice in early childhood programs* (Rev. ed.). Washington, DC: National Association for the Education of Young Children.

Brownell, R. (2000). *Expressive one-word picture vocabulary test manual.* Novato, CA: Academic Therapy Publications.

Burchinal, M.R., Peisner-Feinberg, E., Pianta, R.C., & Howes, C. (2002). Development of academic skills from preschool through second grade: Family and classroom predictors of developmental trajectories. *Journal of School Psychology, 40*, 415–436. doi:10.1016/S0022-4405(02)00107-3

Curby, T.W., Rimm-Kaufman, S.E., & Ponitz, C.C. (2009). Teacher–child interactions and children's achievement trajectories across kindergarten and first grade. *Journal of Educational Psychology, 101*(4), 912–925. doi:10.1037/a0016647

Denham, S.A., Bouril, B., & Belouad, F. (1994). Preschoolers' affect and cognition about challenging peer situations. *Child Study Journal, 24*, 1–21.

Denham, S.A., & Burton, R. (2003). *Social and emotional prevention and intervention programming for preschoolers.* New York, NY: Kluwer-Plenum.

Dickinson, D.K. (2001). Book reading in preschool classrooms: Is recommended practice common? In D.K. Dickinson & P.O. Tabors (Eds.), *Beginning literacy with language: Young children learning at home and school* (pp. 175–204). Baltimore, MD: Paul H. Brookes Publishing Co.

Dickinson, D.K., McCabe, A., Anastasopoulos, L., Peisner-Feinberg, E., & Poe, M. (2003). The comprehensive language approach to early literacy: The interrelationships among vocabulary, phonological sensitivity, and print knowledge among preschool-age children. *Journal of Educational Psychology, 95*, 465–481. doi:10.1037/0022-0663.95.3.465

Dickinson, D.K. & Neuman, S.B. (Eds.) (2006). *Handbook of early literacy research, Vol. 2.* New York, NY: Guilford Press.

Dickinson, D.K., & Smith, M.W. (1994). Long-term effects of preschool teachers' book readings on low-income children's vocabulary and story comprehension. *Reading Research Quarterly, 29*, 104–122. doi:10.2307/747807

Dickinson, D.K., & Sprague, K. (2001). The nature and impact of early childhood care environments on the language and early literacy development of children from low-income families. In S. Neuman & D. K. Dickinson (Eds.), *Handbook of early literacy* (pp. 263–292). New York, NY: Guilford Press.

Dickinson, D.K., & Tabors, P.O. (2001). *Beginning literacy with language: Young children learning at home and school.* Baltimore, MD: Paul H. Brookes Publishing Co.

Domitrovich, C.E., Cortes, R., & Greenberg, M.T. (2000). *The teacher style rating scale technical report.* (Unpublished manuscript). University Park, PA: Pennsylvania State University.

Domitrovich, C.E., Cortes, R., & Greenberg, M.T. (2007). Improving young children's social and emotional competence: A randomized trial of the preschool PATHS curriculum. *Journal of Primary Prevention, 28,* 67–91. doi:10.1007/s10935-007-0081-0

Domitrovich, C.E., Gest, S.D., Gill, S., Bierman, K.L., Welsh, J.A., & Jones, D. (2009a). Fostering high-quality teaching with an enriched curriculum and professional development support: The Head Start REDI Program. *American Educational Research Journal, 46,* 567–597.

Domitrovich, C.E., Gest, S.D., Gill, S., Jones, J., & Sanford DeRousie, R. (2009b). Implementation quality: Lessons learned in the context of the head start REDI trial. *Early Childhood Research Quarterly, 25,* 284–298.

Domitrovich, C.E., Gest, S.D., Jones, D., Gill, S., & DeRousie, R.S. (2010). Implementation quality: Lessons learned in the context of the Head Start REDI trial. *Early Childhood Research Quarterly, 25,* 284–298. doi:10.1016/j.ecresq.2010.04.001

Domitrovich, C.E., Greenberg, M.T., Kusche, C., & Cortes, R. (2005). *The preschool PATHS curriculum.* South Deerfield, MA: Channing Bete Publishing.

Domitrovich, C.E., Moore, J.A., & Greenberg, M.T. (in press). Maximizing the effectiveness of social-emotional interventions for young children through high quality implementation of evidence-based interventions. In B. Kelly and D. Perkins (Eds.), *A handbook of implementation science for psychology in education: How to promote evidence-based programmes and practices.* Cambridge, MA: Cambridge University Press.

Durlak, J. A. (2010). The importance of doing well in whatever you do: A commentary on the special section, "Implementation research in early childhood education." *Early Childhood Research Quarterly, 25,* 348-357.

Dusenbury, L., Brannigan, R., Hansen, W.B., Walsh, J., & Falco, M. (2005). Quality of implementation: Developing measures crucial to understanding the diffusion of preventive interventions. *Health Education Research: Theory and Practice, 20*(3), 308–313. doi:10.1093/her/cyg134

Elkind, D., & Whitehurst, G.J. (2001). Young Einsteins: Much too early, much too late. *Education Matters, 1,* 8–21.

Garner, P.W., & Waajid, B. (2008). The associations of emotion knowledge and teacher–child relationships to preschool children's school related developmental competence. *Journal of Applied Developmental Psychology, 29,* 89–100. doi:10.1016/j.appdev.2007.12.001

Gest, S.D., Holland-Coviello, R., Welsh, J.A., Eicher-Catt, D.L., & Gill, S. (2006). Language development sub-contexts in head start classrooms: Distinctive patterns of teacher talk during free play, mealtime and book reading. *Early Education and Development, 17,* 293–315.

Girolametto, L., Weitzman, E., & Greenberg, J. (2003). Training day care staff to facilitate children's language. *American Journal of Speech-Language Pathology, 12,* 299–311. doi:10.1044/1058-0360(2003/076)

Girolametto, L., Weitzman, E., Lefebvre, P., & Greenberg, J. (2007). The effects of in-service education to promote emergent literacy in child care centers: A feasibility study. *Language, Speech, and Hearing Services in Schools, 38,* 72–83. doi:10.1044/0161-1461(2007/007)

Gottman, J., Katz, L.F., & Hooven, C. (1997). *Meta-emotion.* Hillsdale, NJ: Erlbaum.

Haskins, R., & Loeb, S. (2007). A plan to improve the quality of teaching in American schools. *Future of Children, 17,* 1–8.

Holland-Coviello, R. (2005). *Language and literacy environment quality in early childhood classrooms: Exploration of measurement strategies and relations with children's development* (Unpublished doctoral dissertation). University Park, PA: Pennsylvania University Press.

Howes, C., Burchinal, M.R., Pianta, R.C., Bryant, D., Early, D., Clifford, R., & Barbarin, O. (2008). Ready to learn? Children's pre-academic achievement in pre-kindergarten programs. *Early Childhood Research Quarterly*, *23*, 27–50.

Howes, C., & Smith, E.W. (1995). Relations among child care quality, teacher behavior, children's play activities, emotional security, and cognitive activity in child care. *Early Childhood Research Quarterly*, *10*, 381–404. doi:10.1016/0885-2006(95)90013-6

Hughes, J.N., & Kwok, O. (2006). Classroom engagement mediates the effect of teacher-student support on elementary students' peer acceptance: A prospective analysis. *Journal of School Psychology*, *43*, 465–480. doi:10.1016/j.jsp.2005.10.001

Izard, C.E., King, K.A., Trentacosta, C.J., Morgan, J.K., Laurenceau, J.P., Krauthamer-Ewing, E.S., & Finlon, K.J. (2008). Accelerating the development of emotion competence in head start children: Effects on adaptive and maladaptive behavior. *Development and Psychopathology*, *20*, 369–397. doi:10.1017/S0954579408000175

Izard, C.E., Trentacosta, C.J., King, K.A., & Mostow, A.J. (2004). An emotion-based prevention program for head start children. *Early Education and Development*, *15*, 407–422. doi:10.1207/s15566935eed1504_4

Joseph, G., & Strain, P.S. (2003). Enhancing emotional vocabulary in young children. *Young Exceptional Children*, *6*, 18–27. doi:10.1177/109625060300600403

Justice, L.M., Mashburn, A.J., Hamre, B.K., & Pianta, R.C. (2008). Quality of language and literacy instruction in preschool classrooms serving at-risk pupils. *Early Childhood Research Quarterly*, *23*, 51–68. doi:10.1016/j.ecresq.2007.09.004

Justice, L.M., & Pullen, P.C. (2003). Promising interventions for promoting emergent literacy skills: Three evidence-based approaches. *Topics in Early Childhood Special Education*, *23*, 99–113. doi:10.1177/02711214030230030101

Kontos, S., & Wilcox-Herzog, A. (1997). Influences on children's competence in early childhood classrooms. *Early Childhood Research Quarterly*, *12*, 247–262. doi:10.1016/S0885-2006(97)90002-8

La Paro, K.M., & Pianta, R.C. (2003). *Classroom Assessment Scoring System*. Charlottesville, VA: University of Virginia.

Ladd, G.W., Birch, S.H., & Buhs, E.S. (1999). Children's social and scholastic lives in kindergarten: Related spheres of influence? *Child Development*, *70*, 1373–1400. doi:10.1111/1467-8624.00101

Landry, S.H., Swank, P.R., Smith, K.E., Assel, M.A., & Gunnewig, S.B., (2006). Enhancing early literacy skills for preschool children: Bringing a professional development model to scale. *Journal of Learning Disabilities*, *39*, 306–324. doi:10.1177/00222194060390040501

Lonigan, C.J., Burgess, S.R., & Anthony, J.L. (2000). Development of emergent literacy and early reading skills in preschool children: Evidence from a latent-variable longitudinal study. *Developmental Psychology*, *36*, 596–613. doi:10.1037//0012-1649.36.5.596

Lonigan, C.J., Wagner, R.K., Torgesen, J.K., & Rashotte, C. (2007). *The test of preschool early literacy*. Austin, TX: Pro-Ed.

Lynch, K.B., Geller, S.R., & Schmidt, M.G. (2004). Multi-year evaluation of the effectiveness of a resilience-based prevention program for young children. *The Journal of Primary Prevention*, *24*, 335–353. doi:10.1023/B:JOPP.0000018052.12488.d1

Mashburn, A.J., & Pianta, R.C. (2006). Social relationships and school readiness. *Early Education and Development*, *17*, 151–176. doi:10.1207/s15566935eed1701_7

Mashburn, A.J., Pianta, R.C., Hamre, B., Downer, J., Barbarin, O, Bryant, D., Burchinal, M., … Howes, C. (2008). Measures of classroom quality in pre-kindergarten and children's development of academic, language, and social skills. *Child Development*, *79*, 732–749.

McClelland, M.M., Acock, A.C., & Morrison, F.J. (2006). The impact of kindergarten learning-related skills on academic trajectories at the end of elementary school. *Early Childhood Research Quarterly, 21,* 471–490. doi:10.1016/j.ecresq.2006.09.003

Miller, A.L., Gouley, K.K., Seifer, R., Dickstein, S., & Shields, A. (2004). Emotions and behaviors in the head start classroom: Associations among observed dysregulation, social competence, and preschool adjustment. *Early Education and Development, 15,* 147–165. doi:10.1207/s15566935eed1502_2

National Association for the Education of Young Children. (2010). *Where we stand on curriculum, assessment, and program evaluation.* Retrieved October 28, 2010, from http://www.naeyc.org/files/naeyc/file/positions/StandCurrAss.pdf

National Institute of Child Health and Human Development Early Child Care Research Network. (1998). Early child care and self-control, compliance and problem behavior at twenty-four and thirty-six months. *Child Development, 69,* 1145–1170.

National Institute of Child Health and Human Development Early Child Care Research Network. (2000). The relation of child care to cognitive and language development. *Child Development, 71,* 960–980. doi:10.1111/1467-8624.00202

National Institute of Child Health and Human Development Early Child Care Research Network. (2004). Multiple pathways to early academic achievement. *Harvard Educational Review, 74,* 1–28.

Nelson, K.E., & Welsh, J.A. (1998). Progress in multiple language domains by deaf children and hearing children: Discussions with a rare event transactional model. In R. Paul (Ed.), *Exploring the speech–language connection* (pp. 179–225). Baltimore, MD: Paul H. Brookes Publishing Co.

Peisner-Feinberg, E.S., Burchinal, M.R., Clifford, R.M., Culkin, M.L., Howes, C., Kagan, S.L., & Yazejian, N. (2001). The relation of preschool child-care quality to children's cognitive and social developmental trajectories through second grade. *Child Development, 72,* 1534–1553. doi:10.1111/1467-8624.00364

Raver, C.C., Jones, S.M., Li-Grining, C.P., Metzger, M., Champion, K.M., & Sardin, L. (2008). Improving preschool classroom processes: Preliminary findings from a randomized trial implemented in head start settings. *Early Childhood Research Quarterly, 23,* 10–26. doi:10.1016/j.ecresq.2007.09.001

Raver, C.C., Jones, S.M., Li-Grining, C.P., Zhai, F., Bub, K., & Pressler, E. (in press). CSRP's impact on low-income preschoolers' pre-academic skills: Self-regulation as a mediating mechanism, *Child Development.*

Raver, C.C., Jones, S.M., Li-Grining, C.P., Zhai, F., Metzger, M.W., & Solomon, B. (2009). Targeting children's behaviour problems in preschool classrooms: A cluster-randomized controlled trial. *Journal of Consulting and Clinical Psychology, 77,* 302–316. doi:10.1037/a0015302

Ribordy, S., Camras, L., Stafani, R., & Spacarelli, S. (1988). Vignettes for emotion recognition research and affective therapy with children. *Journal of Clinical Child Psychology, 17,* 322–325. doi:10.1207/s15374424jccp1704_4

Rimm-Kaufman, S.E., Pianta, R.C., & Cox, M.J.(2000). Teachers' judgments of problems in the transition to kindergarten. *Early Childhood Research Quarterly, 15,* 147–166. doi:10.1016/S0885-2006(00)00049-1

Roopnarine, J., & Johnson, J. (Eds.) (2009). *Approaches to early childhood education* (5th ed.). Columbus, OH: Pearson Merrill Prentice Hall.

Sarama, J., & Clements, D.H. (2009). *Early childhood mathematics education research: Learning trajectories for young children.* New York, NY: Routledge.

Scarborough, H. (2001). Connecting early language and literacy to later reading (dis) abilities: Evidence, theory and practice. In S. Neuman & D. Dickinson (Eds.), *Handbook of emergent literacy research* (pp. 97–110). New York, NY: Guildford Press.

Senechal, M., & LeFevre, J. (2002). Parental involvement in the development of children's reading skill: A five-year longitudinal study. *Child Development, 73*, 445–460. doi:10.1111/1467-8624.00417

Shure, M.B., & Spivack, G. (1982). Interpersonal problem-solving in young children: A cognitive approach to prevention. *American Journal of Community Psychology, 10*, 341–356. doi:10.1007/BF00896500

Snow, C.E., Burns, B.S., & Griffin,P. (Eds.). (1998). *Preventing reading difficulties in young children.* Washington, DC: National Academy Press.

Vargha, A., & Delaney, H.D. (2000). A critique and improvement of the CL common language effect size statistics of McGraw and Wong. *Journal of Educational and Behavioral Statistics, 24*, 101–132. doi:10.2307/1165329

Wasik, B.A., & Bond, M.A. (2001). Beyond the pages of a book: Interactive book reading and language development in preschool classrooms. *Journal of Educational Psychology, 93*, 243–250. doi:10.1037//0022-0663.93.2.243

Wasik, B.A., Bond, M.A., & Hindman, A. (2006). The effects of a language and literacy intervention on head start children and teachers. *Journal of Educational Psychology, 98*, 63–74. doi:10.1037/0022-0663.98.1.63

Webster-Stratton, C., Reid, M.J., & Hammond, M. (2001). Preventing conduct problems, promoting social competence: A parent and teacher training partnership in head start. *Journal of Clinical Child and Adolescent Psychology, 30*, 283–302. doi:10.1207/S15374424JCCP3003_2

Webster-Stratton, C., Reid, J., & Hammond M. (2004). Treating children with early-onset conduct problems: Intervention outcomes for parent, child, and teacher training. *Journal of Clinical Child and Adolescent Psychology, 33*, 105–124. doi:10.1207/S15374424JCCP3301_11

Webster-Stratton, C., Reid, M.J., & Stoolmiller. M. (2008). Preventing conduct problems and improving school readiness: Evaluation of the incredible years teacher and child training programs in high-risk schools. *Journal of Child Psychology and Psychiatry, 49*, 471–488. doi:10.1111/j.1469-7610.2007.01861.x

Whitebook, M., Howes, C., & Phillips, D. (1990). *Who cares? Child care teachers and the quality of care in America (Final report of the National Child Care Staffing Study).* Oakland, CA: Child Care Employee Project.

Whitehurst, G.J., Arnold, D.S., Epstein, J.N., & Angell, A.L. (1994). A picture book reading intervention in day care and home for children from low-income families. *Developmental Psychology, 30*, 679–689. doi:10.1037//0012-1649.30.5.679

Whitehurst, G.J., Epstein, J.N., Angell, A.C., Payne, A.C., Crone, D.A., & Fischel, J.E. (1994). Outcomes of an emergent literacy intervention in head start. *Journal of Educational Psychology, 86*, 542–555. doi:10.1037//0022-0663.86.4.542

4

Early Literacy Intervention Intensity and Its Relation to Child Outcomes

Laura M. Justice and Anita S. McGinty

Curricular interventions are designed to increase teachers' focus on specific developmental acquisitions (i.e., the "what" of the intervention) through the use of specific instructional practices or techniques (i.e., the "how" of the intervention). For instance, an early literacy intervention that we have studied extensively, called print-referencing intervention, helps teachers systematically address children's print-knowledge acquisition (i.e., the "what," reflected in a scope and sequence of instructional targets and lesson plans) through the instructional practice of print referencing (i.e., the "how," reflected in manualized directions for drawing children's attention to print during shared reading; Justice, Kaderavek, Fan, Sofka, & Hunt, 2009; Justice, McGinty, Piasta, Fan, & Kaderavek, 2010; Justice & Sofka, 2010). Through the manualized materials and teacher-training workshops, teachers are provided professional development (PD) support regarding the what and how of the intervention, and use of the intervention appears to have causal effects on children's literacy development in the short- and long-term (Justice & Ezell, 2002; Justice et al., 2009, 2010). Yet a critical component of the intervention that may be influential to children's intervention gains is that of intervention intensity (i.e., the "how much"). For instance, McGinty and colleagues (McGinty, Justice, Piasta, Kaderavek, & Fan, in press) showed variation in children's learning within classrooms using print-referencing intervention and found this variation could be explained as a function of differences across classrooms in intervention intensity (i.e., weekly number of intervention sessions, number of times teachers used the practice of print referencing during an intervention session). Such findings suggest that PD employed to support educators' use of specific early literacy interventions ought to emphasize issues related to intervention intensity (the "how much") as strongly as issues related to the targets (the "what") and techniques (the "how") of a program.

The study of intervention intensity involves, by necessity, determining the theorized *locus of learning* within an intervention (Warren, Fey, & Yoder, 2007). The locus of learning is the presumed mechanism responsible for bringing about change in the child's (or adult's) learning. For example, in curricular interventions the use of specified instructional practices (e.g., print referencing) typically represents the active ingredients of the intervention, as the moments in which teachers use specific instructional practices are considered the moments in which children's learning occurs (see Warren et al., 2007). Thus, understanding the intensity with which these instructional practices are used over the course of an intervention is central to studying and understanding the relation of intervention intensity to children's learning. In interventions where the adult's learning is the focus, intervention intensity may refer to other practices, such as the number of hours spent in self-study or number of times a consultant visits the classroom, should these be theorized active ingredients of a program targeting adult change.

In the following section we provide an example of how the concept of intervention intensity may apply to adult learning and child learning within a complex, multitiered intervention. Further, we illustrate the importance of having conceptual alignment among an intervention's targets, techniques, and measures of intervention intensity. Following this section we provide a more detailed look at intervention intensity, considering various terms used within the literature, and present a framework, taken from the field of communication disorders, that may be useful to adopt in the study of intervention intensity within early literacy interventions. Finally, we provide an overview of evidence from our own work, suggesting that intervention intensity may be an important contributor to children's learning within early literacy interventions. Our goal in highlighting our work and the related work of colleagues is to bring the issue of intervention intensity to the forefront and suggest a programmatic emphasis be placed on this topic, as it potentially provides a route that enhances the precision and power of early literacy and early childhood interventions.

INTERVENTION INTENSITY: AN EXAMPLE

As stated earlier, effective early literacy interventions, upon manualization, typically include specification of these three parameters at the least: 1) techniques, 2) targets, and 3) intensity. Put simply, techniques are the "how" of an intervention, targets are the "what," and intensity is the "how much" (Justice, Sofka, & McGinty, 2007). For purposes of illustration of how these parameters of intervention may be differentiated from one another, we can consider an early literacy intervention described recently in several reports, the MyTeachingPartner (MTP)–Language and Literacy Curricula (MTP-L/L) and MTP–Consultancy (MTP-C) (Mashburn, Hamre, Downer, Justice, & Pianta, 2010; Pianta, Mashburn, Downer, Hamre, & Justice, 2008). Examining these two related interventions allows us to consider how intervention intensity may relate to behavior change at two levels—the child level and the teacher level—and examine how definitions of intervention intensity may differ within these respective interventions.

According to published descriptions, the MTP-L/L is a curricular intervention with the goal of enhancing children's phonological awareness, alphabet knowledge, print awareness, vocabulary knowledge, narrative skill, and social communication. This aspect of the MTP intervention involves teachers' use of a battery of *techniques* (or instructional practices), such as open-ended questions and explicit vocabulary models, which are scripted in structured lesson plans. In terms of *intensity*, teachers are asked to implement an MTP activity each day for at least 10 minutes over an academic year.

A second aspect of the MTP intervention, MTP-C, involves a consultancy program designed to enhance the quality with which teachers interact with children across the day and targets the levels of emotional, organizational, and instructional support teachers provide (i.e., the "what" of the intervention). The practices of this intervention (i.e., the "how"), which are theorized to bring about change in teacher behavior, include teacher self-reflection activities and consultation sessions. Self-reflection activities include teachers' review of videos of their own instruction and reflective journaling (in an online system), and teachers must complete a set number of activities every 2 weeks (i.e., the "how much"). A second practice of the intervention involves consultation sessions, which are designed to support teachers in improving their global practices as well as their implementation of MTP-L/L activities, and each session is designed to last 30 minutes. (see Mashburn et al., 2010). Intensity specifications for the MTP-C are thus reflected in the number of practices teachers engage in that are theorized to support their own change, including the number of self-reflection activities conducted in 2 weeks and the time (weekly and/ or total) they work with consultants in one-to-one sessions. It is important to note that although the ultimate goal of MTP-C is to support *children's* learning, the locus of learning (Warren et al., 2007) within the MTP-C intervention occurs at the teacher level and, thus, intensity specifications occur around practices designed to bring about teacher change.

The MTP-L/L and MTP-C both have specific criteria regarding the "what," "how," and "how much" of the intervention. However, as with

many interventions, empirical tests of casual effects have involved implementation of the entire package (including MTP-L/L and MTP-C), rather than systematic evaluation of how each component (i.e., the "what,"
"how," and "how much" of each intervention) may independently contribute to teacher or child change. Thus it is difficult to isolate any one practice
within an intervention as a causal agent, and it is even more difficult to
consider how *intensity* of that practice may relate to learning or behavior
change. For instance, we cannot strongly claim that teacher use of MTP
activities for 10 minutes a day for an academic year, as specified, is a critical determinant of how much children may gain from teacher use of the
intervention, as variations in intensity of implementation have not been
systematically compared for effects on children's gains (e.g., systematic
comparisons of 5 minutes per day versus 10 minutes per day). Nonetheless,
some correlational findings would suggest that aspects of intensity might
be quite relevant to the benefits children receive from the MTP-L/L or
MTP-C interventions. In fact, studies have found that the amount of time
teachers spend implementing MTP-L/L activities in their classrooms and
engaging in consultancy activities have a positive and significant association to children's vocabulary growth during an academic year of preschool
(Mashburn et al., 2010).

Such findings are important, as they imply that intensity deserves significant attention as a critical component of intervention implementation
not just with MTP, but with any intervention that teachers are asked to
use in their classroom. Yet these findings raise a number of questions. For
example, the time in consultancy (i.e., the intensity of the MTP-C) was
related to children's gains, but how much teacher change (the intended
locus of control with respect to consultancy practices) was needed to bring
about a benefit for children? As another example, the finding that the use
of MTP-L/L activities was related to children's vocabulary growth might
be interpreted to show that greater use of MTP is always better than less
use and that teachers should therefore always strive for more time spent in
MTP implementation. However, it is important to study, and then relay
to teachers, how much implementation is enough: Is there a threshold of
implementation at which point children's learning gains begin to plateau?
At the same time, it is also relevant to consider whether alternative schedules of implementation, such as 60 minutes of activities in 1 day versus
10 minutes over 5 days, are equally effective with respect to supporting
children's development.

As an analogy, one might think about whether college students preparing for a test should study for 60 minutes over 1 day or 10 minutes a day
over 6 days. Some basic research on learning suggests that intense bursts of
practice, with time in between for cognitive assimilation, bring about the
most effective learning (Cepeda, Vul, Rohrer, Wixted, & Pashler, 2008); to
what extent would these findings apply to a preschool classroom and young

children's learning within a curricular intervention? These data also show that initial looks at intervention intensity notwithstanding, there are critical questions about intervention intensity that have not been given sufficient attention within the early literacy research and practice communities. One way to bring this topic to the forefront, as we believe it should be, is to adopt a common terminology that allows for unpacking the multiple components of intensity. Taking such a fine grained look at intervention intensity may be quite important, as cumulative intensity may be less important than the configuration of intensity (i.e., 10 minutes 5 times a week versus 25 minutes twice a week) to learning. Therefore, to examine intervention intensity more closely, we will borrow the framework proposed by Warren and colleagues (2007) for the study of early communication interventions, which are very similar to early literacy interventions and thus should provide an appropriate and useful framework.

INTERVENTION INTENSITY: A CLOSER LOOK

Critical to this framework of intervention intensity is the need to establish the locus of learning, as we mentioned at the start of this chapter. The locus of learning can be stipulated at two levels. The macro level is the broader context in which learning takes place, such as an MTP learning activity or an adult–child book reading session. Often, discussions of intervention intensity have focused almost exclusively on the macro level of implementation. For example, teachers who implement a shared-book reading program might be asked to implement sessions four times a week (Wasik, Bond, & Hindman, 2006). The molecular level is the more fine-grained action proposed to lead directly to the child's learning or adults' skill development (Warren et al., 2007). At the molecular level is the moment-by-moment use of specified practices (e.g., number of times adults use print referencing in a shared-reading session or number of observations an adult makes about his or her own teaching), as these practices are thought to bring about child learning or teacher change and are the presumed active ingredient of the intervention. For example, teachers who implement a shared-reading program might be asked to elaborate on the meanings of words 10 times within each shared-reading session; each time the teacher provides a word elaboration, the teacher and child are engaged in an "episode" (i.e., moment where the teacher uses a practice thought to be an "active ingredient" of child development) in which children's learning theoretically occurs (Biemiller & Boote, 2006). Thus measuring the episodes of practice use within a given intervention session reflects a molecular aspect of intervention intensity.

To provide another example, in language intervention, an important practice that has a direct influence on children's grammatical development is *recasting*, in which a child's omission of an obligatory grammatical form is immediately followed by the adult utterance containing the omitted form (e.g., from Proctor-Williams, Fey, & Loeb, 2001; Child: He need it. Adult: He needs it). The adult recast—with its immediate and contingent linkage to the child's preceding utterance—is the presumed locus of learning, or episode, in grammatically focused language intervention. It is interesting, however, that although the density of recasts within an intervention session has been positively correlated with children's grammar gains (Hassink & Leonard, 2010), systematic manipulation of recast density has not shown that increasing recast density within treatment sessions increases children's gains (Proctor-Williams & Fey, 2007).

It is important to note that the framework of intervention intensity we consider in this chapter specifies intensity parameters at both the macro and molecular levels of intervention, as well as the interaction between the two. Drawing from Warren and colleagues (2007), the four measurable components of intervention intensity we discuss include 1) intervention dose (episodes per intervention session), 2) intervention frequency (number of intervention sessions in a standard unit of time, a week), 3) intervention duration (length of intervention from start to finish), and 4) cumulative intervention intensity (combination of previous parameters). These four components are represented in Table 4.1. In the remainder of this section, we go through each one of these intensity parameters in detail.

Intervention Dose

Intervention dose refers to the number of times within an intervention session an episode occurs. As stated earlier, an episode is a moment in which

Table 4.1. Four components of intervention intensity with examples from print-referencing intervention

Intensity component	Definition	Example
Dose	Number of times within an intervention session an episode occurs	Parent asks nine questions about print within a read-aloud session (print-related questions are presumed *locus of learning*).
Frequency (also dose frequency)	Number of sessions (i.e., lessons, activities) that occur per week as part of the intervention protocol	Parent implements three read-aloud sessions per week.
Duration	Overall length of time an intervention will be implemented (e.g., 3 months versus 9 months)	Parent implements read-aloud program for 12 weeks at home.
Cumulative intervention intensity	Product of dose by frequency by duration; represents the actual exposure to presumed locus of learning	Parent implements the locus of learning with a cumulative intervention intensity of 324 (child is exposed to 324 print-related questions over time).

an adult uses a specific practice of a curricular—or PD—intervention (i.e., the use of a vocabulary elaboration technique or a teacher's use of a standardized observation protocol to reflect on his or her teaching). Through the use of that practice, learning is thought to occur. Thus, the measurement of intervention dose captures the number of episodes that occur within a period of time (i.e., per minute) or within a meaningful event of the intervention (i.e., a shared-reading session). In the area of language intervention, for example, a low intervention dose can be measured as a recast density of 0.2 per minute, or as 6 recasts within a 30-minute intervention session; similarly a high intervention dose can be measured as a recast density 0.5 per minute or 15 recasts within a 30-minute intervention session (Proctor-Williams & Fey, 2007).

Studies that focus on intervention dose provide a direct test of the relationship between "active ingredients" of an intervention and children's learning; further, such studies may lead to an improved understanding of how learning occurs within natural settings. For example, correlational evidence has suggested that a higher dose of recasting within language intervention sessions facilitates greater improvements in language ability for children with language impairments (Hassink & Leonard, 2010), yet this has not been substantiated in experimental trials that specifically compare different levels of intervention dose (Proctor-Williams & Fey, 2007). Many of the common conceptions that we have about how children learn, such as the assumption that more exposure to the active ingredients of an intervention is better for children's learning, may, in fact, be erroneous. These data suggest that compressing as much learning as possible into short periods of time may not be beneficial to young children, and such findings are actually consistent with evidence from basic laboratory-based studies on human learning (e.g., see Rohrer & Pashler, 2007). Within the literature on human learning and memory there is evidence to suggest that distributing smaller doses of learning opportunities over time—with large gaps between opportunities—may have specific benefits to both short- and long-term learning (Cepeda et al., 2008). Studies on intervention dose, therefore, may help bridge the gap between the evidence we have on human learning and memory with the evidence we have on applied interventions. Indeed, the study of intervention dose requires taking a very molecular view of an intervention, and this precision may be important when attempting to link principles of learning (observed within tightly controlled laboratory settings) to the design and implementation of educational interventions.

Intervention Frequency

Intervention frequency (also called dose *frequency;* Warren et al., 2007) refers to the number of sessions (i.e., lessons, activities) that occur per week as part of the intervention protocol. This macrolevel aspect of intervention intensity is, typically, the level of intensity at which most early literacy interventions are specified; however, interventions are highly variable in the frequency with which they occur. Indeed, some interventions may involve one or two lessons or activities per week (e.g., Wasik et al., 2006), whereas others may involve daily lesson implementations (e.g., DeBaryshe & Gorecki, 2007). In general, interventions that occur only once or twice per week are considered to be of a low frequency, whereas those that occur more often are considered to be of a high frequency (O'Connor, 2000; Ukrainetz, Ross, & Harm, 2009). Until recently, differences in intervention frequency have not been systematically studied in the area of early literacy intervention, although there have been two recent exceptions. Ukrainetz and colleagues (2009) examined gains in phonological awareness when the program was conducted at a low intervention frequency (one time per week, similar to the notion of distributed practice) versus a high intervention frequency (three times per week). The intervention dose (i.e., number of episodes per session) was controlled so that observed effects could only be attributed to differences in intervention frequency. It is interesting to note that with respect to this particular intervention, there was no short- or long-term benefit to receiving the intervention at a high intervention frequency versus a low intervention frequency: Child outcomes were similar irrespective of how many sessions occurred per week.

Intervention Duration

Intervention duration refers to the overall length of the time an intervention will be implemented (e.g., 3 months versus 9 months). In early literacy interventions, some implementations involve a relatively short duration (e.g., 6 weeks; Justice, Chow, Capellini, Flanigan, & Colton, 2003), whereas others are of a much longer duration (e.g., 2 years; O'Connor, 2000). In general, there has been little systematic experimental examination of how duration may be associated with children's outcomes, and thus many assessments of intervention duration and its linkages to children's language and literacy development are based on meta-analysis, in which effect-size estimates are considered as a function of treatment duration.

Although one might presume that interventions of a longer duration would be associated with greater improvements for children, the evidence is actually not so straightforward. For example, the report of the National Institute of Child Health and Human Development (NICHD, 2001) suggested that there are threshold effects in interventions for phonological awareness, such that moderate durations of intervention are as effective as longer durations of intervention. On the other hand, in a systematic review of language-intervention research for children with language and speech disorders, Law, Garrett, and Nye (2004) suggested that treatments that were of longer duration (> 8 weeks) seemed to result in stronger effects on children's speech and language outcomes, but they emphasized that because information about dosage was not included in the studies reviewed, the results should be viewed as tentative. As their review points out, unless dosage is carefully controlled, it is almost impossible to make claims about treatment duration on child outcomes.

Frequency and duration therefore concern how often children receive the dose and over what length of time. Some researchers refer to these aspects of intensity as treatment scheduling, or simply the schedule to which implementation adheres in terms of days per week (frequency) and the length of implementation (duration; Ukrainetz et al., 2009). When researchers and practitioners talk about intervention intensity, they typically are referring to frequency and duration. For example, studies describing implementation of high-intensity interventions typically involve daily administration and therefore high-frequency implementation of the intervention (Duhon, Mesmer, Atkins, Greguson, & Olinger, 2009; O'Connor, 2000). In general, many constituents presume, largely on theoretical grounds, that high-intensity and longer duration interventions lead to improved learning for children, particularly for those who appear to learn more slowly than other children. To some extent, such conclusions are based on comparisons of effect-size estimates across sets of studies to draw conclusions about how intervention frequency and duration may be associated with children's gains (Law et al., 2004; NICHD, 2001). Nonetheless, as we have noted, studies that involve planned comparisons based on manipulations of frequency and/or duration within the study of education are rare, and those that do exist do not uniformly show that increases in intervention frequency and/or duration lead to increases in children learning (Proctor-Williams & Fey, 2007; Ukrainetz et al., 2009).

Cumulative Intervention Intensity

Cumulative intervention intensity, which is the product of intervention dose multiplied by intervention frequency multiplied by intervention duration (or, more simply, dose × frequency × duration). Obviously, to characterize the cumulative intervention intensity of an intervention, we need fairly precise information about the intervention in terms of dose and frequency and duration. Some research studies provide an adequate characterization of all such parameters, and we therefore can calculate cumulative intervention intensity. Biemiller and Boote (Study 2, 2006), for example, implemented large-group vocabulary intervention in kindergarten, first-grade, and second-grade classrooms. The proposed locus of learning is children's exposure to teachers' explicit elaborations/explanations of word meanings as embedded within storybook reading sessions. Careful analysis of the research description suggests the following intensity parameters:

- Intervention dose: 7–10 word meanings discussed per session

- Intervention frequency: 4 30-minute sessions per week (plus an introductory session)

- Intervention duration: 2 weeks

On the basis of these data, one can propose that the cumulative intervention intensity for this intervention (and that which is associated with the vocabulary gains presented by the authors) is somewhere between 56 and 80 learning episodes. It is unclear—and cannot be assumed—that children will make similar gains in vocabulary development as discussed by these authors in the context of variations from this cumulative intervention intensity. For instance, if teachers implement this intervention but use a different frequency of implementation (two sessions per week over a longer duration), one cannot simply extrapolate that children's vocabulary gains will be similar as that seen with the implementation frequency and duration presented by the authors in their study description.

INTENSITY OF PRINT-REFERENCING INTERVENTION: EMERGING FINDINGS

There is a considerable amount of literature on intervention intensity within fields outside of early childhood education and early literacy intervention, most prominently in the pharmaceutical therapies but also across many foci within the health and behavioral sciences. For example, variations in intervention intensity as applied to drug addiction, depression, attention-deficit disorders, and aphasia have all been studied (Cherney, Patterson, Raymer, Frymark, & Schooling, 2008; Lemak & Alexander, 2001). In general findings suggest that intensity is a parameter of intervention that requires systematic attention at the level of any other parameter (techniques, materials) and that basic assumptions regarding intensity (that more of something is always better) need to be carefully tested using causally sensitive research designs.

In our own work on print-referencing intervention, which has involved the systematic development and then subsequent trialing of an intervention approach from feasibility study (e.g., Ezell, Justice, & Parsons, 2000) to large-scale effectiveness trials (e.g., Justice et al., 2010), we have become increasingly interested in understanding how intensity components (i.e., dose, frequency, duration) may relate to children's gains when exposed to this intervention. We know, quite decisively, that exposure to the intervention has positive effects on children's early literacy development (e.g., Justice & Ezell, 2000, 2002), but how much exposure is needed for these benefits to occur? For example, does a higher dose of print references within a book-reading session (i.e., more episodes per session) lead to greater learning gains compared with a lower dose? Does a higher intervention frequency (i.e., more sessions per week) lead to better gains compared with a lower intervention frequency? In recent years we have addressed these issues and will share our findings here. In doing so, we hope to provide examples of the kinds of questions we are addressing (as well as the methods) so as to stimulate other research teams to do the same in the interventions they may be developing or trialing.

There are three primary reasons for our interest in exploring issues of intensity as it relates to print-referencing intervention. First, implementing an intervention for a long period of time may lead to attrition (program non-completion). In one study of print-referencing intervention in which parents of children with specific language impairment were asked to implement the intervention for 12 weeks (four reading sessions per week) in their homes, we reported an approximately 25% attrition rate (Justice et al., 2010). We cannot help but wonder if completion might have differed if the intervention was shorter in duration. Would more children have received the intervention if it had been 8 weeks or 4 weeks? Related to this issue is that some key constituents, such as teachers, may be very reluctant to begin a high-duration intervention in the first place. By analogy, consider your own willingness to sign up for a low-calorie 12-week diet program versus a 6-week program. At least some people would shy away from anything that required them to eat a low-calorie diet for 3 months, and therefore they would not participate in the program at all. Systematic study of intensity may help us learn whether a longer duration intervention is really necessary. What if children achieve similar learning gains in a 6-week program compared with a 12-week program, as research on phonological awareness intervention has suggested may be a tenable theory (Ukrainetz et al., 2009)?

Second, some studies of treatment intensity, particularly studies of intervention frequency but also studies of dosage, have not shown that more of an intervention is always better. For example, as already mentioned, research on recast density has not found that children gain more in high-density interventions compared with low-density interventions. Children with language impairment who completed an intervention in which instructional episodes were provided at a high dose made language gains that were remarkably similar to those who received the intervention in which instructional episodes were provided at a low dose (Proctor-Williams & Fey, 2007). Perhaps even more compelling are the results reported for children with typical language skills, who also participated in the intervention program. Typically developing children who received a low dose of the intervention made significantly greater gains than those who received the high dose, a finding that was not anticipated by the authors but that could be readily interpreted based on the literature previously discussed regarding human learning and memory, as well as studies suggesting the importance of distributing (or spacing) instructional episodes within language interventions (e.g., Childers & Tomasello, 2002). It stands to reason that children may potentially benefit from a lower dose print-referencing intervention than a higher dose intervention, based on such prior evidence.

Finally, print-referencing intervention is at a point where it is moving to at-scale applications. The principle, in general, of heightening children's explicit attention to print during book-reading interactions has been discussed in teacher- and parent-training manuals (e.g., Weitzman & Greenberg, 2010), practitioner-directed articles (e.g., Lane & Wright, 2007), and policy reports (e.g., What Works Clearinghouse, 2007). Any practice that is taken to scale will be employed with a wide level of variation, and it is typically the case that the effect-size estimates reported in more tightly controlled efficacy trials attenuate in larger scale implementations. Nonetheless, it is important to note what aspects of print-referencing intervention are most influential to children's gains. Is there a certain threshold of exposure that should be achieved for benefits to occur? Many other interventions are moving to at-scale applications as well. For example, coaching of teachers within the early childhood classrooms is gaining momentum as a practice. How much coaching is needed to bring about change in classroom quality and, in turn, children's gains? Prior research on coaching has presented mixed outcomes related to its effectiveness (e.g., Assel, Landry, Swank, & Gunnewig, 2007); it may be that issues related to intensity are contributing to the ambiguity of this intervention, such that the amount of coaching is inadequately distributed over time to bring about significant change in teachers' practice.

Intervention Overview: Locus of Learning

As already mentioned, to discuss the intensity of an intervention it is necessary to identify the locus of learning. In print-referencing intervention, the presumed locus of learning is when the child comes into direct contact with print on the pages of a text; this is the place where the young child learns about the features, forms, and function of print (see Justice & Ezell, 2002). This contact can be facilitated using a variety of techniques, including both nonverbal (pointing to print within the text) and verbal (questioning the child about print within the text); both are equally facilitative for affecting children's direct contact with print in texts (Justice, Pullen, & Pence, 2008) and are viewed as active ingredients of this approach to intervention and are specified when we discuss intervention dose.

Here are examples of one parent's verbal references to print observed within a one-to-one parent–child shared reading; this shows how references to print can be used to orient the child to various aspects of print within the text being read (from Justice, Weber, Ezell, & Bakeman, 2002):

- Do you want to follow the words with your finger?

- Can you find the words that look alike on this page?

- Do you recognize any of these letters?

- *And he went to the dump to make a fuss...* What rhymes?
- Here, *s-t* makes the /st/ sound.
- Do you see the word *bear* on this page?

To promote children's contact with print within classroom-based reading sessions, teachers regularly read books with children and use nonverbal and verbal techniques to promote their contact with print. The most recent instantiation (Justice & Sofka, 2010) involves teachers' implementation of a 30-week book-reading program in their classrooms over an academic year. Teachers are provided a set of 30 print-salient storybooks to use over the intervention period. Print-salient storybooks are those in which the print has a marked design characteristic, as is the case in storybooks containing speech bubbles or font changes. In implementing this intervention, teachers follow a *specified scope* and *sequence* of instruction that is addressed within the group book-reading context; teachers use the book-reading context and the assigned storybooks to explicitly draw children's attention to forms and functions of print within the storybooks and, in turn, increase children's knowledge about print. Parameters of intensity as presented to teachers during PD are discussed below. Several larger scale studies have shown that this manualization of the intervention (e.g., use of the 30 print-salient books, adherence to the specific scope and sequence, and implementation intensity as specified below) has causally interpretable effects on children's short-term literacy development (Justice et al., 2009, 2010), with effects subsequently maintained through first grade on standardized measures of both reading and spelling (Piasta, Justice, McGinty, & Kaderavek, in press).

Intervention Dose

Teachers who implement the print-referencing intervention are asked to address two specific print-related targets in each classroom-based reading session 2–3 times. Thus, the recommended dosage is 4–6 learning episodes per session. In prior implementations, largely with parents (e.g., Justice & Ezell, 2000), we recommended slightly higher dosages per session; however, we have found that many parents actually exceed the recommended dosage quite a bit, and therefore we have decreased the recommendations over time.

Intervention Frequency and Duration

During each week of the program, teachers read a print-salient storybook to their pupils in four whole-group reading sessions. As noted previously, teachers are provided the books to be used. Note also that teachers are free to conduct any additional book reading they desire beyond the ones specified for intervention. The total duration of the intervention is 30 weeks; thus, teachers implement a total of 120 intervention reading sessions.

Cumulative Intervention Intensity

Recall that cumulative intervention intensity is the product of dose $\times$ frequency $\times$ duration. This equates to the total number of learning episodes children experience when receiving the intervention. In general, implementation of print-referencing intervention as we specify it to teachers involves

4–6 episodes per session $\times$ 4 sessions per week $\times$ 30 weeks

Therefore the cumulative intervention, as specified to teachers, is 480–720 episodes distributed over an academic year. In actuality we find that teachers implement a far greater number of episodes per session than is requested. That is, teachers tend to hit the specified two targets per reading session as requested (two to three times per target), but they also address a range of other print-related targets as well at a relatively high rate of occurrence. On average we observe teachers implementing this intervention to reference print about 20 times per session (e.g., McGinty, Breit-Smith, et al., 2011). Consequently, the actual cumulative intensity as teachers implement the intervention may be closer to 2,400 episodes distributed over an academic year, although teachers show considerable variability. That is, in actuality, some teachers implement a relatively high dose of intervention (i.e., high-density implementation), whereas others implement a relatively low dose of intervention (i.e., low-density implementation). Because of this natural variation among teachers in intervention dosage—which then leads to differences over time in cumulative intervention intensity—we are able to systematically explore how variations in intensity may contribute to children's literacy development over time.

Intensity Effects on Children: What Parameters Matter?

In two 2011 studies, we attempted to isolate the effects of dose (number of episodes embedded within intervention sessions) and frequency (number of sessions per week) on children's literacy gains over a 30-week period of print-referencing implementation by classroom teachers (McGinty et al., in press-a, -b). These intensity studies are embedded in a larger project designed to determine the causally interpretable effects of print-referencing intervention on preschool-age children. All of the materials used in the larger study are available in a printed volume, making replication of findings readily available (Justice & Sofka, 2010). In the larger study, 84 teachers working in targeted-enrollment preschool programs, including Head Start and state-funded prekindergarten programs, were randomly assigned to one of three intervention conditions, as described in the following sections.

Condition 1: High-Frequency Print-Referencing Intervention   Teachers assigned to this condition implemented the intervention for a 30-week period at a frequency of four sessions per week (120 sessions in total over the academic year). The recommended dose of implementation, as discussed previously, is four to six episodes per reading session, although many teachers used a much higher rate. The dose and frequency of this condition are similar to those used in a series of smaller scale efficacy trials (Justice & Ezell, 2000, 2002).

Condition 2: Low-Frequency Print-Referencing Intervention

Teachers assigned to this condition implemented the intervention for a 30-week period at a frequency of two sessions per week (60 sessions in total over the academic year). As with the high-frequency teachers, the recommended dose of implementation was four to six episodes per reading session, although many teachers used a much higher rate, as observed among the high-frequency teachers as well. This planned variation in intervention frequency allows us to determine whether a "more" frequent implementation is a causal agent in children's growth.

Condition 3: Normal Book Reading

Teachers assigned to this condition received the same books as teachers in the print-referencing intervention conditions and read these on a high-frequency implementation schedule: four readings per week over a 30-week period. However, these teachers did not receive any intervention materials. Although these teachers did tend to implement a very small dose of print-referencing behaviors into their reading sessions, they occurred at a significantly lower dose than the trained print-referencing teachers.

Role of Dose

In 2011, we conducted a study, embedded within the larger project, that specifically examined the role of dose and frequency to child outcomes. As we have noted, teachers who implemented the print-referencing intervention (both low- and high-frequency conditions), showed considerable variability in the number of learning episodes they embedded within each intervention session (i.e., natural variation in dose). McGinty and colleagues (2011) examined whether the dose of print referencing delivered would actually explain the intervention effect (i.e., explain the difference in child outcomes between those in the high-frequency condition versus the normal book reading condition, $N = 59$; see Justice et al., 2010) and whether the importance of dose may differ across different classroom environments. The outcome of interest was children's growth over the academic year on a composite measure of print knowledge, comprising measures of alphabet knowledge, print concepts, and name-writing skills. In the statistical models generated for this study, the average dose observed was calculated as the average as seen across six reading sessions evenly spaced across the academic year. On average, the dose of print referencing was approximately 20 episodes per shared-reading intervention session. However, it is important to note that there was variation around this mean (standard deviation $[SD] = 16.8$), such that some teachers delivered a very high dose across sessions, whereas others used a very low dose. To consider whether the relation of intervention dose to children's gains may vary across classrooms, we measured the quality of the literacy environment (e.g., number of books in the room, presence of a writing center) and the quality of the instructional environment (e.g., emotional support, instructional support, and classroom management as based on the Classroom Assessment Scoring System™ (CLASS™; Pianta, La Paro, & Hamre, 2008).

The findings of the study, with respect to the influence of dose on children's print-knowledge gains, are quite interesting. First, the effect of the intervention was fully explained by the dose of print referencing delivered by intervention teachers, as opposed to teachers conducting normal book readings. However, once other aspects of the classroom were added to the model, including the classroom literacy environment and quality of the instructional environment, dose no longer had a statistically significant relation to young children's print-knowledge gains. We did find a significant interaction between the quality of the instructional environment and intervention dose. In fact, dose appeared to be instrumental to children's learning when the quality of the instructional environment was low or average (which, in fact, describes the majority of preschool classrooms). In such settings, it does appear that higher delivering intervention sessions with higher doses of print-referencing episodes are positively related to children's literacy gains.

It is important to recognize, however, that this benefit was not apparent in classrooms in which instructional quality was high. In these classrooms, there was no difference in children's outcomes, regardless of the dose of print-referencing episodes delivered. These findings suggest that the "active ingredients" of an intervention may have a complex association to children's outcomes and that "how much" of that active ingredient needs to be delivered (i.e., the dose of the intervention) may not be consistent across all settings. The reason we find this interesting is that it argues the importance of considering intervention dose contextually, in relation to other features of children's classroom environments (or characteristics of children themselves) that may be relevant to their learning. Obviously more attention is needed to further understand the relationship between dose and classroom environment, but it implies that intervention dose cannot be considered in a vacuum. Rather it exhibits a significant interplay with other features of the classroom context.

Role of Intervention Frequency

As mentioned earlier, in the larger project investigating print-referencing intervention, teachers implemented both high-frequency (i.e., four times a week) and low-frequency (i.e., two times a week) implementations of the intervention, such that some children participated in 120 sessions over a 30-week period, whereas others participated in 60 sessions. In a 2011 study, we systematically examined these two conditions more closely, considering how this planned variation in frequency, as well as the natural variation of intervention dose delivered across classrooms, related to children's print-knowledge gains. Because teachers in both the high- and the low-frequency implementations varied substantially in the dose of print-referencing episodes they delivered per intervention session, we could consider how these two aspects of intervention intensity independently and collectively related to children's learning (McGinty, Justice, et al., in press). An important feature of this study is that teachers were randomly assigned to high- and low-intensity implementations. Thus, unlike other correlational studies of intensity parameters (as in our previously reported study; McGinty et al., 2011), with this random-assignment design we can draw causal inferences about how intervention frequency, as a particular parameter of intervention, might relate to children's gains.

As with the dose study discussed previously, we found the results of this study quite interesting. What we found is that intervention frequency had a significant effect on children's learning, but only when the dose of print-referencing episodes per session was relatively low. Further, we found that a relatively high dose of print-referencing episodes would fully compensate for differences between the high-dose frequency and low-dose frequency conditions. In other words, we could not isolate the independent effects of intervention intensity from intervention dose, as there was significant interplay between these two parameters of intervention. As a rule, we found 1) high-intensity intervention (four sessions per week for 30 weeks) leads to greater print-knowledge gains for children when the dose in individual sessions is relatively low, and 2) low-intensity intervention (two sessions per week for 30 weeks) is nearly as effective as a high-intensity intervention when the dose in individual sessions is relatively high.

These findings present a compelling case for studying intensity much more thoroughly. Coupled with our dose findings, it appears that we cannot make strong assumptions about intensity and how it will affect children's learning. For instance, high-dose implementation (loading a great number of learning episodes within individual intervention sessions) is only linked to elevated gains for children's literacy development when classroom quality is low or average. High-intensity intervention (conducting a large number of sessions over time) with low-dose implementation has similar effects on children's literacy development as low-intensity intervention with high-dose implementation, suggesting flexibility in how the cumulative intensity of the intervention is delivered. Taken together, the complexities of such findings suggest that we cannot make strong causal claims about how a given intervention must be implemented. Rather, intensity must be seen as a multidimensional construct characterized by substantial interplay among its various parameters (e.g., dose, intensity, duration, cumulative intervention intensity) and with respect to the broader context in which an intervention is implemented.

IMPLICATIONS FOR PROFESSIONAL DEVELOPMENT OF EARLY EDUCATORS

Early childhood educators are held to similar standards as educators working in the later grades with respect to accountability; that is, educators are asked to use empirically validated practices that have positive effects on children's learning. In the last decade, a large volume of research has identified various practices and programs that appear to yield positive effects on young children's literacy development. PD of educators is the predominant venue for helping educators learn about these new practices and programs and utilize them in their classrooms.

Typically, such PD focuses on helping teachers learn specific techniques, such as how to use certain types of questions that lead to multiturn conversations or how to model rhyming patterns to promote children's phonological awareness. These techniques are believed to be the active ingredients of the intervention and serve as the locus of learning. Often, it seems that the message to educators is that using more of these techniques is better than using fewer, particularly when educators' fidelity of implementation is being monitored (e.g., Mashburn et al., 2010; Pence, Justice, & Wiggins, 2008). Educators are asked to achieve a certain threshold of implementation when, in fact, very little is known about what threshold of implementation is needed to bring about the desired changes in children's skills.

The content of this chapter argues not only that intensity is an important part of implementation of early literacy intervention but also that it warrants very careful study so that educators know how much of a specific technique (or teaching/learning episode) is needed to support children's learning and if common conceptualizations of intervention intensity are appropriate and adequate. Given the state of research today on the matter of intensity, educators asked to engage daily in a specific practice with children does, in fact, yield better outcomes for children than, say, engaging in this practice only once or twice per week. Early childhood educators are asked to address a broad range of learning outcomes for their children and to do so, in many cases, in half-day programs where they see children for only several hours each day and instructional time is measured against a host of other needs (e.g., mealtime, outdoor play, toileting). Ensuring that "recommended doses" of intervention implementation are, in fact, what is needed to bring about meaningful changes in children's learning is one way that researchers might honor the multifaceted and competing demands of the early childhood educator.

Until a more sophisticated knowledge base is achieved with respect to the intensity of early literacy and other types of intervention, PD for early childhood educators should include attention toward the following:

Educate early childhood educators about the components of intensity— namely dose, frequency, duration, and cumulative intervention. In such conversations, educators should be guided to identify the active ingredients of specific interventions so that they can identify for themselves where variations in implementation might make sense, theoretically. For instance, educators who learn that the use of open-ended questions in dialogic reading (Whitehurst et al., 1994) is considered an active ingredient of this language-focused intervention might be able to embed that technique into other activities, such as mealtime conversations, rather than perceiving it as a technique that can only be implemented in one particular learning context.

Delineate for educators what is and is not known about the intensity of a specific intervention, with respect to dose, frequency, duration, and cumulative intervention intensity. In many instances, such information can be extracted from the literature. Educators should receive information about the intensity of interventions as they have been discussed in the literature, and they can be supported to consider how the intensity components might be derived differently in their own classrooms so as to achieve effects reported in the literature. For example, if a particular intervention is causally associated with vocabulary development in children in the context of 100 learning episodes distributed over ten 30-minute large-group sessions, educators might consider how this cumulative intervention intensity might be achieved in alternative ways (e.g., 100 learning episodes distributed over twenty 15-minute sessions).

Support educators to monitor their own implementation of interventions across the various intensity components. By helping early childhood educators learn about the different components of intensity—such as the importance of the learning episode as the place in which children's learning takes place—they can be supported to track their own implementation of these active ingredients in more explicit ways. Today, educators' implementation of many early literacy interventions (and others as well) is tracked at fairly crude levels, such as whether they implemented lesson plans at a desired rate. It is likely more important that implementation is tracked at a molecular level, to ensure that children have access to the loci of learning that are presumed so important. This might include macro monitoring (e.g., tracking the number of instructional sessions per week) as well as micro monitoring (e.g., tracking the number of instructional episodes within a session to include consideration of specific children's experiences/opportunities). If the field of early childhood education is going to achieve the desired capacity of helping all children arrive at school ready to learn, PD must help early childhood educators understand all the active ingredients of interventions, including how intensity contributes to children's learning over time.

REFERENCES

Assel, M.A., Landry, S.H., Swank, P.R., & Gunnewig, S. (2007). An evaluation of curriculum, setting, and mentoring on the performance of children enrolled in prekindergarten. *Reading and Writing, 20,* 463–494. doi:10.1007/s11145-006-9039-5

Biemiller, A., & Boote, C. (2006). An effective method for building meaning vocabulary in primary grades. *Journal of Educational Psychology, 98,* 44–62. doi:10.1037/0022-0663.98.1.44

Cepeda, N.J., Vul, E., Rohrer, D., Wixted, J.T., & Pashler, H. (2008). Spacing effects in learning: A temporal ridgeline of optimal retention. *Psychological Science, 19,* 1095–1102. doi:10.1111/j.1467-9280.2008.02209

Cherney, L., Patterson, J.P., Raymer, A., Frymark, T., & Schooling, T. (2008). Evidence-based systematic review: Effects of intensity of treatment and constraint-induced language therapy for individuals with stroke-induced aphasia. *Journal of Speech, Language, and Hearing Research, 51,* 1282–1299. doi:10.1044/1092-4388(2008/07-0206)

Childers, J.B., & Tomasello, M. (2002). Two-year-olds learn novel nouns, verbs, and conventional actions from massed or distributed exposures. *Developmental Psychology, 38,* 967–978. doi:10.1037//0012-1649.38.6.967

DeBaryshe, B.D., & Gorecki, D.M. (2007). An experimental validation of a preschool emergent literacy curriculum. *Early Education and Development, 18,* 93–110. doi:10.1080/10409280701274741

Duhon, G.J., Mesmer, E.M., Atkins, M.E., Greguson, L.A., & Olinger, E.S. (2009). Quantifying intervention intensity: A systematic approach to evaluating student response to increasing intervention frequency. *Journal of Behavioral Education, 18,* 101–118. doi:10.1007/s10864-009-9086-5

Ezell, H.K., Justice, L.M., & Parsons, D. (2000). A clinic-based book reading intervention for parents and their preschoolers with communication impairment. *Child Language Teaching and Therapy, 16,* 121–140.

Hassink, J.M., & Leonard, L.B. (2010). Within-treatment factors as predictors of outcomes following conversational recasting. *American Journal of Speech-Language Pathology, 19,* 213–224. doi:10.1044/1058-0360(2010/09-0083)

Justice, L.M., Chow, S.M., Capellini, C., Flanigan, K., & Colton, S. (2003). Emergent literacy intervention for vulnerable preschoolers: Relative effects of two approaches. *American Journal of Speech-Language Pathology, 12,* 320–332. doi:10.1044/1058-0360(2003/078)

Justice, L.M., & Ezell, H.K. (2000). Enhancing children's print and word awareness through home-based parent intervention. *American Journal of Speech-Language Pathology, 9,* 257–269.

Justice, L.M., & Ezell, H.K. (2002). Use of storybook reading to increase print awareness in at-risk children. *American Journal of Speech-Language Pathology, 11,* 17–29. doi:10.1044/1058-0360(2002/003)

Justice, L.M., Kaderavek, J.N., Fan, X., Sofka, A., & Hunt, A. (2009). Accelerating preschoolers' early literacy development through classroom-based teacher-child storybook reading and explicit print referencing. *Language, Speech, and Hearing Services in Schools, 40,* 67–85. doi:10.1044/0161-1461(2008/07-0098)

Justice, L.M., McGinty, A., Piasta, S.B., Kaderavek, J.N., & Fan, X. (2010). Print-focused read-alouds in preschool classrooms: Intervention effectiveness and moderators of child outcomes. *Language, Speech, and Hearing Services in Schools, 41,* 504–520. doi:10.1044/0161-1461(2010/09-0056)

Justice, L.M., Pullen, P.C., & Pence, K. (2008). Influence of verbal and nonverbal references to print on preschoolers' visual attention to print during storybook reading. *Developmental Psychology, 44,* 855–866. doi:10.1037/0012-1649.44.3.855

Justice, L.M., & Sofka, A. (2010). *Calling attention to print: Building young children's knowledge of print.* New York, NY: Guilford Press.

Justice, L.M., Sofka, A., & McGinty, A. (2007). Targets, techniques, and treatment contexts in emergent literacy intervention. *Seminars in Speech and Hearing, 28,* 14–24. doi:10.1055/s-2007-967926

Justice, L.M., Weber, S., Ezell, H.K., & Bakeman, R. (2002). A sequential analysis of children's responsiveness to parental references to print during shared story-book reading. *American Journal of Speech-Language Pathology, 11,* 30–40.

Lane, H.B., & Wright, T. (2007). Maximizing the effectiveness of reading aloud. *The Reading Teacher, 60,* 668–675. doi:10.1598/RT.60.7.7

Law, J., Garrett, Z., & Nye, C. (2004). The efficacy of treatment for children with developmental speech and language delay/disorder: A meta-analysis. *Journal of Speech, Language, and Hearing Research, 47,* 924–943. doi:10.1044/1092-4388(2004/069)

Lemak, C.H., & Alexander, J.A. (2001). Managed care and outpatient substance abuse treatment intensity. *Journal of Behavioral Health Services and Research, 28,* 12–29. doi:10.1007/BF02287231

Mashburn, A., Hamre, B., Downer, J., Justice, L.M., & Pianta, R.C. (in press). Teacher utilization of professional development resources and children's language and literacy development during pre-kindergarten. *Journal of Applied Developmental Psychology.*

McGinty, A.S., Breit-Smith, A., Fan, X., Justice, L.M.,& Kaderavek, J.N. (2011). Does intensity matter? Preschoolers' print knowledge development within a classroom-based intervention. *Early Childhood Research Quarterly, 26,* 255–267.

McGinty, A.S., Justice, L.M., Piasta, S.B., Kaderavek, J., & Fan, X. (in press). Does context matter? Explicit print instruction during reading varies in its influence by child and classroom factors. *Early Childhood Research Quarterly.*

National Institute of Child Health and Development. (2001). *Report of the National Reading Panel. Teaching children to read: An evidence-based assessment of the scientific research literature on reading and its implications for reading instruction* (NIH Publication No. 00-4769). Washington, DC: United States Government Printing Office.

O'Connor, R.E. (2000). Increasing the intensity of intervention in kindergarten and first grade. *Learning Disabilities Research and Practice, 15,* 43–54. doi:10.1207/SLDRP1501_5

Pence, K., Justice, L.M., & Wiggins, A. (2008). Preschool teachers' fidelity of implementation for a language-rich preschool curriculum. *Language, Speech, and Hearing Services in Schools, 39,* 329–341. doi:10.1044/0161-1461(2008/031)

Pianta, R.C., La Paro, K., & Hamre, B. (2008). *Classroom Assessment Scoring System Pre-K,[TM] (CLASS[TM]).* Baltimore, MD: Paul H. Brookes Publishing Co.

Pianta, R.C., Mashburn, A., Downer, J., Hamre, B., & Justice, L.M. (2008). Effects of web-mediated professional development resources on teacher-child interactions in pre-kindergarten classrooms. *Early Childhood Research Quarterly, 23,* 431–451. doi:10.1016/j.ecresq.2008.02.001

Piasta, S., Justice, L.M., McGinty, A., & Kaderavek, J. (in press). Increasing young children's contact with print during shared reading: Longitudinal effects on literacy achievement. *Child Development.*

Proctor-Williams, K., & Fey, M.E. (2007). Recast density and acquisition of novel irregular past tense verbs. *Journal of Speech, Language, & Hearing Research, 50,* 1029–1047. doi:10.1044/1092-4388(2007/072)

Proctor-Williams, K., Fey, M.E., & Loeb, D.F. (2001). Parental recasts and production of copulas and articles by children with specific language impairment and typical language. *American Journal of Speech-Language Pathology, 10,* 155–168. doi:10.1044/1058-0360(2001/015)

Rohrer, D., & Pashler, H. (2007). Increasing retention time without increasing study time. *Current Directions in Psychological Science, 16,* 183–186.

Ukrainetz, T.A., Ross, C.L., & Harm, H.M. (2009). An investigation of treatment scheduling for phonemic awareness with kindergartners at risk for reading difficulties. *Language, Speech, and Hearing Services in Schools, 40,* 86–100. doi:10.1044/0161-1461(2008/07-0077)

Warren, S.F., Fey, M.E., & Yoder, P.J. (2007). Differential treatment intensity research: A missing link to creating optimally effective communication interventions. *Mental Retardation and Developmental Disabilities Research Reviews, 13,* 70–77. doi:10.1002/mrdd.20139

Wasik, B. & Bond, M., & Hindman, A. (2006). The effects of a language and literacy intervention on Head Start children and teachers. *Journal of Educational Psychology, 98* (1), 63–74. doi:10.1037/0022-0663.98.1.63

Weitzman, E., & Greenberg, J. (2010). *ABC and beyond: Building emergent literacy in early childhood settings.* Toronto, Ontario: The Hanen Centre.

What Works Clearinghouse. (2007). *WWC intervention report: Interactive shared reading.* Retrieved April 20, 2011, from http://ies.ed.gov/ncee/wwc/pdf/WWC_ISBR_011807.pdf

Whitehurst, G., Arnold, D.S., Epstein, J.N., Angell, A.L., Smith, M., & Fischel, J.E. (1994). A picture book reading intervention in day care and home for children from low-income families. *Developmental Psychology, 30,* 679–689. doi:10.1037//0012-1649.30.5.679

II

Factors Facilitating and/or Moderating Implementation

5

Extending Models of Emotion Self-Regulation to Classroom Settings

Implications for Professional Development

C. Cybele Raver, Clancy Blair, and Christine Li-Grining

Work by Pianta, Hamre, and others has clearly broken new ground in education by considering the importance of the emotional climate of the classroom for young children's emotional and behavioral adjustment and early learning. But what contributes to some teachers' skill in maintaining a positive emotional climate, while other teachers are found across small and large samples of classrooms to resort to harsh, angry, and hostile emotional tones or to emotionally detached, withdrawn styles of interaction? This chapter builds on earlier work that highlighted the importance of considering teachers' psychological development (e.g., Hamre & Pianta, 2004) when predicting classroom emotional climate. Specifically, the following chapter leverages recent advances in affective neuroscience research, as well as recent research on the emotional processes between caregivers and children in the context of poverty, to briefly explore important predictors of teachers' styles of emotional self-regulation.

Given increasing federal, state, and local pressures to improve the quality of instruction in early childhood classrooms, why should policy makers and program administrators be concerned with teachers' styles of emotional self-regulation? In our view, the instructional quality that we may observe in any given educational setting is likely to reflect a complex set of transactions between teachers and students that may be alternately highly emotionally rewarding or stressful to both the adults and the children in that classroom.

In this chapter we consider the evidence to support this hypothesis. We also consider evidence regarding the corollary proposition that efforts to improve instructional quality through professional development (PD) may be strengthened by taking these psychological and emotional processes into account. In the context of this review, we outline 1) ways that models of coercive versus positive adult–child interaction can be extended to include teachers' emotion regulatory processes in the context of poverty, 2) ways that teachers' emotion dysregulation may interfere with their attention deployment and social information processing, and 3) ways that teachers' emotion dysregulation may heighten their work-related stress (e.g., by affecting the information both encoded and remembered by teachers in classroom contexts and also by indirectly affecting children's proneness to engaging in negative and acting-out behaviors). We then go on to consider the implications of these patterns of emotion regulation and dysregulation among teachers for prevention science and intervention in educational contexts.

Before turning to the theoretical bases and empirical evidence for models of emotion dysregulation in the classroom, it is important to step back and place our interest in modeling the sources and sequelae of teacher–student conflict in perspective: Extant research on teachers' relationships with children in nationally, regionally, and locally sampled studies suggest that most teachers engage in positive interactions with students in their early educational classrooms, with the emotional climate rated as generally positive and teachers reporting high levels of reward and satisfaction in their jobs (Burchinal et al., 2008; Ross, Moiduddin, Meagher, & Carlson, 2008). Our experience and the experience of other intervention trials that have targeted improvements in classroom climate and classroom management demonstrate that, on the whole, teachers can and do improve their skills in working proactively and supportively with children over the school year (see Domitrovich et al., 2009; Morris, Raver, Lloyd, & Millenky, 2009; Pianta, Mashburn, Downer, Hamre, & Justice, 2008; Raver et al., 2009). That said, theoretically driven frameworks that help us better understand the emotional and cognitive processes that lead to conflict and difficulties that a small proportion of teachers face may support intervention that targets improvement in classroom quality in the long run.

MODELS OF ADULT–CHILD
CONFLICT IN THE CLASSROOM

Work by Hamre, Pianta, and colleagues has demonstrated that children's experience of with chronic levels of conflict with teachers is an important predictor children's later adjustment, academic achievement, and risk of disciplinary problems as late as eighth grade (Downer, Rimm-Kaufmann, & Pianta, 2007; Hamre & Pianta, 2001). Yet what leads to teachers' episodes of conflict with young children, and what are the implications of those episodes of conflict for teachers' own emotions and behavior, inside and outside the classroom? Teachers clearly differ markedly from one another in their socioemotional competence versus difficulty when working with their students during these episodes of conflict (see Jennings & Greenberg, 2009). Biosocial and transactional models of coercive cycles of adult–child conflict in the context of socioeconomic disadvantage (see Dishion et al., 2008; Afrank, Cramer, & Patterson, Snyder, 2005; Raver, Garner, & Smith-Donald, 2007) may be helpful in understanding ways that conflicts may arise and the consequences of those conflicts for teachers' emotional states, cognitions, and behaviors in classrooms.

Outlining coercive family processes, Patterson (1995, 2002) offers theoretical and empirical insights on ways that adult caregivers may initially engage in low levels of negative interaction that inadvertently reinforce rather than limit children's negative behavior. Over time adults and children both find themselves resorting to increasingly hostile and emotionally negative efforts to control the outcome of a given interaction, leading to escalating (or "high-amplitude") conflict. Notably, a given teacher, or parent, may become caught in these coercive cycles of interaction in ways that are magnified in stressful social contexts: She may have trouble maintaining a calm and collected perspective on child behavior as she, herself, becomes emotionally dysregulated (Arnold, McWilliams, & Arnold, 1998; Raver, 2004).

Specifically, teachers in early education earn low salaries, on average, and are often low- to moderate-income parents themselves (Phillips, Mekos, Scarr, McCartney, & Abbott-Shim, 2000). Classroom and school contexts represent work environments that may be alternately stressful or supportive, and those contexts may play an important role in shaping teachers' responses to the chronic stresses posed by managing children's disruptive behavior (Chang, 2009; Curbow, 1990; Li-Grining et al., 2010). Extant research suggests conflict may be in the eye of the beholder: Research on children's behavior problems suggests that there are substantial discrepancies in the ways that teachers, parents, and independent observers rate children's disruptive behaviors. For example, in a 2009 study of more than 100 children in a large community-based preschool sample who were identified by either a parent or teacher as manifesting behavioral difficulty, less than 20% of those children were identified by *both* parent and teacher as behaviorally problematic (De Los Reyes, Henry, Tolan, & Wakschlag, 2009). Such findings suggest that child behavior may be situationally specific, with teachers becoming caught in episodes of conflict with children in ways that may differ substantially from children's interactions with their parents. These findings also highlight ways that children's behavioral disruptiveness may be a major, but not sole contributor to the ways that teachers perceive and respond to episodes of conflict in the classroom (De Los Reyes & Kazdin, 2004).

Is there evidence to suggest that either teachers' own psychological characteristics or those of their workplaces matter in teachers' attributions of conflict with children? Recent studies have found support for ways that teachers' and programs' characteristics serve as robust predictors of teachers' subjective evaluations of conflict with children (Mashburn, Hamre, Downer, & Pianta, 2006). For example, findings from data collected from a stratified random sample of 100 state-funded prekindergartens within five states by Hamre, Pianta, Downer, and Mashburn (2008) suggest that, although the bulk of conflict perceived by teachers with their young students could be attributed to children's displays of problem behavior, teachers' feelings of self-efficacy and depressive symptoms were also significant predictors of conflict (Hamre et al., 2008). The length of teachers' work day and classroom emotional climate were also predictive of teachers' reports of conflict, suggesting that teachers' perceptions of the quality of their relationships with children were part and parcel of the emotional processes involved in everyday interactions.

TEACHERS' INFORMATION PROCESSING, EMOTION, EMOTION DYSTREGULATION, AND ATTENTION DEPLOYMENT

Extant research on parent–child conflict suggests that adults who maintain hostile attributional biases regarding child misbehavior are often likely to respond to episodes of negative interactions with children in emotionally irritable ways. That is, adults' attributions about children's intentions and actions can be thought of as "verbal-cognitive rules about the sources of child misbehavior that are used to guide discipline efforts" (Snyder et al., 2005, p. 31) that are invoked more or less automatically in the course of ongoing adult–child interaction. Close attention to teachers' experiences in classroom contexts suggests that the challenges of maintaining classroom order when managing children's negative or acting-out behaviors can be experienced by teachers as emotionally intense, where some teachers feel overwhelmed by worries of not being liked and respected and feelings of lack of control and uncertainty in having to make "on the spot" decisions with little support from supervisors (Chang, 2009). A second feature of adults' negative attributional bias during negative interaction is that they have been found to be less attentive to surface features of children's behavior, leading those adults to select disciplinary or management strategies that are largely ineffective (Thijs & Koomen, 2009). In short, in the heat of conflict, adult cognitions and emotion regulation are argued to work in concert to either limit or, in some instances, enhance adults' contingent responsiveness and proactive socialization of child self-control and compliance.

The idea that levels of emotional arousal and attributions concerning the behavior of others can enhance or derail teachers' abilities to reflect and engage in positive and purposeful interactions with their students is supported by research at the neurobiological level. Research on the coordination of neural circuitry in what is referred to as the brain's limbic system (associated with emotional arousal and the physiological response to stress) and neural circuitry located in the frontal cortex (referred to as executive functions) provides support for a bidirectional model of cognition–emotion interaction at the neurophysiological level (see Blair & Ursache, 2010; Holmes & Wellman, 2009; Zelazo & Cunningham, 2007). Specifically, when stressful, emotionally arousing events stimulate structures of the brain's limbic system, they initiate the release of neuroendocrine hormones, including those associated with the faster acting adrenal autonomic nervous system component such as norepinephrine and those associated with the slower acting hypothalamic-pituitary-adrenal (HPA) axis component such as cortisol. In brief, changes in levels of neuroendocrine hormones that occur in response to stress (corticosteroids, adrenal hormones) influence the levels of synaptic activity in neural circuitry in ways that either increase the likelihood of our reflective, reasoned responses to stimulation or our reliance on more highly reactive automatized responses to environmental cues. At moderate levels of arousal, neuroendocrine hormones rise to levels associated with increased executive function abilities and reflective processing of information. At very high levels of arousal, however, neuroendocrine hormone levels rise to a point at which they begin to inhibit activity in prefrontal brain regions and compromised executive function. High levels of those neuroendocrine hormones also increase activity in posterior brain regions associated with robust memory formation of emotionally arousing events and with the initiation of automatic highly routinized responses to stimulation (Arnsten & Li, 2005).

The previously outlined integrated model highlights the role that stress plays in potentially promoting or inhibiting a person's ability to be thoughtful and purposeful in interactions with others. It also calls attention to the ways individuals can fall into specific patterns of interacting with the world and handling stressful situations that over time become self-reinforcing for good or ill. As such, it helps to focus our conceptual and empirical inquiry on how one remains attentive and mentally "present," using executive functions to structure experience and manage his or her own and others' behaviors. Research in cognitive neuroscience suggests a classic tripartite division of executive functions into domains of working memory, inhibitory control, and the ability to flexibly and volitionally shift the focus of attention when needed. Working memory, for example, refers to the ability to hold information in mind and to operate on it and integrate it with other information—that is, to hold it in the focus of attention and resist distraction and inhibit an automatic or prepotent response tendency. As such, information in working memory, a teacher's ability to remember a positive strategy for working with a sad or frustrated child, is in a state that is vulnerable to interference; therefore, the ability to inhibit automatic shifting of attention to distracting information and to inhibit an automatic but inappropriate response such as in the context of a busy classroom are key components of executive function that can be sorely missed when it is most needed (Blair, 2010). Applied to classroom contexts, such a model of executive function and stress arousal is helpful in understanding the disparity between what teachers may know (or may have recently learned) and how they may act when trying to handle episodes of conflict with their students. In addition, research on executive function and stress suggests that the interaction of stress arousal and executive function abilities relies on the fast and flexible deployment of attention in ways that may quickly modulate emotional arousal to maintain an effective balance between emotion and cognition and that assist the individual in resisting distracting stimuli that interfere with meeting goals (see Blair & Dennis, 2010, for further discussion). Neuroimaging studies with laboratory-based attention tasks, such as flanker and Stroop-like assessments, indicate that such tasks, which induce conflict between stimulus and response, quickly activate the anterior cingulate cortex (Dennis & Chen, 2009; Fan, Hof, Guise, Fossella, & Posner, 2007). The anterior cingulate cortex is a central component of corticolimbic neural circuitry that serves as an intermediary between prefrontal cortex networks associated with executive functions and limbic networks associated stress arousal. Applied to an adult's behavior in classroom contexts, it is not too difficult to imagine ways that flexible deployment of attention would be important (and also easily disrupted) for teachers who are trying to keep a group of 15–20 preschoolers seated quietly on a rug during circle time while also completing a lesson plan or activity. Some teachers might be better able to ignore minor acting-out and disruptive behavior on the part of a few children at the back of the classroom so that they can use class time productively, whereas other teachers may inadvertently become distracted by those negative behaviors, with the plan for the day's lesson diverted or derailed. Research on attention in the context of threatening or emotionally upsetting stimuli suggests that adults who are already experiencing feelings of dysphoria have difficulty disengaging their attention from emotionally negative cues and re-orienting their attention to positive cues in the environment, relative to nondysphoric adults (see Chen & Dennis, 2009; De Raedt & Koster, 2010). In short, evidence suggests that under very high levels of negative emotional arousal, adults' ability to process information may literally "short-circuit," curtailing their use of reflective cognitive processing and flexible attention deployment to less salient situational and environmental cues. Applied to classroom contexts, a teacher who is herself becoming emotionally dysregulated by one child's repeated disruptive behavior may also be less able to pay attention to (and therefore less likely to reinforce) more subtle, positive, and compliant behaviors by other children (e.g., children sitting quietly during circle time).

Put another way, acute stressors can overload adults' (and children's) neuroendocrine systems in ways that literally blow the fuse on their use of more reflective, higher order executive function. In addition, under conditions of chronic stress, resting levels or set points for humans' stress-response systems are altered to high or low resting levels or set points that ultimately impair their ability to flexibly regulate those neuroendocrine systems in response to stress. Difficulties in regulating those neuroendocrine systems cannot only render the individual more liable to difficulties with emotion regulation and executive function, but also to stress-related disease (McEwen, 2000).

Since the year 2000, findings across two disparate literatures focusing on parents' increased HPA axis reactivity in the context of interpersonal conflict and stress exposure on the one hand (Pendry & Adam, 2007; Schechter et al., 2004), and employees' increased HPA axis reactivity in the context of stressful work environments on the other hand (see Chandola, Heraclides, & Kumari, 2009; Pruessner, Hellhammer, & Kirschbaum, 1999), support the ways that this model may function for teachers in the midst of chronically emotionally stressful interactions in the classroom. Although some studies have found evidence of altered HPA reactivity (as indexed by elevated basal levels of cortisol) for *children* who experience high conflict with teachers in early educational contexts (see Rappolt-Schlichtmann et al., 2009; Watamura, Kryzer, & Robertson, 2009), little work has examined *preschool teachers'* HPA axis reactivity in those same stressful classroom conditions. Some evidence suggests that burnout and work-related emotional exhaustion are associated with significant disruptions in primary and secondary teachers' HPA axis functioning (Bellingrath, Weigle, & Kudielka, 2008), suggesting that this is a promising area for future research.

What are the implications of such an integrated model of dysregulation for teachers in classroom contexts? In the immediate context of working with young children, it suggests that teachers who experience high levels of negative emotional arousal may also have a more difficult time focusing their attention on multiple details of their classroom, including the activity and behavior of the other children. In short, classrooms may become more chaotic as teachers who are caught in cycles of negative interaction with one or two children may be less able to effectively scan, monitor, and support the behavior and learning of the larger group of less disruptive children. Alternately, teachers who are able to regain emotional equilibrium during conflict with an individual child are likely to be able to more flexibly deploy their attention to other children's behavior, "catching" and reinforcing children's positive behavioral control.

In addition, the stress of repeated or chronic conflict with children may cyclically reinforce adults' biased cognitive schema as they fall back on more reactive rather than more reflective styles of cognitive processing of information about the situation, the child with whom they are having difficulty, and the possible solutions they might be able to deploy to work more effectively with that child. It also suggests that teachers may extend those biased attributions toward their workplace and their own feelings of efficacy, in what Jennings and Greenberg (2009) have termed a "burnout cascade" (see also, Chang, 2009). In short, due to the ways that the neuroendocrine system and the prefrontal cortex work together to coordinate emotion, attention, and memory, teachers may feel increasingly demoralized and less effective as teachers, having attended to, encoded, and remembered incidents of conflict as the toughest part of their work day (Blasé, 1986). In the longer run, we (and others) speculate that teachers who face chronic job stress are at high risk not only for problems with the regulation of emotion, attention, and stress physiology that will be associated with difficulty in building supportive and effective relationships and interactions with children, but they may also be at increased risk for physical health problems that interfere with job performance and classroom quality. McEwen's (2009) work on allostatic load among adults facing chronic stress suggests that those same stressors that contribute to burnout may lead to wear and tear on adults' immune system function and cardiovascular health. Implications for classroom processes suggest that teachers' compromised health might lead to more sick days, in addition to greater turnover, further destabilizing classroom processes, as children and administrators try to adjust to shifting patterns among teaching staff.

TEACHERS' EMOTION DYSREGULATION AND BURNOUT

Models of emotion regulation can be leveraged to provide some insight into the ways in which interactions between teachers and students may be substantially magnified by work-related stressors. In previous work, we have argued that models of parenting and poverty-related risk could be expanded to consider the work-related stressors imposed by low-wage, menial work, where mothers' transitions to low-wage work with low levels of control were associated with increases in parents' use of harsh, negative parenting at home with their children (Raver, 2003). Research on burnout among teachers suggests strong support for the extension of this hypothesis to classroom contexts: Lack of job control and low resources on the job have consistently been argued to erode teachers' ability to maintain emotionally positive and responsive styles of instruction and care when working with the young children in their classroom (Chang, 2009; Curbow, 1990). Models of burnout are particularly well suited to our effort to better understand emotion regulatory processes between teachers and students, given that burnout is characterized by Maslach (e.g., Maslach & Jackson, 1981) as composed of several components, including an affective dimension (feelings of emotional exhaustion) and a cognitive dimension (attributional bias of depersonalization, desensitization, and callousness toward those individuals whom the teacher is serving, e.g., children). In CSRP analyses, we tested the hypothesis that both personal and work-related stressors would be related to Head Start teachers' maintenance of a positive emotional climate in the classroom, finding that teachers with higher levels of personal stressors (being the primary earner in a single household with a large number of children) was associated with substantially lower levels of classroom behavioral management on the CLASS and lower social interaction on the Early Childhood Environment Rating Scale—Revised Edition (ECERS-R; Li-Grining et al., 2010). Of particular interest, we did not find any evidence that teachers' work-related stressors were significant predictors of classroom quality using the CLASS. These findings are congruent in some ways, and different in others, from findings from previous research (Allhusen et al., 2004; Pianta et al., 2005).

IMPLICATIONS FOR IMPLEMENTATION OF INTERVENTION I: TEACHER'S REGULATORY STYLE AS MODERATOR

Recent findings from several innovative randomized controlled trial (RCT) efficacy trials have suggested that it may be critical to focus a theoretically informed lens on emotion and behavior dysregulation on the part of both adults and children when we ask teachers to try new strategies of instruction or new curricula. Teachers' styles of emotion self-regulation may be an important but underrecognized factor in the extent to which a new intervention is taken up and implemented, thereby potentially amplifying or attenuating the efficacy of programs that target teachers' instructional and classroom management practices. Prevention and educational intervention researchers consistently highlight the importance of teachers' psychological characteristics, more generally, when implementing new approaches designed to support child achievement or behavioral skill: The teacher's interest, willingness, and skill in taking up the intervention is, in almost all cases, the key to getting a given intervention "off the ground" (Baker, Kupersmidt, Voegler-Lee, Arnold, & Willoughby, 2010). This may be particularly true for interventions that target children's socioemotional development. Jennings and Greenberg (2009) point out, for example, the necessity of having teachers themselves serve as outstanding role models of socially competent behavior so that they interact with children in emotionally regulated and respectful ways when implementing a socioemotional learning curriculum (SEL).

In 2010, the CSRP research team tested the hypothesis that teachers' psychosocial stressors might not only erode classroom quality over time, but also serve as a barrier to take up the intervention. The concern might be twofold: That treatment effects might be estimated from boosting the skills of our sample's least stressed teachers, and that treatment might not be reaching the teachers who most need support and additional training (Li-Grining et al., 2010). Instead we found the opposite to be true in our study: Teachers who faced higher levels of work-related stress attended the most trainings and were most highly engaged in intervention (net of levels of personal stress) compared with their less work-stressed colleagues

(Li-Grining et al., 2010). Our findings were similar to those of Domitrovich et al. (2009), who found that teachers who reported higher levels of emotional exhaustion were more involved, rather than less involved, in implementing a new classroom-based intervention with high-fidelity. We speculate that teachers were drawn to opportunities to learn new techniques or approaches that might alleviate key sources of stress, such as children's acting-out behaviors and teachers' own sense of isolation.

On the other hand, we did find that teachers who were more stressed in both the work and personal domains of their lives spent fewer mental health consultant (MHC) classroom visits working on building positive relationships with students and developing empathy for children with the highest levels of behavioral difficulty. This suggests some support for what we might term the "teacher stressor cycle" hypothesis, where teachers' hostile attributional biases reinforce their emotional exhaustion, which in turn reinforces their emotional withdrawal, which then feeds back into continued, negative attributional biases. Within such a scenario, it might be hard for teachers to overcome the hurdle of feeling detached from the children whom they perceive (often correctly) to be exhibiting the most difficult behavior to manage. This has significant implications for one of the major goals of many interventions that focus on promoting self-regulation—that of building more positive teacher–student relationships (Rimm-Kaufman, Storm, Sawyer, Pianta, & LaParo, 2006).

In addition, teachers' psychological characteristics may be implicated in their feelings of stress, serving as moderators of treatment impact. For example, just as some children may be more emotionally reactive to the stress of new contexts such as day care (as indicated by rising levels of cortisol over the course of a given day in out-of-home care), so too may teachers differ in their profiles of emotional and HPA axis reactivity (Dettling, Gunnar, & Gonzella, 1999; Watamura et al., 2009). Adam (2005) considered adult women's cortisol response to a higher number of work and family responsibilities, but to our knowledge, collection of cortisol has not been used to examine the ways that preschool teachers may show increases in HPA reactivity as a function of their "emotional work" with young children and represents an interesting area of inquiry that has not yet been extensively explored. Importantly, it may be those teachers who are under greatest environmental and caregiving stress who benefit most from careful implementation of interventions designed to support their skills in managing their classrooms and building self-regulatory as well as child-regulatory skills.

In addition, there may be situational conditions or characteristics of the classroom that reflect "history" effects as well as individual differences across adult caregivers. For example, just as Gunnar and colleagues have found that children have higher reactivity during the beginning of the school year (as indicated by physiological markers of stress, i.e., cortisol levels), teachers' ability to manage their own emotions and their capacity to provide emotional support to their students might vary at times of transition (Dettling et al.,

1999; Gunnar, Tout, De Haan, Pierce, & Stanbury, 1997). The collection of physiological data from adults in early childhood care settings using designs similar to those applied with children may help us to understand temporal variations in teachers' capacity to manage their own and their students' emotions. In addition, opportunities for PD may be most effective during periods that are moderately, rather than highly, stressful.

In considering ways that adults' self-regulation may moderate intervention, it is also important to keep in mind that extant research on the role of stress and attention suggests a curvilinear, rather than a linear, function. A key axiom (termed the Yerkes-Dodson Principle) in cognitive neuroscience is that stress affects learning in ways that represent a U-shaped curve: Teacher cognition, attention, and motivation to learn new instructional practices might be most easily recruited during periods of moderate stress, but may be depleted in conditions of high stress (Blair, 2010). That is, teachers may be most engaged when they feel moderate levels of challenge, experiencing moderate stress as a motivating, rather than limiting, force in their environments. In contrast, when classrooms become too chaotic and work environments feel too stressful, teachers may be less able to engage in new trainings or consultative sessions offered by interventionists. Some evidence from school-based intervention supports this model, with several researchers emphasizing the importance of schools' and teachers' "readiness for change" (Gottfredson, 2001).

IMPLICATIONS FOR INTERVENTION II: TARGETING TEACHERS' EMOTION REGULATION AS A KEY MEDIATOR

Several investigators have squarely addressed the prospect of teachers' emotion dysregulation as a key target of intervention. Efforts to help teachers reduce their levels of stress and gain greater self-regulation in the context of intervention have been both explicit goals of some intervention and likely mechanisms of change (even if not explicitly identified as a goal) in others.

At the behavioral level, Webster-Stratton, Reid, and Hammond (2004) and others have specifically targeted teachers' management of episodes of conflict with children to reduce the likelihood that they escalate to the point of emotion dysregulation on the part of both the adults and children (Ialongo et al., 1999; Lochman & Wells, 2003). These behaviorally anchored classroom management models have been embedded in multicomponent preventive interventions that are designed to support positive behavior in young children across home and school contexts. Similar approaches have been used in classroom settings where children with emotional and behavioral disorders are served (see Hester, Hendrikson, & Gable, 2009).

Other models have explicitly anchored their intervention effort in models of emotion and behavior self-regulation on the part of both children and adults. For example, in CSRP, we anchored a multicomponent model of intervention in a theoretical framework that focused on emotion and behavior regulatory processes between teachers and children. As one mechanism to reduce children's behavior problems, we provided 30 hours of intensive training in strategies teachers could employ to provide their classrooms with more effective regulatory support and better classroom management (Raver et al., 2008). We also drew from the complementary theoretical "burnout" model outlined earlier, whereby teachers were hypothesized to be at risk for emotion dysregulation as a result of trying to meet too many classroom demands with too little support (Brouwers & Tomic, 2000). Our review of this second body of literature raised our level of concern regarding treatment dosage and fidelity: We worried that teachers might be unlikely to take new, proactive steps to support children's behavioral self-regulation if they themselves felt unsupported (Woolfolk, Rosoff, & Hoy, 1990). This framework led us to include two additional components to the model. As part of a model of classroom- and child-centered consultation, a weekly MHC provided 20 weeks of consultation as a "coach" in supporting teachers while they tried new techniques learned in the teacher training (Donohue, Falk, & Provet, 2000; Gorman-Smith, Beidel, Brown, Lochman, & Haaga, 2003). As an additional program component, MHCs also spent a significant portion of the school year (in winter) conducting stress-reduction workshops to help teachers reduce stress and limit burnout.

How might the coach–teacher relationship have helped teachers' emotion self-regulation in the context of PD? We speculate that this supportive relationship may have provided needed positive affective reinforcement (in the form of praise) to help shift teachers' negative attributions and to shape their development of new skills. Coaches' perspectives on classroom dynamics may have helped shift teachers' views of their own skills as well as their attributions about some children as chronically "bad" versus "good." By carefully observing teachers and children and providing regular feedback on teachers' successes and challenges in implementing newly learned classroom management strategies, coaches may also have helped teachers redirect their own attention, problem solving, and self-monitoring when managing children's disruptive behaviors (with the hope that teachers would continue self-monitoring once the coaches left at the end of the school year). In short, we hoped the coaches' regular feedback would help caregivers in proactive ways; that they might cognitively restructure their attributions about negative child behavior as well as lower their emotion negativity in the context of conflict with children. Lastly, we also included a clear emphasis on stress reduction for teachers. Although these components represent only preliminary attempts to support teachers' regulatory style, they were promising, and our hunch is that teachers were more willing to take the risk of trying new strategies of classroom management when given support from coaches for managing their own feelings of frustration and distress.

A second approach has been to focus directly on adults' stress reduction through mindfulness training. Also termed mindfulness meditation (MM), this focus on mindfulness is designed to help adults (including parents, teachers, and military personnel) handle high levels of stress (Jha, Stanley, Kiyonaga, Wong, & Gelfand, 2010; Kabat-Zinn, 2003; Segal, Williams, & Teasdale, 2002). When applied to parents, Duncan, Coatsworth, and Greenberg (2009) argue that bringing "mindful awareness" to parent–child interactions can substantially help adult caregivers avoid making biased attributions or appraisals and "attend to their child's needs, while exercising self-regulation and wise choice in their actions" (p. 256). Adults are given basic behavioral tools to monitor their own escalating negative appraisals and feelings of frustration in the context of dyadic interaction and to attenuate prolonged reactivity to negative stimuli. Importantly, multiple 2009 randomized trials with parents suggest that mindfulness training supports adult caregivers' reports of parent–child relationship quality, and parents' self-reported mental health (Coatsworth, Duncan, Greenberg, & Nix, 2009, reported in Duncan et al., 2009). Recent work using experimental paradigms suggests clear neuroaffective benefit of such training, with adults randomly assigned to 7 weeks of MM compared with adults in control groups. Those practicing mindfulness training were found to show improved cognitive control (indexed by performance on working memory tasks), higher positive affect and lower negative affect (as reported on the a commonly used self-report measure, the PANAS), and attenuated reactivity to emotion stimuli during a lab-based task when compared with other adults who were randomly assigned to a wait-list control condition (Jha et al., 2010; Ortner, Kilner, & Zelazo, 2007). These studies (as well as others) have also reported that individuals randomly assigned to a mindfulness condition have been found to exhibit higher immune function and to report lower feelings of anxiety and negative affect, compared with those young adults who were randomly assigned to a control condition (see Davidson et al., 2003).

SUMMARY AND FUTURE DIRECTIONS

There are a wide array of approaches that we did not review in this chapter, including interventions that target teachers' psychological feelings of empowerment, efficacy, and internal working models. However, one lesson from our own work, from work by Dishion and colleagues (in "Family Check Up" interventions with parents, 2008), and work by Pianta and colleagues (in MyTeachingPartner interventions with teachers, 2008), is that teachers may feel most empowered when they are able to successfully enact new behavioral repertoires, breaking those very cycles of coercive interaction that we discussed earlier. Specifically, interventions by Dishion, Pianta, Bierman, Greenberg, and others share the following in common: They are based on concrete, actionable steps that teachers can take that lead to immediate improvement in individual children's behaviors or improvements in classroom processes, which may be reinforcing in their own right. When combined with regular feedback from coaches, consultants, or mentors, teachers may be better able to attend to and remember the link between their own actions and the incremental improvements in child behavior and classroom climate that the coach or consultant helps the teacher to perceive. In so doing, teachers may be able to experience the physiologic as well as cognitive and affective benefits of new strategies of self-regulation and regulation of child behavior.

In an effort to identify pathways that might be amenable to intervention, this chapter has provided a thumbnail sketch of the neuroendocrine, affective, and cognitive processes that may underlie teacher–child conflict. We have made the case that, in the heat of conflict, adult cognitions and emotion regulation work in concert to limit, or in some instances enhance, adults' contingent responsiveness and proactive socialization of child self-control and compliance. Our second aim was to consider the self-regulatory, relational, and organizational hurdles that teachers face when asked to take the risk of adopting new approaches to working with young children. In so doing, we hope to have shed light on ways that adults may benefit from PD in both the short and long run. Empirical examination of models of adult self-regulation in classroom contexts (in ways that integrate a clearer understanding of teachers' stress physiology, emotion, attention, and executive function) represents an intriguing area for future research. We look forward to testing ways that teachers may not only be better able to support children's learning but may themselves be in better emotional, behavioral, and physiological shape when given high levels of regulatory support in the context of intervention.

REFERENCES

Adam, E. (2005). Momentary emotion and cortisol levels in the everyday lives of working parents. In B. Schneider & L. Waite (Eds.), *Being together, working apart: Dual-career families and the work-life balance* (pp. 105–133). New York, NY: Cambridge University Press.

Allhusen, V., Belsky, J., Booth-LaForce, C.L., Bradley, R., Brownwell, C.A., Burchinal, M., ... NICHD Early Child Care Research Network (2004). Does class size in first grade relate to children's academic and social performance or observed classroom processes? *Developmental Psychology, 40,* 651–664. doi:10.1037/0012-1649.40.5.651

Arnold, D.H., McWilliams, L., & Arnold, E.H. (1998). Teacher discipline and child misbehavior in day care: Untangling causality with correlational data. *Developmental Psychology, 34,* 276–287. doi:10.1037//0012-1649.34.2.276

Arnsten, A.F.T., & Li, B.M. (2005). Neurobiology of executive functions: Catecholamine influences on prefrontal cortical functions. *Biological Psychiatry, 57*(11), 1377–1384. doi:10.1016/j.biopsych.2004.08.019

Baker, C.N., Kupersmidt, J.B., Voegler-Lee, M.E., Arnold, D.H., & Willoughby, M.T. (2010). Predicting teacher participation in a classroom-based, integrated preventive intervention for preschoolers. *Early Childhood Research Quarterly, 25,* 270–283. doi:10.1016/j.ecresq.2009.09.005

Bellingrath, S., Weigle, T., & Kudielka, B.M. (2008). Cortisol dysregulation in school teachers in relation to burnout, vital exhaustion, and effort-reward-imbalance. *Biological Psychology, 78,* 104–113. doi:10.1016/j.biopsycho.2008.01.006

Blasé, J.J. (1986). A qualitative analysis of sources of teacher stress: Consequences for performance. *American Educational Research Journal, 23,* 13–40. doi:10.2307/1163040

Blair, C. (2010). Stress and the development of self-regulation in context. *Child Development Perspectives, 4*(3), 181–188.

Blair, C. & Dennis, T. (2010). An optimal balance: Emotion-cognition integration in context. In. S. Calkins & M. Bell (Eds.), *Child development at the intersection of cognition and emotion* (pp. 17–36). Washington, DC: American Psychological Association.

Blair, C & Ursache, A. (2010). A bidirectional model of executive functions and self-regulation. In K.D. Vohs & R.F. Baumeister (Eds.), *Handbook of self-regulation: Research, theory, and applications* (2nd edition). New York, NY: Guilford Press.

Brouwers, A. & Tomic, W. (2000). A longitudinal study of teacher burnout and perceived self-efficacy in classroom management. *Teaching and Teacher Education, 16,* 239–253.

Burchinal, M., Howes, C., Pianta, R., Bryant, D., Early, D., Clifford, R., & Barbarin, O. (2008). Predicting child outcomes at the end of kindergarten from the quality of pre-kindergarten teacher-child interactions and instruction. *Applied Developmental Science, 12,* 140–153. doi:10.1080/10888690802199418

Chandola, T., Heraclides, A., & Kumari, M. (2009). Psychophysiological biomarkers of workplace stressors. *Neuroscience and Behavioral Reviews, 35,* 51–57. doi:10.1016/j.neubiorev.2009.11.005

Chang, M. (2009). An Appraisal perspective of teacher burnout: Examining the emotional work of teachers. *Educational Psychology Review, 21,* 193–218. doi:10.1007/s10648-009-9106-y

Coatsworth, J.D., Duncan, L.G., Greenberg, M.T., & Nix, R.L. (2009). *Changing parents' mindfulness, child management skills, and relationship quality with their youth: Results from a randomized pilot intervention trial.* Manuscript under review.

Curbow, B. (1990). Job stress in child care workers: A framework for research. *Child and Youth Care Quarterly, 19,* 215–231. doi:10.1007/BF01083941

Davidson, R.J., Kabat-Zinn, J., Schumacher, J., Rosencranz, M., Muller, D., Santorelli, S.F., ... Sheridan, J.F. (2003). Alterations in brain and immune function produced by mindfulness meditation. *Psychosomatic Medicine, 65,* 564–570. doi:10.1097/01.PSY.0000077505.67574.E3

De Los Reyes, A., & Kazdin, A.E. (2004). Measuring informant discrepancies in clinical child research. *Psychological Assessment, 16,* 330–334. doi:10.1037/1040-3590.16.3.330

De Los Reyes, S., Henry, D.B., Tolan, P.H., & Wakschlag, L.S. (2009). Linking informant discrepancies to observed variations in young children's disruptive behavior. *Journal of Abnormal Child Psychology, 37,* 637–652.

De Raedt, R., & Koster, E.H. (2010). Understanding vulnerability for depression from acognitive neuroscience perspective: A reappraisal of attentional factors and a new conceptual framework. *Cognitive, Affective, and Behavioral Neuroscience, 10*(1), 50–70.

Dennis, T.A., & Chen, C. (2009). Trait anxiety and conflict monitoring following threat: An ERP study. *Psychophysiology, 46,* 122–131. doi:10.1111/j.1469-8986.2008.00758

Dettling, A.C., Gunnar, M.R., & Gonzella, B. (1999). Cortisol levels of young children in full day childcare centers: Relations with age and temperament. *Psychoneuroendocrinology, 24,* 519–536. doi:10.1016/S0306-4530(99)00009-8

Dishion, T.J., Connell, A., Weaver, C., Shaw, D., Gardner, F., & Wilson, M. (2008). The family check-up with high-risk indigent families: Preventing problem behavior by increasing parents' positive behavior support in early childhood. *Child Development, 79,* 1395–1414. doi:10.1111/j.1467-8624.2008.01195

Domitrovich, C.E., Gest, S.D., Gill, S., Bierman, K.L., Welsh, J.A., & Jones, D. (2009). Fostering high-quality teaching with an enriched curriculum and professional development support: The Head Start REDI program. *American Educational Research Journal, 46*(2), 567–597. doi:10.3102/0002831208328089

Donohue, P., Falk, B., & Provet, A.G. (2000). *Mental health consultation in early childhood.* Baltimore, MD: Paul H. Brookes Publishing Co.

Downer, J.T, Rimm-Kaufman, S.E., & Pianta, R.C. (2007). How do classroom conditions and children's risk for school problems contribute to children's behavioral engagement in learning? *School Psychology Review, 36,* 413–432.

Duncan, L.G., Coatsworth, J.D., & Greenberg, M.T. (2009). A model of mindful parenting: Implications for parent-child relationships and prevention research. *Clinical Child and Family Psychology Review, 12*(3), 255–270. doi:10.1007/s10567-009-0046-3

Fan, J., Hof, P.R., Guise, K.G., Fossella, J.A., & Posner, M.I. (2007). The functional integration of the anterior cingulate cortex during conflict processing. *Cerebral Cortex, 18*(4), 796–805. doi:10.1093/cercor/bhm125

Gorman-Smith, D., Beidel, D., Brown, T.A., Lochman, J., & Haaga, A.F. (2003). Effects of teacher training and consultation on teacher behavior towards students at high risk for aggression. *Behavior Therapy, 34,* 437–452. doi:10.1016/S0005-7894(03)80029-1

Gottfredson, G.D. (2001). Fostering the scientific practice of vocational psychology. *Journal of Vocational Behavior, 59*(2), 192–202. doi:10.1006/jvbe.2001.1825

Gunnar, M.R., Tout, K., De Haan, M., Pierce, S., & Stanbury, K. (1997). Temperament, social competence, and adrenocortical activity in preschoolers. *Developmental Psychobiology, 31,* 65–85. doi:10.1002/(SICI)1098-2302(199707)31:1<65::AID-DEV6>3.0.CO;2-S

Hamre, B.K., & Pianta, R.C. (2001). Early teacher-child relationships and the trajectory of children's school outcomes through eighth grade. *Child Development, 72,* 625–638. doi:10.1111/1467-8624.00301

Hamre, B.K., & Pianta, R.C. (2004). Self-reported depression in nonfamilial caregivers: Prevalence and associations with caregiver behavior in child-care settings. *Early Childhood Research Quarterly, 19,* 297–318. doi:10.1016/j.ecresq.2004.04.006

Hamre, B.K., Pianta, R.C., Downer, J.T., & Mashburn, A.J. (2008). Teachers' perceptions of conflict with young students: Looking beyond problem behaviors. *Social Development, 17,* 115–136. doi:10.1111/j.1467-9507.2007.00418

Hester, P.P., Hendrickson, J.M., & Gable, R.A. (2009). Forty years later—The value of praise, ignoring, and rules for preschoolers at risk for behavior disorders. *Education and Treatment of Children, 32*(4), 513–535.

Holmes, A., & Wellman, C.L. (2009). Stress-induced prefrontal reorganization and executive dysfunction in rodents. *Neuroscience and Biobehavioral Reviews, 33*(6), 773–783. doi:10.1016/j.neubiorev.2008.11.005

Ialongo, N.S., Werthamer, L., Kellam, S.G., Brown, C.H., Wang, S., & Lin, Y. (1999). Proximal impact of two first-grade preventive interventions on the early risk behaviors for later substance abuse, depression, and antisocial behavior. *American Journal of Community Psychology, 27,* 599–641.

Jennings, P.A., & Greenberg, M.T. (2009). The prosocial classroom: Teacher social and emotional competence in relation to student and classroom outcomes. *Review of Educational Research, 79,* 491–507. doi:10.3102/0034654308325693

Jha, A.P., Stanley, E.A., Kiyonaga, A., Wong, L., & Gelfand, L. (2010). Examining the protective effects of mindfulness training on working memory capacity and affective experience. *Emotion, 10*(1), 54–64. doi:10.1037/a0018438

Kabat-Zinn, J. (2003). Mindfulness-based interventions in context: Past, present, and future. *Clinical Psychology: Science and Practice, 10*(2), 144–156. doi:10.1093/clipsy.bpg016

Li-Grining, C., Raver, C.C., Champion, K., Sardin, L., Metzger, M.W., & Jones, S.M. (2010). Understanding and improving classroom emotional climate in the "real world": The role of teachers' psychosocial stressors. *Early Education and Development*, 21(1), 65–94. doi:10.1080/10409280902783509

Lochman, J.E., & Wells, K.C. (2003). Effectiveness of the coping power program and of classroom intervention with aggressive children: Outcomes at a 1-year follow-up. *Behavior Therapy*, 34, 493–515. doi:10.1016/S0005-7894(03)80032-1

Mashburn, A.J., Hamre, B.K., Downer, J.T., & Pianta, R.C. (2006). Teacher and classroom characteristics associated with teachers' ratings of prekindergartners' relationships and behaviors. *Journal of Psychoeducational Assessment*, 24(4), 367–380. doi:10.1177/0734282906290594

Maslach, C. & Jackson, S.E. (1981). The measurement of experienced burnout. *Journal of Organizational Behavior*, 2, 99–113. doi:10.1002/job.4030020205

McEwen, B.S. (2000). The neurobiology of stress: From serendipity to clinical relevance. *Brain Research*, 886, 172–189. doi:10.1016/S0006-8993(00)02950-4

Morris, P., Raver, C.C., Lloyd, C., & Millenky, M. (2009). *Can teacher training in classroom management make a difference for children's experiences in preschool? A preview of findings from the foundations of learning demonstration*. New York, NY: MDRC.

Ortner, C.N., Kilner, S.J., & Zelazo, P.D. (2007). Mindfulness meditation and reduced emotional interference on a cognitive task. *Motivation and Emotion*, 31, 271–283. doi:10.1007/s11031-007-9076-7

Patterson, G.R. (1995). Coercion as a basis for early age of onset for arrest. In J. McCord (Ed.), *Coercion and punishment in long-term perspectives* (pp. 81–105). New York, NY: Cambridge University Press.

Patterson, G.R. (2002). The early development of coercive family process. In J.B. Reid, G.R. Patterson, & J. Snyder (Eds.), *Antisocial behavior in children and adolescents: A developmental analysis and model for intervention* (pp. 25–44). Washington, DC: American Psychological Association.

Pendry, P. & Adam, E.K. (2007). Associations between parents' marital functioning, maternal parenting quality, maternal emotion and child cortisol levels. *International Journal of Behavioral Development*, 31, 218–231. doi:10.1177/0165025407074634

Phillips, D., Mekos, D., Scarr, S., McCartney, K., & Abbott-Shim, M. (2000). Within and beyond the classroom door: Assessing quality in child care centers. *Early Childhood Research Quarterly*, 15(4), 475–496. doi:10.1016/S0885-2006(01)00077-1

Pianta, R.C., Howes, C., Burchinal, M., Bryant, D., Clifford, R., Early, D., & Barbarin, O. (2005). Features of pre-kindergarten programs, classrooms, and teachers: Do they predict observed classroom quality and child-teacher interactions? *Applied Developmental Science*, 9, 144–159. doi:10.1207/s1532480xads0903_2

Pianta, R.C., Mashburn, A., Downer, J.T., Hamre, B.K., & Justice, L. (2008). Effects of web-mediated professional development resources on teacher-child interactions in pre-kindergarten classrooms. *Early Childhood Research Quarterly*, 23, 431–451. doi:10.1016/j.ecresq.2008.02.001

Pruessner, J., Hellhammer, D.H., & Kirschbaum, C. (1999). Burnout, perceived stress, and cortisol responses to awakening. *Psychosomatic Medicine*, 61, 197–204.

Rappolt-Schlichtmann, G., Willett, J. B., Ayoub, C.C., Lindsley, R., Hulette, A. C., & Fischer, K.W. (2009). Poverty, relationship conflict, and the regulation of cortisol in small and large group contexts at child care. *Mind, Brain, and Education*, 3(3), 131–142. doi:10.1111/j.1751-228X.2009.01063

Raver, C.C. (2003). Does work pay psychologically as well as economically? The role of employment in predicting depressive symptoms and parenting among low-income families. *Child Development*, 74, 1720–1736.

Raver, C.C. (2004). Childcare as a work support, a child-focused intervention, and a job. In A.C. Crouter & A. Booth (Eds.), *Work-family challenges for low-income parents and their children* (pp. 179–190). Mahwah, NJ: Erlbaum.

Raver, C.C., Garner, P.W., & Smith-Donald, R. (2007). The roles of emotion regulation and emotion knowledge for children's academic readiness: Are the links
causal? In R.C. Pianta, M.J. Cox, & K.L. Snow (Eds.), *Kindergarten transition and
early school success* (pp. 121–148). Baltimore, MD: Paul H. Brookes Publishing Co.

Raver, C.C., Jones, S.M., Li-Grining, C.P., Metzger, M.W., Smallwood, K., & Sardin, L. (2008). Improving preschool classroom processes: Preliminary findings
from a randomized trial implemented in Head Start settings. *Early Childhood
Research Quarterly, 23,* 10–26. doi:10.1016/j.ecresq.2007.09.001

Raver, C.C., Jones, S.M., Li-Grining, C.P., Zhai, F., Metzger, M., & Solomon,
B. (2009). Targeting children's behavior problems in preschool classrooms: A
cluster-randomized controlled trial. *Journal of Consulting and Clinical Psychology,
77,* 302–316. doi:10.1037/a0015302

Rimm-Kaufman, S.E., Storm, M.D., Sawyer, B.E., Pianta, R.C., & LaParo, K.M.
(2006). The teacher belief Q-sort measure of teachers' priorities in relation to
disciplinary practices, teaching practices, and beliefs about children. *Journal of
School Psychology, 44,* 141–165.

Ross, C., Moiduddin, E., Meagher, C., & Carlson, B. (2008). *The Chicago program evaluation project: A picture of early childhood programs, teachers, and preschool-age children
in Chicago* (Final External Report). Princeton, NJ: Mathematica Policy Research.

Schechter, D.S., Zeanah, C.H., Myers, M.M., Brunelli, S.A., Liebowitz, M.R.,
Marshall, R.D., ... Hofer, M. A. (2004). Psychobiological dysregulation in vi-
olence-exposed mothers: Salivary cortisol of mothers with very young children
pre- and post-separation stress. *Bulletin of the Menninger Clinic, 68*(4), 319–336.
doi:10.1521/bumc.68.4.319.56642

Segal, Z.V., Williams, J.M.G., & Teasdale, J.D. (2002). *Mindfulness-based cognitive therapy
for depression: A new approach for preventing relapse.* New York, NY: Guilford Press.

Snyder, J., Cramer, A., Afrank, J, & Patterson, G.R. (2005). The contributions of
ineffective discipline and parental hostile attributions of child misbehavior to the
development of conduct problems at home and school. *Developmental Psychology,
41,* 30–41.

Thijs, J., & Koomen, H.M.Y. (2009). Toward a further understanding of teachers' reports of early teacher-child relationships: Examining the role of behavior appraisal and attributions. *Early Childhood Research Quarterly, 24,* 186–197.
doi:10.1016/j.ecresq.2009.03.001

Watamura, S.E., Kryzer, E.M., & Robertson, S.S. (2009). Cortisol patterns at
home and child care: Afternoon differences and evening recovery in children
attending very high quality full-day center-based child care. *Journal of Applied
Developmental Psychology, 30*(4) 475–485. doi:10.1016/j.appdev.2008.12.027

Webster-Stratton, C., Reid, M.J., & Hammond, M. (2004). Treating children with
early-onset conduct problems: Intervention outcomes for parent, child, and
teacher training. *Journal of Clinical Child and Adolescent Psychology, 33,* 105–124.
doi:10.1207/S15374424JCCP3301_11

Woolfolk, A.E., Rosoff, B., & Hoy, W.K. (1990). Teachers' sense of efficacy and
their beliefs about managing their students. *Teaching and Teacher Education, 6,*
137–148. doi:10.1016/0742-051X(90)90031-Y

Zelazo, P.D., & Cunningham, W.A. (2007). Executive function: Mechanisms underlying emotion regulation. In J.J. Gross (Ed), *Handbook of emotion regulation*
(pp. 135–158). New York, NY: Guilford Press.

6

Implications of Information Processing Theory for Professional Development of Early Educators

Jason T. Downer, Faiza Jamil,
Michelle F. Maier, and Robert C. Pianta

Each day that early educators arrive in the classroom, they face the challenge of navigating a complex set of classroom dynamics in order to foster children's learning and development. They are often simultaneously juggling long-term learning objectives with real-time, in-the-moment needs and cues of children. This complexity only increases as racial/ethnic and linguistic diversity expand, and inclusion efforts place children with varying learning needs in the same classroom, thus intensifying the difficulty of simultaneously addressing both socioemotional and academic learning. The daunting nature of classroom teaching is well reflected in the following quote from Shulman (2004), who notes that

> The more time I spend in classrooms with teachers—talking with them, observing, watching videotapes, talking some more, reflecting on my own teaching—the more I peel off layer upon layer of incredible complexity. After 30 years of doing such work, I have concluded that classroom teaching...is perhaps the most complex, most challenging, and most demanding, subtle, nuanced, and frightening activity that our species has ever invented. In fact, when I compared the complexity of teaching with that much more highly rewarded profession, "doing medicine," I concluded that the only time medicine even approaches the complexity of an average day of classroom teaching is in an emergency room during a natural disaster. (p. 504)

Handling the nuances of the moment within changing classroom dynamics while trying to remain focused on learning objectives can place great demands on teachers' cognitive skills—such as memory, attention, and information processing speed. In particular, overload of cognitive capacities and skills can occur when the external demands of a situation and need for active, internal processing of incoming information overburden a teacher's cognitive capacity.

Recent applications of information processing theory, and the dual-process model of cognition in particular, to teaching indicate the central role that both deliberate and automatic cognitive processing play in teachers' real-time, classroom-based decision making and ultimately their application of effective practices (Feldon, 2007; Gregoire, 2003). This focus on the basic psychological processes of attention and memory has exciting implications for teacher training within preservice and in-service professional development (PD) contexts. In particular, dual process theory provides support for a growing trend in early educator training toward the use of video-based learning and feedback mechanisms that target authentic repeated practice, development of cognitive schema, and teachers' understanding of how to detect appropriate cues, attend to relevant sensory information, and access the relevant knowledge needed to undertake a suitable course of action—often all without much time or overt conscious awareness.

In this chapter, we briefly summarize the dual process theory of information processing theory as it relates to teaching in early childhood education classrooms and discuss the implications of this theory for pre- and in-service training of early educators. In particular, we provide a case example of applying these cognitive principles to video-based coursework and coaching and report on recent findings from a randomized controlled trial that support this integration of cognitive theory into early educators' training. We conclude with a discussion of next steps in future research on the alignment of cognitive processing models with early education teacher training programs and supports. We also draw a broader set of conclusions about the need for teacher preparation and PD to take into account a larger set of basic psychological processes, which can be measured directly, studied objectively, and altered through PD offerings, as contributors to changes in practice.

APPLICATION OF INFORMATION PROCESSING THEORY TO THE COMPLEXITY OF TEACHING

The cognitively challenging elements of teaching young children are largely overlooked when developing methods to support early educators' work in the classroom. In reality, teaching is in large part a cognitive balancing act that involves drawing relevant pedagogical content and process knowledge from long-term storage as well as actively processing the wide array of sensory information that occurs moment to moment within classrooms. How these cognitive processes work and are manifest in actual teaching practice can be understood through the lens of information processing theory, which essentially considers the human mind to be computer-like, in that it takes incoming data from the senses and applies several cognitive processes to them (Mayer, 2005). The following sections provide a brief overview of information processing theory as applied to teaching in early childhood education settings, with a particular emphasis on how a dual-process model of cognition (Barrett, Tugade, & Engle, 2004) holds direct implications for the support and training of early educators.

Information Processing Theory

In its most basic sense, the human information processing system consists of two primary components—working and long-term memory—and the cognitive processes that connect them to one another and to incoming perceptual information (see Figure 6.1). Perceptual input can come from any of the five senses, though hearing and seeing are the most relevant and active in the case of teaching. Consider for a minute a teacher sitting in a circle with a large group of 4-year-olds. This teacher hears a teaching assistant calling to her from across the room, while at the same time listening to a child answer her question about what he had for breakfast that morning. Simultaneously, the teacher feels a girl leaning into her from the left, notices two children across the circle turned slightly away from the group and whispering, and sees the clock on the wall reaching 9 a.m. Important to note is that this is where the first cognitive process plays a role—attention.

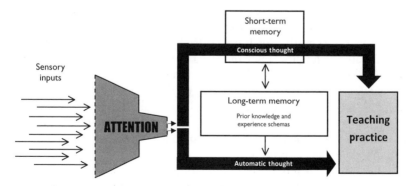

Figure 6.1. Dual-process model of cognition as applied to teaching in early education classrooms. (We acknowledge that this is an oversimplification of the information processing model, for the purpose of a basic illustration of the ways it could be applied to teaching. For more detailed accounts of the model, please refer to Sweller, (2005), and Smith and DeCoster, (2000).

If the teacher pays particular attention to the two whispering children, then this visual information moves along the processing chain, and other sensory inputs go undetected or unprocessed at higher levels.

Working memory then involves the *conscious processing* of perceptual information to determine a course of action. But, importantly, this effortful, controlled processing of information also involves the integration of prior knowledge and experiences, which are stored within long-term memory as part of dynamic and growing organizational networks called *schemas* (Sweller, 2005). These schemas are a resource, resulting in more efficient processing of incoming information and selection of a course of action, because all the relevant pieces of prior knowledge can be quickly accessed as an interconnected whole, instead of an assortment of individual ideas. For example, the teacher from the above example attends to the two children across the circle and consciously recalls that this same pair distracted each other the day before. The teacher pulls from long-term memory the fact that these children, and others before them in similar situations, responded positively to subtle verbal redirection to listen to the group discussion. Therefore, visual input is pulled into working memory through selective attention, this new information is integrated with past knowledge stored within long-term memory (i.e., a schema for subtle redirection), and the result is fluid repetition of a successful practice from the teacher's previous experience.

Dual-Process Model of Cognition

The previous example of how information is processed by a teacher within the classroom environment focuses exclusively on a deliberate, reflective pathway that relies heavily on working memory. In contrast, a dual-process model of cognition adds to the basic information processing system an alternative cognitive pathway—*automaticity*. This pathway involves the fluid, nonconscious processing of incoming information (Wegner, 2002) and eases the cognitive load experienced by working memory, which is only capable of holding and handling a limited amount of information at one time. In particular, when a schema is applied repeatedly over time to deliberately process information as previously described, this application becomes increasingly automatized until eventually the well-used schema within long-term memory operates as a cognitive "shortcut" that helps an individual respond quickly in a given situation without conscious thought, and thereby reduces overall load.

Let's step back into the classroom for an illustration of how this might work. During a whole group book reading activity, the teacher pauses to ask children to describe what they see on each page and predict what might happen next. In this instance, her schema for a group book reading, based on a combination of past experiences and an understanding of children's emergent language/literacy development, revolves around the concept of active involvement and providing opportunities for children to use language and to think. As new sensory information becomes available, the teacher can consciously attend to this information, automatically apply the same schema, or unconsciously activate a different schema in order to arrive at a course of action. For example, let's say that a child is so enthusiastic about an illustration in the book that she leans forward, points excitedly, and begins to wiggle in place. There seem to be many potential directions for the teacher to go in this situation, based on what she sees and hears. If she were to apply the schema described above, she might use an open-ended prompt such as, "Tell me what you see Abby," so that the child becomes engaged in sharing her ideas. Alternatively, the girl's minor misbehavior may activate a schema about classroom management and lead to the teacher stating a rule about raising a hand quietly to which the girl responds. During either scenario, schemas help to unconsciously focus the teacher's attention on the most relevant cues in the classroom environment, as well as apply rules of thumb based on experience, that process incoming data more efficiently. In essence, teaching involves a delicate balance of both effortful and automatic cognitive processes, with each having their pros and cons for supporting effective practice.

Limitations of Conscious and Automatic Processing

One of the biggest shortcomings of conscious thought is the fact that there are limits to working memory (Sweller, 2005). Namely, working memory can only process so much incoming information at one time. Therefore, when the demands of a given classroom situation exceed the processing capacity of working memory, a teacher experiences *cognitive overload* that can negatively affect teaching performance. More specifically, this overload occurs when extraneous load, or anything that is irrelevant to the teaching moment, distracts a teacher from the germane load, or the combination of relevant information from the current situation and from long-term memory that are likely to inform effective practice (Sweller, 1988).

There are two ways that an imbalance of extraneous and germane cognitive load can result in poor teaching performance. First, the experience of overload leads to limited flexibility in the moment. For example, when working memory is tapped out, a teacher's attentional resources are greatly diminished, so they are less effective at noticing and then responding to the individual needs of certain children (Schempp, Tan, Manross, & Fincher, 1998; Webb, Diana, Luft, Brooks, & Brennan, 1997). In addition, teachers who are overreliant on conscious processing of information have a difficult time adapting to unique, unanticipated situations (Borko & Putnam, 1996) because their processing resources are already fully engaged, such as an inexperienced or early career teacher. A second implication of cognitive overload is the increased risk of applying "fast and frugal" reasoning that can be grounded in misleading schemas, such as stereotypes and biases (Gigerenzer, Czerlinski, & Martignon, 2002, p. 559). For example, if a boy is constantly crawling over peers in the dress-up area in the midst of a busy part of the morning, the teacher may draw on stereotypes of boys' behavior to determine her response, rather than individualizing to that particular child. She might think "These active boys just won't ever listen," get frustrated, and reprimand the child. This snap judgment and action due to limited availability of cognitive resources, however, could come at the expense of remembering that this boy had been at the doctor's office all morning and therefore had a lot of pent-up energy. If accessed, this contextual information may have allowed for a more individualized and effective response to the misbehavior. In other words, an important role for conscious processing is to serve as a check on automaticity when new sensory information requires the revision of a schema to ensure optimal teaching performance.

Grounded in this dual-process model of cognition, teachers will be most effective in helping children to learn in early education settings if support and training help them to increase the "functional span of their working memory" (Feldon, 2007, p. 129) by developing elements of automaticity into their practice. In other words, the target of PD needs to include a focus on helping teachers spend fewer cognitive resources attending to irrelevant information, while also organizing and processing information within working memory more efficiently. If successful, improving the efficiency of conscious processing will free up working memory space to be able to handle complex situations and unexpected occurrences, as well as meet the individual needs of young children. The following section builds from this basic premise and provides a set of implications for how PD for early childhood educators can be used to maximize the dual processes of cognition in the classroom.

RELEVANCE OF THE DUAL-PROCESS MODEL OF COGNITION TO TEACHER TRAINING AND PROFESSIONAL DEVELOPMENT

The dual-process model of cognition implies that the goal of early childhood educator training and PD should be to improve the efficiency of educators' conscious processing, by facilitating the creation of comprehensive schemas about effective teacher practices that are not biased by personal perceptions or irrelevant sensory information, thus freeing up capacity to consciously process relevant, novel sensory information to act intentionally in the present moment. The theory also indicates that PD can be tailored to individual teachers, based on their experience. For the novice teacher, training and PD should support the creation of schemas based on unbiased, research-based practices (Artino, 2008). For the more experienced teacher, training and PD might help them actively identify, question, and modify the biased or inappropriate schemas they currently utilize to automatically guide behavior (Artino, 2008).

The next few sections describe how training and PD can facilitate the creation of unbiased schemas from which teachers can generate rules of thumb that lead to effective and efficient classroom decisions and practices. Training and PD can accomplish this goal, first, by providing teachers with new content and pedagogical knowledge as well as a comprehensive framework for implementing effective teaching practices. Second, PD can encourage numerous opportunities for accessing and applying relevant schemas in the classroom. Finally, PD can help teachers to self-monitor their cognitive processing and provide explicit feedback in order to ensure that inappropriate schemas are challenged and then updated with relevant information so that future automatic processing leads to the most effective teaching practices. We provide examples of these implications from teacher education literature when possible, as well as relevant illustrations from other fields in which information processing theory is more extensively applied.

Provide Content Knowledge and Schemas

Regardless of whether teachers are using effortful or automatic cognitive processing at any given moment, they are drawing upon schema and relevant prior knowledge to determine how to respond to the situation. Therefore, the schema utilized need to be appropriate, unbiased, and effective for the particular situation in which they are deployed. Training and PD can assist teachers in the creation of their own comprehensive and unbiased schemas by providing research-based, task-relevant information (van Merriënboer, Kirschner, & Kester, 2003), content and pedagogical knowledge, and an explicit framework for conceptually organizing this new information to form appropriate connections with their prior knowledge. Training and PD should help teachers develop these schemas so that they focus available cognitive resources on processing information relevant for effective teaching (germane load) rather than on irrelevant issues (extraneous load) that arise in the classroom (Artino, 2008; Feldon, 2007). In addition, the new information provided should be comprehensive and take into consideration the wide range of classroom experiences the teacher may encounter. This helps guard the teacher against creating faulty, stereotyped schemas (Feldon, 2007).

During training and PD, having new information presented in an organized manner that is explicitly connected to teachers' existing knowledge helps teachers establish a large and well-integrated knowledge structure which, in turn, facilitates information retrieval and efficiency during actual classroom interactions (Greitzer, Kuchar, & Huston, 2007). Individuals tend to organize and sort new information in terms of what they already have in their knowledge base. Clearly showing teachers how the new information provided in training relates to their preexisting experiences and knowledge will facilitate easier integration into schemas (Greitzer et al., 2007). As schemas are created with both new and existing knowledge, this allows for "chunking," the creation of many elements of knowledge into a single, comprehensive unit that helps guide task performance and behavior. Because it is only one piece of information in working memory terms, the data are processed more efficiently and require less mental effort, thus reducing teachers' cognitive load (Feldon, 2007; van Merriënboer et al., 2003).

Research has shown that providing individuals with new content knowledge and a larger conceptual framework can result in modification of schemas as well as in behavior change. For example, the PD program Cognitively Guided Instruction (CGI) provides teachers with knowledge and a framework about how students think about mathematics (Carpenter, Fennema, & Franke, 1996). The main tenet of CGI is to allow teachers to create their own ways of organizing the knowledge provided and make associations between the knowledge and their teaching (i.e., to construct schemas). One case study of three primary school mathematics teachers suggested that CGI allowed those teachers to construct a schema for understanding their students' thinking that they were then able to use when making instructional decisions in the classroom (Franke, Carpenter, Fennema, Ansell, & Behrend, 1998). This resulted in changes in teacher-reported beliefs as well as observed teaching practices (Franke et al., 1998).

Another illustration of how altering schemas can change behavior comes from the field of public health, focused on youth risk behaviors. A curriculum for the prevention of alcohol consumption in 11-year-olds was designed to make a child's mental image of an 11-year-old drinker negative and to decrease the perceived similarity between the self and the mental image of the drinker (Gerrard et al., 2006; Gerrard, Gibbons, Houlihan, Stock, & Pomery, 2008). The curriculum also focused on decreasing the child's willingness to drink by teaching the child about planned and reactive behavior. Providing a negative mental image of a drinker and the new knowledge regarding planned and reactive behavior was found to alter their schemas about drinking by reducing mental images of the favorability of the drinker and subsequently decreasing youths' willingness to drink and consume alcohol.

Practice and Repetition

Although comprehensive schemas allow for efficient cognitive processing and quick decision making, teachers are unlikely to see the benefits of this automatic process in their performance unless they are able to access an appropriate schema for a particular situation. One way to ensure that this happens is through practice and repetition of applying schemas, which leads to behaviors and procedures becoming ingrained and automated (Feldon, 2007; Paas, Renkl, & Sweller, 2004). This automaticity of behavior reduces cognitive load and frees memory use for other more complex elements of that particular task or for other tasks entirely, such as differentiating instruction to individual students (Feldon, 2007). Teacher training and PD, therefore, should provide educators with numerous opportunities to practice applying the schemas they are forming or revising during the PD.

During practice opportunities, it is critical to rehearse utilizing newly acquired information within an "authentic" context; teachers must repeatedly practice whole learning tasks in their entirety, rather than practice separate task elements or skills (van Merriënboer et al., 2003). The assumption is that learning a novel and complex strategy or task in its entirety allows teachers to integrate the knowledge, skills, and attitudes needed for executing the strategy or task effectively in a classroom (Merrill, 2002; van Merriënboer, Kester & Paas, 2006). Within an authentic context, teachers are asked to develop a holistic view of the entire task and focus on integrating its numerous elements. Practice and repetition begin with the simplest task that the teacher might experience in an actual classroom. Task complexity is gradually increased by varying the number of task elements and interactions between task elements that must be processed by the teacher. For example, if a teacher wants to work on her questioning skills so she can promote high-order thinking in her students, she could start by focusing on using fewer closed-ended and more open-ended questions during one particular activity of the day, such as group book reading. Over time as the use of open-ended questioning in this context becomes more automatic, the teacher can focus on implementing that type of questioning during other instructional activities. Eventually, it will be easier for her to use that type of questioning throughout the day in any situation. Such a focus on repeated practice of learning tasks within an authentic framework is more likely to lead to well-integrated, automatic processing because the entire task was practiced, rather than individual elements, and the learning occurred in a real-life situation, allowing for a more effective transfer to real-life teaching situations (van Merriënboer et al., 2003).

Research has shown that repetition and practice of complex tasks result in those behaviors becoming automated. Nowhere is the benefit of consistent practice as apparent as in the discipline of sports training in which athletes repeatedly practice certain exercises so that a motor skill, as well as optimal metabolic functioning for increased physical performance of that skill, becomes automated (Smith, 2003). The positive results of practice, however, have also been shown in education contexts. For example, instructional guidance that focuses on practicing distinct elements of a more complex task (rather than the whole task at once) has been shown to benefit novice learners because it helps them with schema construction (Pollock, Chandler, & Sweller, 2002). In addition, teachers who attended 5-year programs that allowed for more clinical training and coursework at the graduate level feel better prepared to teach and are rated by principals and teaching colleagues as being as confident and effective as senior teachers (Andrew, 1990; Andrew & Schwab, 1995). These teachers are more effective educators because they had extended student teaching in actual schools—practice in an authentic context. This allows teachers to integrate their theoretical, course-based learning and practical learning in the classroom (Darling-Hammond, 1998) into schemas that help automate effective classroom interactions.

Self-Monitoring and Feedback

Although teachers repeatedly practice applying the new schemas they have developed, they also need to focus on monitoring the effectiveness of these efforts. Teacher training and PD should help teachers to self-monitor their conscious processing and subsequent performance and provide individualized feedback to improve the accuracy of the self-monitoring process. Active self-monitoring gives the teacher an opportunity to evaluate her cognitive processing during an authentic task: Are her current schemas relevant to her ongoing classroom experiences and are her decisions based on these schemas leading to effective practice?

Such monitoring allows a teacher to actively contemplate the decision points, or moments during the school day, when a choice is made (automatically or consciously) about how to respond. Active monitoring of actual decision points and their subsequent results can be viewed as a source of continual learning in which the teacher can realize whether the schema employed was biased or unbiased (Franke et al., 1998) and the resulting course of action effective or ineffective. During the school day, teacher self-monitoring is likely to occur in a cyclic pattern in which she fluctuates between gauging if students are engaged and learning and determining whether she should continue with or modify her current teaching strategy (Peterson & Clark, 1978). This self-monitoring in itself is not enough, particularly if the teacher determines that she has not attained the desired outcome (e.g., students are engaged and understanding the material), but she does not know how to change her behavior to achieve that desired result. Unless a teacher has an appropriate, alternative teaching strategy that she determines is better than the one she is currently using, she will not change her behavior (Peterson & Clark, 1978).

Therefore, training and PD should include multiple opportunities for teachers to be observed in actual classrooms and to receive explicit feedback from a colleague, supervisor, or coach regarding how well she is integrating and implementing the knowledge and schemas that were taught. Feedback draws the teacher's attention to cues in the classroom and helps identify teacher decision points and subsequent behavior. When faced with most decision points, teachers, especially those with more experience, often respond automatically, so self-monitoring and feedback has the potential to disrupt the reflexivity of these unconscious cognitive processes and make the automatic schemas explicit (Freitas, Jiménez, & Mellado, 2004). For example, watching and reflecting on a video of oneself teaching allows more objectivity, as the educator can think about what she did and why. If the teacher of the boy crawling over peers in the dress-up area, who was previously described, watched the video of that interaction, she would likely recall that it was a busy morning and she was frustrated and that was why she reprimanded the boy to leave his peers alone. By watching the situation outside of the moment, however, she may observe (or an observer may point out) that she failed to notice other aspects of the classroom: For example, the boy was playing with several girls who were doing the same thing. She may then realize that the decision point that led to her behavior was influenced subconsciously by a biased stereotype regarding boys' behavior.

This kind of reflection and self-monitoring of decision points and behavior can help the educator in several ways. Once the decision points are brought into consciousness, the teacher can determine objectively whether that decision (reprimanding the boy) was effective for that situation. It also allows her to recognize that the quick judgment she made is automated and likely influenced by a biased stereotype. She is now able to brainstorm viable, alternative strategies and responses to address the children's behavior (e.g., suggest the children move the game to another area so as not to bother nonplaying peers). Equipped with feasible alternatives, she is able to practice implementing those alternative strategies the next time a similar situation arises in her classroom—essentially, to override the subconscious stereotyped response with an unbiased response. Correspondingly, when she identifies effective practices in the videos, such as her use of a class-management strategy to successfully transition to outside time, she can work on implementing them more consistently. Finally, self-monitoring and feedback present ways to highlight missed opportunities. For example, either the teacher or other observer might notice that the teacher walks around during individual time but interacts with the children minimally, even when a child shows the teacher what he built with blocks. This can generate a list of the different ways the teacher could engage the boy and extend his learning about building block towers in the future. Importantly, this process of self-monitoring is likely to be most effective if based on an evidence-based standard.

In sum, teacher training and PD based on the dual-process model of cognition has the potential to be very successful in helping early childhood teachers to become more effective educators. By providing educators many opportunities for repeated practice of applying schemas in real-life classrooms, effective self-monitoring, and explicit feedback, PD is likely to create teachers who employ automated schemas consistent with theories endorsed by that training and PD.

A Case Study of Professional Development Focused on Effective Classroom Interactions

Over the past decade, we have developed several PD resources for early childhood educators that capitalize on the cognitive theory previously presented to improve teacher–child interactions in the classroom. This case study describes just one of a growing number of PD approaches that use different combinations of didactic instruction, video-based learning, and coaching to advance teacher effectiveness in the classroom. The following sections will describe the conceptual framing and content of these teacher supports, highlight their alignment with different aspects of cognitive theory, and report findings from two randomized controlled trials that provide evidence in support of integrating cognitive theory into teacher training.

Teaching Through Interactions: Theoretical Foundations of a Professional Development Format

Information processing theory suggests that anchoring PD within a comprehensive, evidence-based framework can help teachers to develop and apply relevant, effective schemas during complex classroom interactions that require quick thinking and responses. In this spirit, all of our PD efforts are closely aligned with the Teaching Through Interactions (TTI; Hamre et al., 2011) framework, which organizes the broad range of moment-to-moment interactions, or proximal processes (Bronfenbrenner & Morris, 1998), that occur between teachers and children into a comprehensive model. Drawing from observations conducted in more than 4,000 classrooms using a standardized and validated observation measure, the TTI framework posits that these important teacher–child interactions fall into three broad domains—Emotional Support, Classroom Organization, and Instructional Support. These domains are then broken down into specific dimensions (e.g., Teacher Sensitivity), which are based on observable features of teacher–child interactions and contribute to a more nuanced understanding of high-quality teaching practice.

The Emotional Support domain of the TTI framework draws from attachment theory (Ainsworth, Blehar, Waters, & Wall, 1978; Bowlby, 1969) and self-determination theory (Connell & Wellborn, 1991; Ryan & Deci, 2000) to suggest that teacher–child interactions characterized by warmth and supportiveness create a sense of security that motivates children to explore and learn (Downer, Sabol, & Hamre, 2010). Recent research findings suggest that children who experience emotionally supportive classroom environments show greater academic growth (O'Connor & McCartney, 2007), better social skills (Brophy-Herb, Lee, Nievar, & Stollak, 2007; Curby et al., 2009), and fewer behavior problems (McClelland, Cameron, Wanless, & Murray, 2007). The Classroom Organization domain of the TTI framework is based on research in children's self-regulatory skills (Raver, 2004;

Tobin & Graziano, 2006), suggesting that instructional planning, proactive management strategies, and engaging materials and activities help dysregulated children develop higher levels of self-regulation (Raver et al., 2008) and spend enough time engaged in instructional activities to learn new skills and concepts (Phillips, Clancy-Minchetti, & Lonigan, 2008). Finally, the Instructional Support domain of the TTI framework finds its theoretical underpinnings in research on children's cognitive and language development, which stresses the importance of learning new ideas in an interconnected, organized way to facilitate easy retrieval for future use and emphasizes the important role that adults play in supporting the development of complex skills (Davis & Miyake, 2004; Skibbe, Behnke, & Justice, 2004; Vygotsky, 1991). There is growing empirical evidence that instructionally supportive classroom interactions promote gains in children's vocabulary, math, language, and social development (Barnett, Yarosz, Thomas, & Hornbeck, 2008; Burchinal et al., 2008; Curby et al., 2009; Pence, Justice, & Wiggins, 2008; Peterson & French, 2008).

From a dual-process perspective, the TTI framework serves as a detailed schema through which teachers can organize, understand, and respond to a range of classroom interactions. And, because TTI is based on research indicating that children's interactions with their peers and with adults play an integral role in their academic learning and social and emotional development (see Hamre & Pianta, 2010, for a review), it can guide teachers to decisions and behaviors that are effective, rather than maladaptive. When teachers are faced with complex situations in the classroom, this framework allows them to quickly identify and focus on the germane elements of what is happening, while ignoring irrelevant aspects of the situation (e.g., Fisk & Eggemeier, 1988; Klein & Calderwood, 1991). The automated processing of important classroom interactions using the TTI framework allows new information to be handled more efficiently in working memory, using fewer attentional resources and leaving more resources free to focus on the unique aspects of the situation, such as the needs of individual students (Feldon, 2007). Once teachers have encoded this schema for classroom interactions, it not only provides a comprehensive framework into which new knowledge about interactions can be easily incorporated, but it also provides the basis for teachers to develop a more effective and comprehensive set of automatic responses to everyday classroom interactions. This framework is embedded in every component of the PD resources that we have developed and therefore provides teachers with a consistent schema for effective teaching.

Teaching Through Interactions
Professional Development: Content and Structure

The TTI framework serves as the foundation to a multicomponent suite of web-mediated PD resources that target teacher–child interactions. Developed over a 10-year period, these resources include 1) the National Center for Research on Early Childhood Education (NCRECE) course, 2) the MyTeachingPartner (MTP) video library, and 3) MTP consultation. Even though the components take different approaches, they all target teacher–child interactions in the classroom as a vehicle for improving teacher effectiveness and child social, emotional, and academic outcomes. Few people will argue that teaching is an incredibly complex task that requires constant monitoring for and evaluation of numerous cues from the classroom environment. In such a situation, in which there is reasonable potential for cognitive overload (Sweller, 1989), these PD components capitalize on the difference between deliberate and automatic cognitive processing by focusing on relevant content and knowledge and allowing teachers to attend to germane cues from the classroom.

Course

Based on the importance of prior knowledge in cognitive theory, the NCRECE course, taught in 14 three-hour sessions, focuses on changing teachers' beliefs, knowledge, and skills in two main areas—effective teacher–child interactions and language and literacy instruction in early childhood classrooms (LoCasale-Crouch, Kraft-Sayre, & Pianta, 2010). The NCRECE course uses the TTI framework to organize the delivery of this explicit knowledge and actively advances the belief that these interactions are essential for learning to occur in the classroom (Hamre et al., 2011). The course helps teachers develop a detailed schema for classroom interactions so they may quickly process germane information about the classroom. It also explicitly aims to increase teachers' content knowledge in the area of teacher–child interactions and children's language and literacy skills, and as a result, reduces intrinsic load (Sweller, 1999). As teachers develop a higher level of expertise in these content areas, attention can be freed up to focus on other unique aspects of a particular teaching situation.

The course also uses analysis of video from real classrooms to help teachers make connections between teacher actions and child behaviors, with a particular focus on teachers' skill at identifying specific and concrete behavioral examples of effective teacher–child interactions. This focus is based on the hypothesis that in order for teachers to transfer their knowledge of effective interactions into their instructional practice, they must first detect teacher–child interactions as they occur in the classroom and assess their effectiveness in the moment of teaching (Hamre, Downer, Jamil, & Pianta, in press). By incorporating authentic examples of effective pedagogy in this way, the course also allows teachers to draw on a wide range of classroom experiences when developing their arsenal of responses to different decision points that arise in the context of teaching and provides them with practice at recognizing important decision points as they arise.

Video Library

Another component of our PD that offers video-based practice is the MTP video library. This library is an online collection of more than 200 video clips of early childhood teachers engaged in effective interactions with their students in the context of everyday classroom instruction. These 1- to 2-minute clips are in a searchable online database organized by TTI framework dimension, and each is accompanied by a detailed behavioral description of the high-quality teacher–child interaction that is taking place in the video (Kinzie et al., 2006; Pianta, Mashburn, Downer, Hamre, & Justice, 2008). The purpose of the video library is to provide teachers with concrete behavioral examples of what the high-quality interactions captured by the TTI framework look like when enacted by others. This is an especially important resource considering the relative isolation of the individual classrooms in which most teaching practice takes place once teachers leave teacher preparation and enter the field.

The MTP video library has the potential for being an especially impor- tant component for reducing the negative effects of cognitive default (Clark, 2001) when the teacher is under a great deal of cognitive load. Whereas less experienced teachers who have limited exposure to classrooms might develop a faulty schema based on their own experiences as students (Lortie, 1975) to which they revert when their working memory is overtaxed, those who have exposure to many classrooms are at an advantage. The video library demonstrates the pedagogy highlighted in the TTI framework in the context of real-world classroom interactions. It also provides access to qual- ity teaching in a large range of classrooms, allowing teachers to develop a de- fault schema that incorporates more effective classroom behaviors. Possibly most important of all, it offers teachers much needed practice at detecting classroom cues and thinking through important decision points outside of the moment of teaching, when they have more cognitive resources available for effortful reflection on their own behavior choices.

Consultation

This reflection and feedback on one's teaching practice is also the cornerstone of MTP consultation. The consultation consists of a regular 2-week cycle of observation-based feedback during which teachers work with consultants to analyze video of their own teaching using the TTI framework (Pianta et al., 2008). Every 2 weeks, teachers capture video of themselves interacting with their students in an instructional context and send it to the consultant, who then edits it into three short clips that highlight the particular TTI dimen- sion that is of interest that week. These clips are then paired with written feedback in the form of prompts that ask teachers to 1) identify instances of effective teaching behaviors, 2) suggest possible alternative behaviors, and 3) and comment on their implementation of instructional activities. Edited video and prompts are posted to a secure web site where they can be accessed by the teacher, and after the teacher responds to the prompts, teachers and consultants meet by phone or videoconference. The purpose of this meeting is to use the prompts and teacher responses as the basis for discussion, problem solving, and creation of an action plan for future instruction. At this point, the cycle starts again, as the teacher integrates the action plan into her practice and records another round of video.

Similar to the video library, the consultation process challenges teachers to use the TTI framework to identify the ways in which teacher actions (in this case, their own) are linked to certain child behaviors. The consultation pushes this process further in that once the connections between teacher and child behaviors are made, it provides a structure within which teachers can plan the repetition of successful interactions and create opportunities to practice more effective responses to situations that they have previously found challenging. Allowing teachers to evaluate themselves outside of the moment of teaching, the MTP consultation uses the type of controlled processing procedures that studies show can produce persistent attitude change (Petty, Cacioppo, Sedikides, & Strathman, 1988). Consultants help teachers in their reflective process by providing feedback prompts that draw teachers' attention to relevant cues in the classroom and helps identify decision points and brainstorm viable responses (Sherin & Han, 2004; van Es & Sherin, 2002). The cyclical process of the consultation, with weekly focus on a particular dimension of the TTI framework, also help teachers practice authentic teaching tasks in their entirety while gradually increasing the complexity of their focus on teacher–child interactions. With each week, a new dimension of the TTI framework is targeted and new skills are incorporated into teachers' instructional practice, though the dimensions of focus from previous weeks continue to be part of the teacher's schema of effective teacher–student interactions.

In summary, the TTI-inspired PD resources attempt to maximize the levels of germane load experienced by teachers in the moment of classroom instruction by providing them with a detailed schema from which they can draw a set of comprehensive rules of thumb for classroom interactions. By reducing the working memory resources required to manage recurring teacher–child interactions, this suite of PD resources allows teachers to focus more of their attention on the challenging and unique features of a teaching situation.

Teaching Through Interactions
Professional Development: Findings and Implications

Though not designed to explicitly test the utility of integrating cognitive theory into PD for early educators, two randomized controlled trials of PD resources based on the TTI model provide broad evidence that integration of cognitive theory into teacher training through a schema-generating framework, repeated practice, and guided self-monitoring is relevant and worthwhile. The first randomized controlled trial included more than 240 state-funded preschool teachers (Pianta et al., 2008). Classrooms in two different study conditions, 1) a Web only condition, in which teachers only had access to the MTP video library, and 2) a Consultation condition, in which teachers participated in the MTP consultation and had access to the video library, were examined for improvements in instructional quality and child outcomes over the course of an academic year. Findings supported the efficacy of MTP consultation (Pianta et al., 2008), with teachers in the Consultation group making significantly greater improvements in the use of classroom interactions when compared with the Web only group. Consultation teachers made greater gains in their sensitivity and response to student cues ($d = .82$), use of interesting and engaging instructional materials and experiences ($d = .77$), and use of interactions to stimulate language development ($d = .97$). The differences between teachers in these two groups were especially pronounced when comparing classrooms that were high in poverty. These findings are pertinent to the current discussion, because classrooms with such high levels of risk have the potential to be exceptionally taxing on teachers' cognitive resources.

As would be expected from cognitive theory, more fine-grained analyses of the data from this study have also suggested an important role of watching video in attaining these effects. For example, teachers in the Web only group who spent more time watching other teachers in the context of instructional videos from the MTP video library also showed higher levels of sensitivity to student needs, more effective use of positive and proactive behavior management strategies, and more productive use of instructional time in the classroom (Pianta et al., 2008). Teachers who made more use of the MTP video library also had children who made greater social development gains over the course of the study year ($d = .23–.36$; Hamre, Pianta, Mashburn, & Downer, in press). This video effect was also observed in the context of the MTP consultation, with children whose teachers who spent more time viewing footage of their own teaching demonstrating greater vocabulary development during prekindergarten ($d = .30$; Mashburn, Downer, Hamre, Justice, & Pianta, 2010). Taken together, these results suggest that watching teaching take place in many contexts can provide not only a larger body of interactions from which to draw in situations of high cognitive load, but also more opportunities to reflect on prior decisions and to practice identifying important decision points.

A more recent study conducted by NCRECE builds on the findings from the first test of MTP resources by examining the effects of the NCRECE course and evaluating the additive effects of experiencing both the course and MTP consultation. In a randomized controlled trial involving more than 440 teachers over the course of 18 months, this study sorted teachers into a Course group and a Control group for an initial phase. Teachers in the Course condition of the NCRECE project demonstrated greater knowledge of (d = .77) and greater skills at detecting (d = .60) teacher–child interactions which are regarded as effective by the TTI framework, when compared with teachers in a control condition (Hamre, Pianta, et al., in press). Course teachers also demonstrated more effective emotional (d = .41) and instructional (d = .66) teacher–child interactions in the context of their own classrooms. This study also highlights the importance of interaction detection skills, in that the effects of the NCRECE course on teachers' actual performance in the classroom are partially mediated by their skill at detecting effective interactions. These early findings support the hypothesis that in order for the knowledge gained during the NCRECE course to actually impact the quality of interactions in a teachers' classroom, teachers must first be able to perceive and evaluate the effectiveness of those interactions in the moment of teaching. Because course teachers have the opportunity to develop a rich schema for classroom interactions based on the TTI framework, they have an efficient means by which to perceive and evaluate these interactions. After this initial phase, teachers were then re-randomized into Consultation and Control groups, but these data are not available to report at this time.

IMPLICATIONS OF A DUAL-PROCESS MODEL OF COGNITION FOR EARLY EDUCATOR PROFESSIONAL DEVELOPMENT

In our search of the literature, insights from the dual-process model of cognition have led to improvements in the training of professionals ranging from athletes to air traffic control officers and appear to hold many promising applications to the training and support of teachers. The relevance of a dual-process model of cognition to teaching opens up many possibilities for future research, as well as practical applications within training and PD programs, a few of which are described here.

Future Research

Thus far, this chapter has shown how early educators' working memory capacity, cognitive load, and retrieval of schemas may facilitate or hinder their ability to implement effective teaching practices. In fact, it appears that these cognitive processes may be key intermediary mechanisms through which preservice education and in-service PD lead to changes in teacher practice and affect student outcomes. Perhaps even more striking is the fact that information processing is only one of a whole set of basic psychological processes that are likely to contribute, uniquely and in various combinations, to patterns of teaching practice. Yet, relatively little is known about how any of these processes affect teachers during their day-to-day interactions with children, thus limiting understanding of potential targets for PD aimed at producing effective teaching. It is certainly beyond the scope of this chapter to address how other psychological processes, such as motivation (Gregoire, 2003) or emotional arousal and stress (see Raver et al., Chapter 5), may directly influence teachers' classroom practice, or indirectly transform it through negative influences on the cognitive processes detailed in this chapter. However, in demonstrating the centrality of one psychological process, the dual-process model of cognition, to effective teaching, it is clear that there remains ample room in the field for expanding our understanding of how PD for early educators can benefit from taking into consideration basic psychological processes.

One major hindrance to the examination of these psychological processes is the lack of appropriate assessment tools, with a tendency toward overreliance on teacher self-report. Remaining with the dual-process model of cognition as an example, many studies have examined teacher attitudes and beliefs as proxies for specific cognitive processes (e.g., schemas) that may be related to teacher behavior and practices in the classroom. Despite what teachers report they believe, studies have shown that they do not necessarily practice what they preach (e.g., Cohen, 1990; Feldon, 2007; Gregoire, 2003; Simmons et al., 1999). It has been proposed that teachers' automatic and unconscious schemas underlie this discrepancy between what teachers, through self-reports, say they endorse and what they are actually observed to do in practice (Feldon, 2007; Gregoire, 2003). In other words, automatic processing can take over in the classroom and may be informed by schemas that differ from what a teacher states as a belief outside the moment of teaching. It is, therefore, critical not to rely solely on distal proxies, such as self-report of attitudes and beliefs, but instead design measurement tools that attempt to directly assess teachers' cognitive processes, which shape what they actually do, subconsciously and consciously, in the classroom.

This type of direct assessment could be done with general adult measures of cognition, such as subtests from intelligence tests that tap into working memory or selective attention, though these would only provide assessments of cognitive processing outside the relevant context of classroom-based teaching. Alternatively, measures could be developed to assess the application of cognitive processing to authentic teaching scenarios. For example, the case study described previously used a newly developed tool, called the Video Assessment of Interactions and Learning (VAIL; Jamil & Pianta, 2011), to measure teachers' knowledge of and skills in detecting the kinds of effective teacher–child interactions embedded in the TTI framework. Teachers watched short video clips of other teachers in the classroom and were asked to identify effective teaching strategies. Responses were deemed "correct" when they matched with strategies known to have positive effects on child outcomes and were described by the teachers in specific objective, behavioral terms. This video assessment protocol aims to measure whether teachers have developed a schema about effective teacher–child interactions and the skill to apply this schema (consciously or subconsciously) by selectively attending to relevant behaviors and interactions by children and teachers in real classrooms. Certainly, this is not the same as observing the teacher's decision making in his or her own classroom. However, the VAIL is an example of trying to measure the cognitive processes that not only help teachers pay attention to, organize, and understand what happens in classrooms but also assist them in efficiently making choices in the best interest of helping children learn. As more direct assessments of the full range of psychological processes are developed and applied within a teaching context, it will open up a world of possibilities for designing studies that aim to better understand some of the psychological mechanisms through which PD can lead to improved teaching.

Practice Innovations

In addition to the general implications for teacher preparation and PD noted in previous sections, the dual-process model of cognition suggests several intriguing directions for innovative practice. One particularly interesting venture involves the application of virtual-reality technology to provide teachers with authentic classroom-based learning opportunities before they even enter an actual classroom. Faculty in the College of Education and School of Electrical Engineering and Computer Science at the University of Central Florida have partnered with the Haberman Education Foundation, Lockheed Martin Corporation, and Simiosys L.L.C., to develop and test a virtual classroom environment (Dieker, Hynes, Hughes, & Smith, 2007). Developed for use in teacher preparation with novice teachers, the virtual classroom provides repeated opportunities for prospective teachers to stand in front of a group of students and teach, while having to handle realistic issues of keeping students with a range of abilities and personalities engaged in learning. This virtual classroom approach to preparing teachers draws from the dual-process model of cognition by offering repetition and room to make mistakes, as well as guided feedback immediately afterward, without impacting the learning and behavior of actual students.

As touched on earlier, the dual-process model of cognition also provides clear direction for how to differentiate PD and training opportunities for novice and experienced teachers. Rather than a one-size-fits-all approach to providing PD, it is apparent that longstanding experienced teachers are in a different place cognitively than their preservice or early career counterparts. Whereas, novice teachers may benefit most from additional practice in the application of schemas for effective teaching (as noted above in the virtual reality example), teachers with years of experience in early childhood classrooms have already automatized much of what they do with children moment to moment. Though many of these reflexive actions may lead to well-organized, warm, and stimulating teacher–child interactions, it is also possible that these teachers develop schemas over time that hold some bias and lead to less optimal learning environments for young children. Therefore, it seems crucial that experienced teachers seek out and are provided with PD opportunities, such as coaching and consultation that bring to light and challenge their preexisting schemas so that ongoing decisions in the classroom are intentional and aligned with contemporary best practices for supporting the development of preschoolers.

CONCLUSION

Ironically, the dual-process model of cognition has been used for decades to inform the development of educational interventions and tailor learning opportunities for students (Merrill, 2002; van Merriënboer et al., 2006; Velmahos et al., 2004). Yet, only recently has this cognitive theory been applied to the act of teaching (Feldon, 2007) in an effort to identify cognitive precursors to effective teaching practice that can serve as the targets of preservice preparation and in-service PD for early educators. This chapter brings attention to several cognitive processes that have direct implications for developing PD to support effective teaching, and in doing so also seeks to open the larger box of unexplored basic psychological processes that play a role in everything adults do and hold great promise in further understanding what leads to effective practice in preschool classrooms and how we can build PD systems to support teachers in these efforts.

REFERENCES

Ainsworth, M.D., Blehar, M.C., Waters, E., & Wall, D. (1978). *Patterns of attachment: A psychological study of the strange situation.* Hillsdale, NJ: Erlbaum.

Andrew, M.D. (1990). Differences between graduates of 4-year and 5-year teacher preparation programs. *Journal of Teacher Education, 41,* 45–54. doi:10.1177/002248719004100206

Andrew, M.D., & Schwab, R.L. (1995). Has reform in teacher education influenced teacher performance? An outcome assessment of graduates of an eleven-university consortium. *Action in Teacher Education, 17,* 43–53

Artino, A.R. (2008). Cognitive load theory and the role of learner experience: An abbreviated review for educational practitioners. *Association for the Advancement of Computing in Education Journal, 16,* 425–439.

Barnett, S., Yarosz, D., Thomas, J., & Hornbeck, A. (2008). Educational effectiveness of a Vygotskian approach to preschool education: A randomized trial. *Early Childhood Research Quarterly, 23,* 299–313.

Barrett, L.F., Tugade, M.M., & Engle, R.W. (2004). Individual differences in working memory capacity and dual-process theories of mind. *Psychological Bulletin, 130,* 553–573. doi:10.1037/0033-2909.130.4.553

Borko, H., & Putnam, R.T. (1996). Learning to teach. In D. Berliner & R. Calfee (Eds.), *Handbook of educational psychology* (pp. 673–707). New York, NY: Simon & Schuster Macmillan.

Bowlby, J. (1969). *Attachment and loss, Vol. 1: Attachment.* New York: Basic Books.

Bronfenbrenner, U., & Morris, P.A. (1998). The ecology of developmental processes. In W. Damon, & R.M. Lerner (Eds.), *Handbook of child psychology: Theoretical models of human development* (5th ed., Vol. 1, pp. 993–1029). New York, NY: John Wiley & Sons.

Brophy-Herb, H.E., Lee, R.E., Nievar, M.A., & Stollak, G. (2007). Preschoolers' social competence: Relations to family characteristics, teacher behaviors and classroom climate. *Journal of Applied Developmental Psychology, 28,* 134–148.

Burchinal, M., Howes, C., Pianta, R., Bryant, D., Early, D., Clifford, R., & Barbarin, O. (2008). Predicting child outcomes at the end of kindergarten from the quality of pre-kindergarten teacher–child interactions and instruction. *Applied Developmental Science, 12,* 140–153. doi:10.1080/10888690802199418

Carpenter, T.P., Fennema, E., & Franke, M.L. (1996). Cognitively guided instruction: A knowledge base for reform in primary mathematics instruction. *Elementary School Journal, 97,* 3–20. doi:10.1086/461846

Clark, R.E. (2001). New directions: Cognitive and motivational research issues. In R.E. Clark (Ed.), *Learning from media: Arguments, analysis, and evidence* (pp. 263–298). Greenwich, CT: Information Age Publishing.

Cohen, D.K. (1990). A revolution in one classroom: The case of Mrs. Oublier. *Educational Evaluation and Policy Analysis, 12,* 311–329. doi:10.2307/1164355

Connell, J.P., & Wellborn, J.G. (1991). Competence, autonomy, and relatedness: A motivational analysis of self-system processes. In R. Gunnar & L.A. Sroufe (Eds.), *Minnesota symposia on child psychology* (Vol. 23, pp. 43–77). Hillsdale, NJ: Erlbaum.

Curby, T.W., LoCasale-Crouch, J., Konold, T.R., Pianta, R.C., Howes, C., Burchinal, M., ... Barbarin, O. (2009). The relations of observed pre-K classroom quality profiles to children's achievement and social competence. *Early Education and Development, 20,* 346–372. doi:10.1080/10409280802581284

Darling-Hammond, L. (1998). Teachers and teaching: Testing policy hypotheses from a national commission report. *Educational Researcher, 27,* 5–15. doi:10.2307/1176922

Davis, E.A., & Miyake, N. (2004). Explorations of scaffolding in complex classroom systems. *Journal of the Learning Sciences, 13,* 265–272. doi:10.1207/s15327809jls1303_1

Dieker, L., Hynes, M., Stapleton, C., & Hughes, C. (2007). Virtual classrooms: STAR simulator building virtual environments for teacher training in effective classroom management. *New Learning Technology SALT, 4,* 1–22.

Downer, J., Sabol, T.J., & Hamre, B.K. (2010). Teacher–child interactions in the classroom: Toward a theory of within- and cross-domain links to children's developmental outcomes. *Early Education and Development, 21,* 699–723. doi:10.10 80/10409289.2010.497453

Feldon, D.F. (2007). Cognitive load and classroom teaching: The double-edged sword of automaticity. *Educational Psychologist, 42,* 123–137. doi:10.1080/00461520701416173

Fisk, A.D., & Eggemeier, R.T. (1988). Application of automatic/controlled processing theory to training of tactical command and control skills: I. Background and task analytic methodology. *In 33rd annual proceedings of the Human Factors Society* (pp. 281–285). Santa Monica, CA: Human Factors Society.

Franke, M.L., Carpenter, T., Fennema, E., Ansell, E., & Behrend, J. (1998). Understanding teachers' self-sustaining generative change in the context of professional development. *Teaching and Teacher Education, 14,* 67–80.

Freitas, I.M., Jiménez, R., & Mellado, V. (2004). Solving physics problems: The conceptions and practice of an experienced teacher and an inexperienced teacher. *Research in Science Education, 34,* 113–133. doi:10.1023/B:RISE.0000021000.61909.66

Gerrard, M., Gibbons, F.X., Brody, G.H., Murry, V.M., Cleveland, M.J., & Wills, T.A. (2006). A theory-based dual-focus alcohol intervention for preadolescents:

The strong African American families program. *Psychology of Addictive Behaviors, 20*, 185–195. doi:10.1037/0893-164X.20.2.185

Gerrard, M., Gibbons, F.X., Houlihan, A.E., Stock, M.L., & Pomery, E.A. (2008). A dual-process approach to health risk decision making: the prototype willingness model. *Developmental Review, 28*, 29–61. doi:10.1016/j.dr.2007.10.001

Gigerenzer, G., Czerlinski, J., & Martignon, L. (2002). How good are fast and frugal heuristics? In T. Gilovich, D. Griffin, & D. Kahneman (Eds.), *Heuristics and biases: The psychology of intuitive judgment* (pp. 559–581). New York, NY: Cambridge University Press.

Gregoire, M. (2003). Is it a challenge or a threat? A dual-process model of teachers' cognition and appraisal processes during conceptual change. *Educational Psychology Review, 15*, 147–179.

Greitzer, F.L., Kuchar, O.A., & Huston, K. (2007). Cognitive science implications for enhancing training effectiveness in a serious gaming context. *Journal on Educational Resources in Computing, 7*, 2.1–2.16. doi:10.1145/1281320.1281322

Hamre, B., Downer, J., Jamil, F., & Pianta, R. (in press). Enhancing teacher intentionality: A conceptual model for the development and testing of professional development interventions. In Pianta, R., Justice, L., Barnett, S., & Sheridan, S. (Eds.), *Handbook of early education*. New York, NY: Guilford Press.

Hamre, B.K., & Pianta, R.C. (2010). Classroom environments and developmental processes: conceptualization & measurement. In J. Meece & J. Eccles (Eds.), *Handbook of research on schools, schooling, and human development* (pp. 25–41). New York, NY: Routledge.

Hamre, B., Pianta, R., Burchinal, M., Field, S., LoCasale-Crouch, J., Downer, J., … Scott-Little, C. (in press). A course on effective teacher–child interactions: Effects on teacher beliefs, knowledge, and observed practice. *American Education Research Journal.*

Hamre, B.K, Pianta, R.C., Downer, J.T., Hamagami, A., Mashburn, A., Jones, S., … Brackett, M. (2011). T*eaching through interactions—Testing a developmental framework of teacher effectiveness in over 4,000 classrooms.* Manuscript submitted for publication.

Hamre, B.K., Pianta, R.C., Mashburn, A.J., & Downer, J.T. (in press). Promoting young children's social competence through the preschool PATHS curriculum and MyTeachingPartner professional development resources. *Early Education and Development.*

Jamil, F., & Pianta, R.C. (2011). *A measure of teachers' skills in detecting interactions: The Video Assessment of Interactions and Learning.* Manuscript in preparation.

Kinzie, M.B., Whitaker, S.D., Neesen, K., Kelley, M., Matera, M., & Pianta, R.C. (2006). Innovative web-based professional development for teachers of at-risk preschool children. *Educational Technology and Society, 9*, 194–204.

Klein, G.A., & Calderwood, R. (1991). Decision models: Some lessons from the field. *IEEE Transactions on Systems, Man, and Cybernetics, 21*, 1018–1026. doi:10.1109/21.120054

LoCasale-Crouch, J., Kraft-Sayre, M., & Pianta, R. (2010). Implementation of an early childhood professional development course in nine settings and fifteen sections. Manuscript in preparation.

Lortie, D. (1975). *Schoolteacher: A sociological study.* Chicago, IL: University of Chicago Press.

Mashburn, A.J., Downer, J.T., Hamre, B.K., Justice, L.M., & Pianta, R.C. (2010). Consultation for teachers and children's language and literacy development during pre-kindergarten. *Applied Developmental Science, 14*, 179–196. doi:10.1080/1 0888691.2010.516187

Mayer, R.E. (Ed.). (2005). *The Cambridge handbook of multimedia learning.* Cambridge, MA: Cambridge University Press.

McClelland, M.M., Cameron, C.E., Wanless, S., & Murray, A. (2007). Executive function, behavioral self-regulation, and social-emotional competence: Links to school readiness. In O.N. Saracho & B. Spodek (Eds.), *Contemporary perspectives in early childhood education: Social learning in early childhood education* (Vol. 7, pp. 113–137). Greenwich, CT: Information Age.

Merrill, M.D. (2002). First principles of instruction. *Educational Technology Research and Development, 50,* 43–59. doi:10.1007/BF02505024

O'Connor, E., & McCartney, K. (2007). Examining teacher–child relationships and achievement as part of an ecological model of development. *American Educational Research Journal, 44,* 340. doi:10.3102/0002831207302172

Paas, F., Renkl, A., & Sweller, J. (2004). Cognitive load theory: Instructional implications of the interaction between information structures and cognitive architecture. *Instructional Science, 32,* 1–8. doi:10.1023/B:TRUC.0000021806.17516.d0

Pence, K.L., Justice, L.M., & Wiggins, A.K. (2008). Preschool teachers' fidelity in implementing a comprehensive language-rich curriculum. *Language, Speech, and Hearing Services in Schools, 39,* 329–341. doi:10.1044/0161-1461(2008/031)

Peterson, P.L., & Clark, C.M. (1978). Teachers' reports of their cognitive processes during teaching. *American Educational Research Journal, 15,* 555–565. doi:10.2307/1162648

Peterson, S.M., & French, L. (2008). Supporting young children's explanations through inquiry science in preschool. *Early Childhood Research Quarterly, 23,* 395–408. doi:10.1016/j.ecresq.2008.01.003

Petty, R.E., Cacioppo, J.T., Sedikides, C., & Strathman, A.J. (1988). Affect and persuasion: A contemporary perspective. *American Behavioral Scientist, 31,* 355–371. doi:10.1177/000276488031003007

Phillips, B.M., Clancy-Menchetti, J., & Lonigan, C.J. (2008). Successful phonological awareness instruction with preschool children. *Topics in Early Childhood Special Education, 28,* 3. doi:10.1177/0271121407313813

Pianta, R., Mashburn, A., Downer, J., Hamre, B., & Justice, L. (2008). Effects of web-mediated professional development resources on teacher–child interactions in pre-kindergarten classrooms. *Early Childhood Research Quarterly, 23,* 431–451. doi:10.1016/j.ecresq.2008.02.001

Pollock, E., Chandler, P., & Sweller, J. (2002). Assimilating complex information. *Learning and Instruction, 12,* 61–86. doi:10.1016/S0959-4752(01)00016-0

Raver, C.C. (2004). Placing emotional self-regulation in sociocultural and socioeconomic contexts. *Child Development, 75,* 346–353. doi:10.1111/j.1467-8624.2004.00676

Raver, C.C., Jones, S.M., Li-Grining, C.P., Metzger, M., Smallwood, K., & Sardin, L. (2008). Improving preschool classroom processes: Preliminary findings from a randomized trial implemented in Head Start settings. *Early Childhood Research Quarterly, 23,* 10–26. doi:10.1016/j.ecresq.2007.09.001

Ryan, R.M., & Deci, E.L. (2000). Self-determination theory and the facilitation of intrinsic motivation, social development, and well-being. *American Psychologist, 55,* 68–78. doi:10.1037//0003-066X.55.1.68

Schempp, P.G., Tan, S., Manross, D., & Fincher, M. (1998). Differences in novice and competent teachers' knowledge. *Teachers and Teaching, 4,* 9–20. doi:10.1080/1354060980040102

Sherin, M.G., & Han, S. (2004). Teacher learning in the context of a video club. *Teaching and Teacher Education, 20,* 163–183. doi:10.1016/j.tate.2003.08.001

Shulman, L.S. (2004). *The wisdom of practice: Essays on teaching, learning, and learning to teach.* San Francisco, CA: Jossey-Bass.

Simmons, P.E., Emory, A., Carter, T., Coker, T., Finnegan, B., Crockett, D., ... Labuda, K. (1999). Beginning teachers: Beliefs and classroom actions. *Journal of Research in Science Teaching*, *36*, 930–954. doi:10.1002/(SICI)1098-2736(199910)36:8<930::AID-TEA3>3.3.CO;2-E

Skibbe, L., Behnke, M., & Justice, L.M. (2004). Parental scaffolding of children's phonological awareness skills: Interactions between mothers and their preschoolers with language difficulties. *Communication Disorders Quarterly*, *25*, 189–203. doi:10.1177/15257401040250040401

Smith, D.J. (2003). A framework for understanding the training process leading to elite performance. *Sports Medicine*, *33*, 1103–1126. doi:10.2165/00007256-200333150-00003

Smith, E.R., & DeCoster, J. (2000). Dual-process models in social and cognitive psychology: Conceptual integration and links to underlying memory systems. *Personality and Social Psychology Review*, *4*, 108–131. doi:10.1207/S15327957PSPR0402_01

Sweller, J. (1988). Cognitive load during problem solving: Effects on learning. *Cognitive Science*, *12*, 257–285. doi:10.1016/0364-0213(88)90023-7

Sweller, J. (1989). Cognitive technology: Some procedures for facilitating learning and problem solving in mathematics and science. *Journal of Educational Psychology*, *81*, 457–466. doi:10.1037//0022-0663.81.4.457

Sweller, J. (1999). *Instruction design in technical areas.* Camberwell: Australian Council for Educational Research.

Sweller, J. (2005). Implications of cognitive load theory for multimedia learning. In R.E. Mayer (Ed.), *The Cambridge handbook of multimedia learning* (pp. 19–30). Cambridge, MA: Cambridge University Press.

Tobin, R.M., & Graziano, W.G. (2006). Development of regulatory processes through adolescence. In D.K. Mroczek & T.D. Little (Eds.), *Handbook of personality development* (pp. 263–283). Mahwah, NJ: Erlbaum.

van Es, E.A., & Sherin, M.G. (2002). Learning to notice: Scaffolding new teachers' interpretations of classroom interactions. *Journal of Technology and Teacher Education*, *10*, 571–596.

van Merriënboer, J.J.G., Kester, L., & Paas, F. (2006). Teaching complex rather than simple tasks: Balancing intrinsic and germane load to enhance transfer of learning. *Applied Cognitive Psychology*, *20*, 343–352. doi:10.1002/acp.1250

van Merriënboer, J.J.G., Kirschner, P.A., & Kester, L. (2003). Taking the load off of a learner's mind: Instructional design for complex learning. *Educational Psychologist*, *38*, 5–13. doi:10.1207/S15326985EP3801_2

Velmahos, G.C., Toutouzas, K.G., Sillin, L.F., Chan, L., Clark, R.E., Theodorou, D., & Maupin, F. (2004). Cognitive task analysis for teaching technical skills in an inanimate surgical skills laboratory. *The American Journal of Surgery*, *187*, 114–119. doi:10.1016/j.amjsurg.2002.12.005

Vygotsky, L.S. (1991). Genesis of the higher mental functions. In P. Light, S. Sheldon, & M. Woodhead (Eds.), *Learning to think* (pp. 32–41). Florence, KY: Taylor & Frances/Routledge.

Webb, J.M., Diana, E.M., Luft, P., Brooks, E.W., & Brennan, E.L. (1997). Influence of pedagogical expertise and feedback on assessing student comprehension from nonverbal behavior. *Journal of Educational Research*, *91*, 89–97. doi:10.1080/00220679709597526

Wegner, D.M. (2002). *The illusion of conscious will.* Cambridge, MA: MIT Press.

III

Scaling Up Professional Development

7
History, Scale Up, and Improvements of a Comprehensive, Statewide Professional Development Program in Texas

Susan H. Landry, Tricia A. Zucker,
Emily Solari, April D. Crawford, and Jeffrey M. Williams

The need to provide young children with the learning experiences and skills they need to be successful once they enter kindergarten is a national concern (Bowman, Donovan, & Burns, 2001; National Research Council and Institute of Medicine, 2000). To ensure early school success, the field needs research-proven models of professional development (PD) that support pre-kindergarten (pre-K) teachers to implement instructional activities and provide rich language input that adequately prepares 3- and 4-year-old children for school (Early et al., 2007; Howes, 1997; Howes et al., 2008; LoCasale-Crouch et al., 2007). The call for effective models of early childhood PD has increased over the last decade, as an increasing number of well-conducted studies show null or contradictory associations between preschool teachers' education level and classroom quality and/or children's academic gains (e.g., Blau & Mocan, 2002; Early et al., 2007; Mashburn et al., 2008). PD, on the other hand, that provides pre-K teachers with training in instructional strategies that expose children to the experiences that build the foundational skills necessary for school competence (e.g., early literacy, math) are related to children's gains in learning (e.g., Girolametto, Weitzman, Lefebvre, & Greenberg, 2007; Kontos, Howes, & Galinksy, 1996; Pianta, Mashburn,

Downer, Hamre, & Justice, 2008; Neuman & Cunningham, 2009; Wasik, Bond, & Hindman, 2006; Whitehurst & Lonigan, 1998).

This chapter describes the development, efficacy studies, and scale up of a comprehensive integrated pre-K PD program in Texas. We first outline the development process behind the PD program, with attention to innovations within the conceptual framework designed to bring novel practices, technologies, and knowledge to pre-K teachers. Next, we summarize experimental studies conducted to evaluate the usefulness of the PD program for teachers and students. Then, we elaborate on how we have extended and sustained the program and networks that assist teachers and school communities in implementing the program more systematically and with new tools. Finally, we reflect on key lessons learned in this scale up process.

DEVELOPMENT PROCESSES AND CONSIDERATIONS

Development of the PD program began in 1998 at the Center for Improving the Readiness of Children for Learning and Education (CIRCLE) that is now within the Children's Learning Institute (CLI) at the University of Texas Health Science Center at Houston (UTHSCH). This was a time when many early childhood educators were concerned that too much of an academic focus in these early years was developmentally inappropriate, despite accumulated evidence that teaching early language and literacy skills in appropriate ways is essential for school readiness (International Reading Association & National Association for the Education of Young Children, 1998; Snow, Burns, & Griffin, 1998) and that early experiences shape brain development in ways that lay the foundation for long-term academic success (e.g., Dawson, Klinger, Panagiotides, Hill, & Spieker, 1992). Thus, our goal was to design a PD program that would train pre-K teachers to deliver cognitive instruction in ways that were *playful* but also *planful* and *purposeful*—"the 3 Ps." For most educators, this approach resonated as a meaningful, engaging, and developmentally appropriate way to ensure pre-K children's school readiness in academic and social skills.

A number of issues were considered in the development of the PD program that included, but were not limited to, determining the full range of training experiences and supportive resources necessary for teachers and staff across different educational settings to be effective. As the PD program was ultimately expected to be delivered in early childhood classrooms within public schools, Head Start centers, and for-profit or not-for-profit child care centers, the PD model needed to address the needs of teachers with a range of education experiences and demands from their own unique classroom settings. The resources available to these three different service delivery models continue to be dramatically different, but the design of the PD program needed to be feasible and effective for all types of preschool programs.

Additional issues were considered in the development process that included finding a delivery format that changed teachers' beliefs about appropriate content and pedagogy through a process of engaging them to take responsibility for their own learning in response to the program. We expected that preschool teachers could be facilitated to use effective instructional practices through the following goals: 1) acknowledging teachers' philosophies in order to best fit new information within existing belief systems, 2) ensuring intellectual engagement in the subject matter, 3) situating teacher learning in authentic contexts with opportunities to practice new skills, and 4) extending learning over a period of time (Bransford, Brown, & Cocking, 2000; Putnam & Borko, 2000). To achieve these goals, a highly specified framework of what is needed in preschool classrooms was developed from theory, best practices, and previous intervention research. In order to allow for successful scaling, the design was highly systematic without scripting the PD program and classroom resources to allow input into implementation from teachers and administrators. Training goals were carefully sequenced and spread out over 2 academic years to support transfer of goals into the classroom.

The innovative use of technology was key to developing a program that could provide training courses in evidence-based instructional practices and provide resources for teachers to monitor children's cognitive and social learning progress, all of which needed to be implemented on a large scale with a moderate to high degree of fidelity. In regard to teachers' training courses, the essential elements of high-quality preschool instruction were developed into nine web-based courses that were delivered with both face-to-face small-group trainings (i.e., a trained facilitator uses the web platform for interactive activities and discussion with teachers) and opportunities for guided and independent practice (i.e., teachers access online tutorials, quizzes, classroom application activities, and discussion blogs). The courses, referred to as eCIRCLE (electronic CIRCLE early education training), covered responsive teaching interactions, classroom management (room arrangement, routines, and flexible groupings), the key early literacy areas, language building, shared book reading, building social skills, and early math.

Conceptual Framework

Too often, innovative programs that are taken to scale fail to affect change in meaningful, sustained ways because the design unsuccessfully fit the realities of educational practices and the complex environments of schools (Cohen & Ball, 2007). Through an iterative process including many years of educator input and feedback, we have developed a conceptual framework designed to address these obstacles to scalability.

A Comprehensive Conceptual Framework
with a Concentration on Professional Development

Early childhood is a critical period for building school readiness skills in the areas of language, emergent literacy, early mathematics, and social, emotional, and cognitive development. As shown in Figure 7.1, the conceptual framework for the PD program required five components to support these school readiness skills within a variety of pre-K service delivery systems (including district-based pre-K, Head Start, and not-for-profit or for-profit child care). This illustration highlights PD to emphasize our belief that effective PD is the most essential component for achieving high-quality pre-K programs. Furthermore, the focus of the PD training is on several key principles of responsive instruction (detailed subsequently) that are hypothesized to be the most important mechanisms for achieving high-quality pre-K programs that have a positive impact on children's school readiness. In addition to PD, the conceptual framework includes the provision of teaching and learning resources, tools for making data-driven decisions, technical assistance in developing sustainable solutions, and processes for effective communication among all key stakeholders at classroom, regional, and state levels. Assertions underlying this framework include 1) cognitive readiness can be achieved in ways that support the whole child; 2) research-based, comprehensive curricula are essential classroom tools; 3) responsive teaching promotes social and cognitive development; 4) progress monitoring that informs instruction better ensures school readiness; 5) program effectiveness can be objectively measured and supported with systems for technical assistance and effective communication; and 6) effective PD with ongoing mentoring for teachers assures goals are achieved.

Key Principles of Professional Development Center on Responsive Teacher–Child Interactions   As stated, the cornerstone behind this comprehensive program is hypothesized to be sustained, individualized PD to support novice and experienced pre-K teachers. The conceptual framework for the PD component of the program includes an emphasis on combining highly responsive teacher–child interactions with targeted learning activities and opportunities in language building, phonological awareness, letter knowledge, and early writing, math, and social skills. These five key principles motivated the PD program design: 1) a responsive teaching style, 2) intentional content planning for social-emotional and cognitive areas (e.g., early literacy, math, language), 3) building concepts through unit planning, 4) a balance of teacher-directed and child-directed activities, 5) flexible groupings (one-to-one, small group, large group) of children in learning activities across each day, and 6) use of data to inform instruction (Landry, 2008). The key principles are defined in Table 7.1 and explained in the next sections.

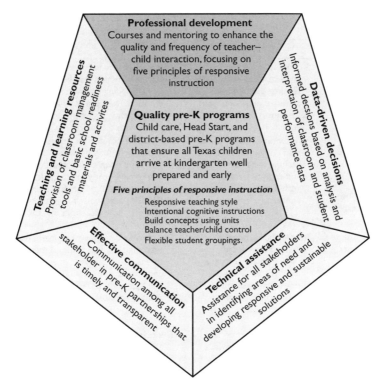

Figure 7.1. The conceptual framework includes five components: 1) professional development (PD), 2) teaching and learning resources, 3) data-driven decisions, 4) technical assistance, and 5) effective communication. Through the PD courses and in-class mentoring, key principles of responsive teaching style promote social and cognitive development. Provision of teaching resources, including a research-based comprehensive curriculum, is an essential teaching tool. Regular progress-monitoring assessments inform instruction to better ensure school readiness. Program effectiveness can be objectively measured and areas of need can be improved. Effective communication between key stakeholders allows cognitive readiness to be achieved in ways that support the whole child.

Responsive Style   Sociocultural theory provides an excellent structure to guide teachers in their efforts to support young children's learning (Vygotsky, 1978). A hallmark of this theory is the importance it places on the child's ability to learn at higher levels with specialized support, referred to as *scaffolding*, from more competent others (e.g., parents, teachers). When that occurs, young children's social and cognitive skills are placed on more positive trajectories (Landry, Smith, Swank, Assel, & Vellet, 2001). This sociocultural theory–guided development of the responsive teaching style. Responsive and appropriate interactions that scaffold children's learning require 1) sensitivity to a child's level of understanding, 2) responses contingent on a child's signals, 3) an ability to maintain and build on a child's focus of interest, 4) rich oral language input, 5) avoidance of excessive restrictions on behavior, 6) provision of choices, and 7) adapting to a child's changing

Table 7.1. Key principles of professional development (PD) to achieve high-quality teacher–child interactions

Key principles	Definition	Example
Responsive style	A responsive interaction style includes consistent teacher use of warm, sensitive, and contingent responses to children's signals.	The teacher attends to a child's nonverbal facial expression that he or she is nervous by responding warmly and labeling the emotion. Then, the teacher suggests two positive choices for the child as he or she copes with the feeling.
Intentional instruction	An intentional instructional plan combines learning in various social-emotional and cognitive areas within one activity or context.	The teacher conducts a simple science experiment that includes rich language input and open-ended questions and requires early mathematics (e.g., measuring with nonstandard units). Children practice self-regulation skills as they follow directions and take turns measuring.
Build concepts	Teachers build students' content knowledge using thematic units and experiences that create rich memories when conceptually related activities occur in close proximity.	The teacher develops a long-term plan for teaching skills using several thematic units to ensure that playful activities provide the context for content and skills instruction and that conceptually linked vocabulary and experiences occur in proximity.
Balance control	A balance of teacher- and child-directed activities provides a fluid daily schedule and uses a gradual release model for scaffolding learning.	The teacher leads a large-group circle-time activity. Then he or she models a new center activity and asks a student to demonstrate the activity for the group so he or she can offer supported practice. Next, children choose learning centers in which they gain independent practice with the new and previously learned activities.
Flexible groupings	Learning activities occur in a variety of groupings (one- to- one, small group, large group) and children move between groups according to learning needs.	The teacher's daily schedule includes large-group activities, small-group teaching during center times, and intentional use of one-to-one conversations and teaching throughout the day. Progress-monitoring data help teachers determine small groups of children with similar needs.

needs. By vigilantly observing and evaluating children's needs and levels of comfort in their environment and providing responsible and responsive care, a teacher establishes a warm and caring environment that helps the child feel comfortable and facilitates the learning process (Peisner-Feinberg et al., 2001). We expected that for effective instruction to occur, this responsive style needed to be combined with an effective plan for teaching the content critical to school readiness.

Intentional Content Planning

The content plan for the PD program required teachers to take advantage of opportunities to combine multiple areas of learning (i.e., math, social skills, language) within a single lesson, activity, or experience (CIRCLE Preschool Early Language and Literacy Including Mathematics Manual, 2009). For example, in an effective "read aloud," teachers builds vocabulary and background knowledge as they highlights characters or key concepts in the book. Their questioning promotes language expression as the children attempt to describe their thoughts about the book. The "give and take" among the children and their ability to cooperate as teachers requests that they wait their turn and listen to each other's responses supports their development of social competence. As the book may be about early math, science, history, or literacy (i.e., alphabet book), the read-aloud activity builds learning in any one of these important areas.

Build Concepts with Thematic Units   Helping teachers understand the "how-to's" of effective planning was the third key ingredient. Theories of learning suggest that children are more likely to build knowledge that sustains if they have repeated experiences in close proximity in time with a new concept (Rovee-Collier, 1995). For example, if teachers introduce a new concept, such as a new vocabulary word, during a shared book reading, children will be more likely to learn this concept at a deeper level if they talk and hear about it in a range of different contexts across the day and week.

Balance Control   Instruction is more effective if it is combined with a teacher-directed activity, as well as with child-directed activities in which children have experiences with new and familiar concepts. At this stage of development, children continue to have a need for increasing autonomy and need to be provided with appropriate choices to exercise their independence (Killen & Smetana, 1999). Providing child-directed activities such as center time gives students practice in planning and carrying out their plans, an approach that is hypothesized to promote development of executive functions (Diamond, Barnett, Thomas, & Munro, 2007).

Flexible Groupings   Children who have opportunities to interact with their teachers in small groups and one- to- one are expected to be more likely to actively engage in learning (Lonigan & Whitehurst, 1998). Regardless of whether teachers have another teacher assistant in the classroom, the PD program trains teachers to utilize flexible groupings that include daily small-group activities.

Complex Environments Require Comprehensive Professional Development Supports

The operating environments of schools involve complex systems that consist of multiple changing factors (such as federal and state policies; district- and school-level initiatives; standards, curriculum, and testing requirements; and funding opportunities) that require developers of scalable programs to

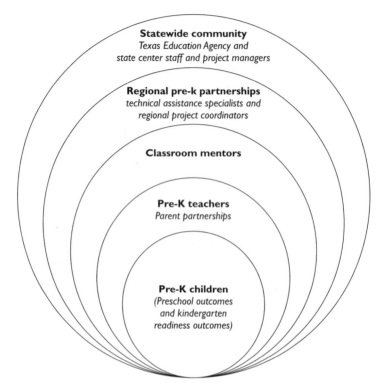

Figure 7.2. Scaling up a professional development (PD) program within an ecological framework requires a partnership among key stakeholders that range from the microsystem level (child, teacher, classroom mentor), to the mesosystem level (regional partnership stakeholders, regional project coordinators, technical assistance specialists), to the exosystem level (State Center staff and project managers, Texas Education Agency).

continuously fine-tune the program design in response to the changes and demands of the environment (Bodilly, Glennan, Kerr, & Galegher, 2004). Ecological theory (Bronfenbrenner & Morris, 2006) provides useful guidance for understanding and intervening in complex education environments in which daily interactions occur that have an impact on children's pre-K learning outcomes. This theory postulates that children's development occurs within nested systems beginning with the *microsystem* (family, school, or any immediate environment of the child), the *mesosystem* (in which microsystems interact with one another, such as parent–teacher interactions), the *exosystem* (external environments that influence development indirectly), and finally the *macrosystem* (larger societal context).

Our PD program engages key constituents at various levels of these systems, such as teachers, mentors, school leaders, regional project coordinators, and state level staff, in building partnerships focused on the goal of ensuring that pre-K teachers can readily prepare their students for kindergarten. Figure 7.2 outlines how the children's microsystems are affected when their pre-K teachers interact with their mentors on a regular basis through facilitated courses and in-class coaching with feedback. The PD program's influence on the classroom is the primary mechanism for change; however, we are studying the effects of coupling the PD program with a family intervention to strengthen teacher–parent partnerships and improve the consistency of adult–children interactions when children are at home and school.

The next levels in Figure 7.2 comprise regional partnerships that include school leaders working with PD project coordinators and technical assistance specialists to ensure that each region has resources to facilitate teachers' coursework and use of resources. Other essential partners influence children's learning more indirectly, such as the State Center for Early Childhood Development (subsequently referred to as State Center) staff and project managers who develop and update PD courses and classroom materials and train project mentors and staff at each level. In addition, exosystem factors such as the funding climate and policies of the Texas Education Agency affect pre-K children's learning. In essence, ecological theory suggests that the child's development results from interactions between the child and his or her school, family, and community over time. Therefore, our PD program seeks to improve children's learning by providing comprehensive supports to teachers and by intervening at all influential, malleable levels of the micro-, meso-, and exosystems.

Conceptual and research models describe the need for a comprehensive set of supports (e.g., PD, research-based curriculum) in order for teachers to assure children develop a range of cognitive and social skills necessary for later school success (e.g., Gallagher, Clifford, & Maxwell, 2004; Sullivan, 1999). Thus, our PD model contains comprehensive supports designed to ensure effective teacher learning over extended periods of time that include practice within the classroom and follow-up feedback on these efforts from a trained mentor (Smylie, Allensworth, Greenberg, Harris, & Luppescu, 2001). Based on adult learning research, the PD program incorporated 1) knowledge about teaching such as the expectations educators have about children, child-development theory, and the content and design of the curriculum; 2) provision of models for teachers to construct knowledge with opportunities for exploration and questioning so that the incorporation of new knowledge into their teaching practices is more likely; 3) making support available for teachers to work with others in their field for fuller engagement with ideas and materials; 4) PD practices that recognize teachers as adult learners and as professionals, utilizing their expertise as well as acknowledging that teachers have different levels of experience; and 5) supporting ample time and follow-up efforts to allow teachers to become fully competent in the new content and strategies and ensure they are able to put them into practice (Bransford et al., 2000).

RESEARCH SUPPORT FOR THE
PROFESSIONAL DEVELOPMENT MODEL

Study 1: Initial Study in Head Start Centers

The genesis for the comprehensive PD program was based on the areas already described and implemented in Texas across 2 years in a quasi-experimental study with more than 750 Head Start teachers in 20 communities (500 received the PD program and 250 control teachers; $n = 5,728$ children) (Landry, Swank, Smith, & Gunnewig, 2006). Teachers received the program in 4-day interactive workshops with sessions on effective practices in: building social skills through teacher responsiveness, language enrichment and scaffolding techniques, shared book reading, building vocabulary and comprehension, print and book awareness, motivation to read, phonological awareness, alphabet knowledge, and written expression. Teachers received weekly in-classroom mentoring from mentors across the state. Details about the coordinator and mentor training, fidelity of implementation procedures, and program effectiveness are described in Landry et al. (2006). For example, findings showed that children's language skills improved significantly after teachers were in the PD program for 2 years in language comprehension (73% of programs) and expression (69% of the programs).

Study 2: Multisite Efficacy Study
Across Service Delivery Systems

In response to the need to further scale up the PD program to a greater number of early childhood teachers and determine its effectiveness for public school pre-K, Head Start, and subsidized child care, the program content was expanded using web-based technology and evaluated in a randomized control trial (Landry, Anthony, Swank, & Monsegue-Bailey, 2009). The previous multiday workshops were adapted to be appropriate for a web-based application, called eCIRCLE. The nine courses covered the following topics: classroom management, best practices and responsive teaching, setting the stage for children's talk, reading aloud, phonological awareness, letter knowledge, mathematics, written expression, and language development. Consistent with theoretical frameworks for effective adult learning (e.g., Bransford et al., 2000), the online courses involved 1) small-group interactive learning facilitated by a trained mentor, 2) extensive videotaped modeling of content-related activities and expert commentaries that allowed teachers to see examples in realistic contexts that were relevant to their classroom experiences, 3) interactive engagement with web-based coursework and web-based assessments of knowledge, 4) opportunity for independent review of all course content, 5) opportunity to practice specific skills within the small group (e.g., role-playing and development of lesson plans), 6) practice of specific instructional activities in one's own classroom and with mentor observation, coaching, and feedback, 7) teacher web-based postings of classroom experiences to facilitate discussion and collaboration among teachers working in the same region, and 8) mentor review and response to postings and group feedback. The eCIRCLE web-based PD program was developed to provide teachers with the appropriate balance between implementing developmentally appropriate activities that are teacher directed and designed to foster development of specific skills and implementing activities that are child directed and designed to allow children to enhance mastery and breadth of skills through active exploration.

Project coordinators and mentors were trained in how to facilitate these courses and received highly detailed facilitator guides. As our previous study (Landry et al., 2006) did not allow for the evaluation of the added benefit of in-classroom mentoring above and beyond the PD training, we developed a web-based eCIRCLE course on the mentoring philosophy and we provided comprehensive procedures for the statewide mentoring staff to facilitate eCIRCLE courses and conduct in-classroom mentoring. Each of the nine courses included an extensive amount of video examples taken in a range of classrooms across the country showing pre-K teachers conducting purposeful and engaging instructional activities related to the skill domain featured in the course. They also included video commentary from teachers and experts about the classroom examples in order to guide learning through careful observation of what the featured teachers were doing and how the children responded. The web-based courses are delivered with small groups of teachers ($n = 15$) usually in a computer lab in a school for 2-hour sessions twice each month across 2 years.

In response to research that has demonstrated the effectiveness of progress-monitoring approaches that inform a teachers' instruction, we developed the CIRCLE-Phonological Awareness, Language, and Literacy Screener (C-PALLS), which now also includes a math and social competence assessment (C-PALLS+) (Landry, Swank, Assel, & King, 2009). This set of brief screening measures is administered by the teacher to individual children early in the school year, in the middle of the school year, and toward the end of the school year. We studied the relative efficacy of this progress-monitoring tool when used in a paper–pencil format and also on a technology platform (e.g., personal digital assistant [PDA], netbook, or laptop). When administered on a technology platform, the software scores the child's responses, gives a learning profile for each child and for the class, provides growth trajectories across the year, and suggests how to group children for small-group instruction. It also is linked to language, literacy, and math supplementary curricula activities within the CIRCLE manual and informs the teacher about which activities are best suited to which children given their learning history.

In order to determine the most effective set of PD resources for pre-K teachers, we conducted a random assignment study in four states: Columbus, Ohio (rural and urban Head Start); Prince George County, Maryland (public school pre-K); Miami, Florida (subsidized child care); and Corpus Christi, Texas (a balance of public school, Head Start, child care). Across the four states, 262 classrooms (n = 1,786 children) were randomly assigned to one of four PD conditions or to a business-as-usual condition. The four PD conditions all included the web-based eCIRCLE courses with two conditions having either pencil–paper progress monitoring or two with PDA progress monitoring with feedback. Within each of the two types of progress-monitoring conditions, one received in-class mentoring and the other did not. Thus, the design was a 2 x 2 such that we could cross mentoring and progress monitoring; the study is described in detail in Landry, Anthony, et al. (2009). This design allowed for the examination of whether our PD web-based program when paired with a pencil–paper monitoring system was more effective than a business-as-usual approach or if there was a significant added benefit to teacher practices and child outcomes if it was paired with a technology-driven monitoring system that gave immediate feedback about how the child's learning progress could be linked to the next instructional steps. In addition, we could determine the added benefit of in-classroom mentoring. To evaluate change in teacher responsiveness and instructional practices we used the CIRCLE Teacher Behavior Rating Scale (TBRS) (Landry, Crawford, Gunnewig, & Swank, 2002). This measure included 50 items measuring the quality and quantity of responsive practices, oral language, book reading, print and letter knowledge, written expression, and phonological awareness observed within a 2-hour observation. The 2006 version also included a mathematics instruction subscale. Lesson planning, centers, and portfolios were also assessed, but only with a quality score (not quantity). The TBRS yielded individual subscale scores and a total composite score. The TBRS was developed to fill a gap in pre-K classroom observation systems, as existing measures did not assess a comprehensive set of early literacy, language, and math instructional practices (Assel, Landry, & Swank, 2007). Gains in the children's skills were measured in English and Spanish (when appropriate) with a battery of standardized language and literacy assessments. The results demonstrated the condition that received the web-based PD courses combined with in-classroom mentoring and instructional planning feedback from technology-based progress monitoring showed the greatest improvements in teaching behavior and children's language and literacy outcomes.

This comprehensive integrated set of PD resources showed the greatest gains for teaching quantity and quality across most subscales of the TBRS. The web-based PD courses with the PDA progress monitoring without mentoring showed comparable TBRS gains only for the book reading and quantity of oral language subscales. All four PD conditions outperformed the control condition on all TBRS subscale scores except oral language and showed greater gains in the total quality and quantity score. Because there were no statistically significant site effects in teacher outcomes, we concluded that the effectiveness of the PD program was comparable for teachers in public schools, Head Start, and subsidized child care in spite of notable differences in teachers' education and resources across these service delivery settings. Examination of the effects of the different PD conditions on gains in child skills generally showed the greatest gains in expressive language skills in the mentoring and PDA progress-monitoring condition, but for global language skills, results differed by site, with Florida and Maryland showing less of a relation between the children's initial language levels if their teachers were in the mentored, PDA condition. For aspects of literacy skills, the mentoring and the PDA conditions generally showed the greatest benefit for letter knowledge, whereas the PDA without mentoring best supported phonological awareness.

Study 3: Statewide Scale Up Study Across All Service Delivery Systems

The next step was to examine the effectiveness of the comprehensive integrated PD program across 11 regional communities in Texas, given the support from this four-state efficacy study for using a comprehensive approach that incorporated the web-based PD courses with a PDA progress-monitoring system and in-classroom mentoring. A random-assignment study was conducted across 11 communities comparing the comprehensive PD model to business-as-usual controls, with each community having balanced representation of public school pre-K, Head Start, and subsidized child care (Landry, Anthony, Swank, & Assel, in press). This was required as part of the state's pre-K initiative to integrate these three service delivery systems into integrated community partnerships; this was expected to strengthen quality, particularly in the child care settings, by pooling resources already established within public schools and Head Start. The study design examined the benefit of 1 versus 2 years of the PD program for gains in teacher practices and child outcomes. In addition, a within-group comparison was conducted on teacher practices and child outcomes for the same group of teachers without (Year-1 controls) and with (Year 2) the program (Landry et al., in press). Each of the 11 regional partnerships had to meet the following criteria: 1) bring together a leadership committee that included members from the three early childhood programs that serve low-income children (i.e., Head Start, subsidized child care, school district) into a partnership to identify common school readiness goals and instructional processes (e.g., all agreed to use the same curriculum), 2) identify a lead agency to coordinate offices for project coordinators and mentors, and 3) agree to random assignment of 20 classrooms within the

partnership to business-as-usual versus participation in the PD program
with stratification across the three types of service delivery system. In addition, the community partnership had to agree to 1) use a research-based
language and literacy curriculum from the state approved list; 2) implement the PD model, including the progress monitoring system, the nine
facilitated online eCIRCLE courses, and in-classroom mentoring; 3) participate in training for multiple levels of partners within the community
(i.e., leadership, mentor, teacher); and 4) participate in meetings throughout the year to ensure effective implementation. Of the 17 communities
that applied, 11 met the above criteria and were accepted into the first year
of the program.

In addition, an advisory panel, mandated by the state legislation and
comprised of the key state agencies involved with young children (e.g., the
Head Start collaborative office, State Department of Family and Protective Services) assisted with program oversight. The State Center also developed a resource panel comprised of national early childhood experts to
inform and advise the project.

In Year 1, 220 classrooms were randomized into the comprehensive
PD program or business-as-usual and pre- and postdata were collected
on 213 teachers and in Year 2, 209 teachers were randomized. Across the
2 years, 6,984 children were included in the program and control classrooms with six per classroom randomly selected for pre- and postassess-
ment evaluation of gains in children's language and literacy skills. In Year
1, assessments were completed for 639 children from control and 626 from
program classrooms. In Year 2, the first-year controls were required by the
state education agency to receive the program, so 800 children had teachers in their first year of the program and 527 children had teachers in the
second year of the program. There were fewer children for second- versus first-year teachers, because communities were only allowed to replace
second-year teachers who did not return in Year 2 with first-year program
teachers. This was necessary to address the question of the benefit of 1
versus 2 years of the program.

The first evaluation looked at differences in gains between control
and program teachers in the Year 1, 4.6-month study period. (Given delays in state funding, the program started in January instead of September, resulting in a 4.6-month program.) The findings of this evaluation
showed that across this period, program teachers showed greater gains in
language-building practices, shared-book reading, and literacy practices,
including phonological awareness and print knowledge activities as well as
responsive interactions and organization and planning (moderate to large
effects). Changes in child skills related to the program were not expected across the 4.6-month period and analyses confirmed this expectation.
Evaluation of differences in the teachers' practices in their first program
year versus those in their second year showed similar teacher changes,

but there were greater increases in children's early literacy and language skills if their teachers were receiving Year 2 of the program. For gains in children's language skills, having a teacher with more training was most beneficial for English language learners (ELLs), for children with lower pretest vocabulary skills, and for younger children. Children of second-year program teachers also showed larger gains in letter knowledge skills, and this was particularly true for children who had the lowest level skills at pretest. Age was important for understanding the significant effects of second-year teachers for phonological awareness, but significant effects were seen for older ELL children and younger English-speaking children. When comparing the same group of teachers without the program (year 1) to themselves with the program (Year 2), we found significant gains in teaching quantity and quality (large effect sizes) on all TBRS subscales when teachers had the program. Effects of teachers having the program were seen for the children's literacy (e.g., print knowledge) and vocabulary gains.

Given the promising findings of these three studies, we plan to continue research on the PD program with a focus on identifying factors that promote scale up and sustainability. Such work can help us understand how nested systems within the educational environments of various service delivery programs change over time to support teachers in effectively implementing high-quality pre-K instruction.

BRINGING THE PROGRAM TO SCALE

Since the time when the third study was conducted with 11 regional communities (2003–2005) the program has been brought to a larger scale across the state; there are more than 100 partnerships in 38 communities. At the start of the 2010–2011 school year, approximately 4,000 classrooms were involved serving more than 70,000 children in what is now referred to as the Texas School Ready! (TSR!) program. Each year new classrooms are recruited as schools to complete the 2-year PD program and begin sustaining change with minimal TSR! support in the third year. With funds from the state education agency, classrooms are provided with a curriculum from the state adopted list, a technology-based progress monitoring system with a PDA or netbook, bimonthly in-classroom mentoring that reduces to monthly in Year 2, and 2 years of the web-based PD courses with a trained mentor from the community to facilitate the courses with groups of 15 teachers across the different service delivery programs.

A statewide infrastructure has been constructed to ensure that the program is conducted with adequate fidelity. This includes a statewide director of the program and eight program managers at the State Center housed in CLI. Nine regional technical assistant specialists oversee project coordinators and mentors in each of their regions. Yearly institute trainings are conducted where the State Center staff work with the region and community coordinators and mentors in a trainer-of-trainer model to problem-solve, update procedures, introduce and train new web-based courses, and analyze regional trends in children's outcome data. State Center staff also analyze statewide data trends to identify aspects of the program that need to be strengthened.

Several resources have been developed to enhance communication of new research evidence to pre-K educators and to exchange ideas for effective practice within the field. A monthly newsletter called the *TSR! Beat* communicates success stories from the field, mentoring tips, and other regional "buzz." A quarterly newsletter for educators, *The Learning Leader,* communicates relevant research findings and ongoing research projects. Finally, annual TSR! Summits gather nationally recognized early childhood experts, policy makers, and researchers to discuss evidence-based practices and issues in pre-K using a webcast to broadcast the summit to viewing parties in all regional communities across the state and to others internationally via the web. The eCIRCLE courses continue to be the primary vehicle for training teachers in evidence-based practices. An advantage of web-based eCIRCLE courses for PD is that they can be readily updated and disseminated across the state as new evidence within the field emerges; many of the language and early literacy web-based courses were updated in 2010-2011 and expanded to incorporate new research. In addition, in response to teacher input and statewide trends in children's learning, three new courses have been added to web-based facilitated training: 1) Social-Emotional Development, 2) Serving Children with Special Needs, and 3) Pre-K Response to Instruction and the Developing Talkers Program.

In addition to these ongoing processes to strengthen and update the PD program, we have further improved the model with four extensive initiatives. These four initiatives addressed the goals of: 1) examining students' school readiness outcomes in kindergarten to assist pre-K classrooms in determining the extent to which their students enter kindergarten with adequate school readiness skills, 2) extending the PD program to match the unique needs of ELL students in classrooms with primarily English instruction and in classrooms with bilingual instruction, 3) advancing the tools and strategies mentors use to encourage reflective teaching, and 4) realizing the potential of flexible groupings by employing a tiered response to instruction framework. Each of these major initiatives fits within the conceptual framework and achieves important steps in a reflective instruction cycle as outlined in Figure 7.3 and detailed here.

Initiative 1: Linking the Professional
Development Model to School Readiness Outcomes

In 2005, the Texas state legislature requested the development of a quality rating system to evaluate how successfully early childhood programs are

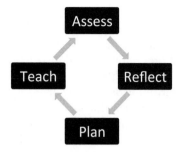

Four major initiatives to improve the professional development (PD) program

	1. School readiness certification system	*2. Extending PD for bilingual students*	*3. Advancing mentoring tools*	*4. Pre-K response to instruction*
Assess...	classrooms by gathering kindergarten child data and pre-K teacher beliefs and knowledge.	bilingual students in both English and Spanish with PM tool.	teachers in fall with COT and monthly with videotaped instruction.	students' response to Tier 1 with PM tool and response to Tier 2 with CBM.
Reflect...	during mentor–teacher certification meeting.	on child's strengths and weaknesses in each language.	on quality of teacher–child interactions across all content areas.	by identifying students who need Tier 2 supports.
Plan...	action steps to improve school readiness outcomes at teacher and school level.	instruction with flexible groupings based on PM data.	with short-term goal reports that address teacher and mentor action items.	instruction for Tier 2 that provides reteaching and additional practice.
Teach...	with more information on classroom's strengths and areas to improve.	using ELL strategies and to improve both English and Spanish skills.	with a focus on improving specific targets of teacher–child interactions.	with tiered groupings and increasingly explicit instruction.

(Note. PM tool = the C-PALLS+ (CIRCLE [Center for Improving the Readiness of Children for Learning and Education]-Phonological Awareness, Language, and Literacy Screener) progress-monitoring assessment used three times per year. ELL = English Language Learners. COT = Classroom Observation Tool completed by mentors in the fall of the academic year to individualize PD goals based on the quality of observed teacher–child interactions. Tier 2 = small group instruction provided as a secondary support when children do not respond adequately with Tier 1 instruction alone. CBM = curriculum-based measures.)

Figure 7.3. A reflective, data-driven instruction cycle guides both professional development (PD) and classroom instruction. Each of the four major program initiatives listed in the top row provided improvements that rely on different types of data (e.g., student progress-monitoring assessments, teacher observation data) to reflect on and plan instruction or PD that more systematically prepares all students to enter kindergarten ready to learn.

preparing their students for school. One of the most important reasons to develop quality rating systems for early childhood programs that are linked to child outcomes is that they support pre-K teachers and leaders in data-driven improvement of programmatic and instructional practices. In addition, the quality rating system should provide programs that are in need of improvement with an individualized training and technical assistance plan. A second compelling reason for identifying effective programs is to provide parents with information they can use to guide their school choice decisions for their children. Although large-scale reports indicate that high-quality early childhood centers can be as cognitively stimulating as home care in middle-class families, working parents of lower income have less access to such high-quality centers (Phillips, Voran, Kisker, Howes, & Whitebook, 1994). Moreover, it is high-quality, early childhood programs that have demonstrated a positive influence on students' school readiness (e.g., Bierman et al., 2008; Hindson et al., 2005; Reynolds, Mavrogenes, Bezruczko, & Hagemann, 1996).

Overview of the School Readiness Certification System   The School Readiness Certification System (SRCS) is a data-driven quality rating system that was developed in conjunction with state educational leadership, national experts in early childhood, and community-based stakeholders (e.g., directors, teachers, parents). The agreed-upon objective was that SRCS should be a statewide system, applicable across service delivery systems, that incorporates information not only from the preschool year, but also from the children once they enter school. SRCS is a 2-year process in which the quality of the pre-K programs is assessed during the first year, and at the beginning of the following school year elementary schools provide kindergarten students' reading and social competency assessments. These kindergarten data are matched by the Texas Education Agency so that the preschool information collected for each program is matched with its students' outcome data. These combined data are used to ascertain which pre-K programs are successfully preparing their students for school.

To accomplish this, a web-based data collection system was created that is easily accessible to programs across the state so they can apply for certification by supplying information about their program, teacher beliefs and knowledge, and children's learning outcomes. The web-based preschool application system gathers information on enrolled students, characteristics of the preschool and classroom facility, teaching practices, and teaching beliefs. Information evaluated within the application is based on characteristics associated with high-quality programs (National Early Literacy Panel, 2008; Snow et al., 1998). For example, information is gathered concerning aspects of the classroom environment (e.g., availability of small group learning areas, space for children to gather for large-group activities, literacy environment; Crosser, 1992; Dunn, Beach, & Kontos,

1994), instructional practices (e.g., intentional language and literacy instruction, time for children to explore new concepts, and opportunities to practice skills with feedback; National Research Council, 2001; Raver & Knitzer, 2002), curriculum (e.g., availability of research based scope and sequence for cognitive and social learning; Assel, Landry, Swank, & Gunnewig, 2007; Whitehurst et al., 1994), assessment approaches (reliable and valid information about students' learning across the year with feedback to teachers to direct instruction; e.g., McConnel, McEvoy, Priest, & Missal, 2000), and quality of available teacher PD (e.g., small group trainings, learning across time, support for opportunities to practice in the classroom; e.g., Elmore, 2002). In addition, the web-based application system contains a mechanism for elementary schools to provide students' scores on their kindergarten literacy skills (e.g., *Texas Primary Reading Inventory* or *Tejas Lee*; Texas Education Agency, 1998, 2002) and social skills (i.e., social competence subscale of the Social Competence and Behavior Evaluation, SCBE-30; Dumas, Martinez & LaFreniere, 1998; Kotler & McMahon, 2002; LaFreniere & Dumas, 1996).

A major goal of SRCS is to determine appropriate criteria for certifying or not certifying classrooms as preparing their students for kindergarten. Because data for all classrooms within a school are not always provided, analysis and certification decisions are made for each classroom, rather than certifying an entire school. A clustering analysis approach (latent profile analysis), in which classrooms are grouped into different categories based on the pattern of their responses, was deemed most appropriate for certifying or not certifying classrooms. Classrooms in the certified group include those that demonstrate both high-quality pre-K programming *and* age-appropriate scores on the kindergarten outcomes. Those classrooms that demonstrate low scores on either the pre-K or kindergarten measures are not certified, and these classrooms are subsequently given feedback on their performance so that they can improve the areas that prevented their certification. In this way, the SRCS serves as an alternative form of program level progress-monitoring data that can enable program enhancement. Moreover, additional mentoring is provided to classrooms that are not certified by trained staff in order to target areas in which improvement is needed.

Initiative 2: Extending the Statewide Model to Meet the Needs of English Language Learners

Given the population of Texas, with many children who come from Spanish-speaking backgrounds, it became apparent that a critical need in the state was increased PD for bilingual teachers and teachers serving ELL students in English immersion programs. In the United States, between 1979 and 2007, the number of students classified as language minority increased from 3.8 to 10.8 million and now make up 12% of the school-age population (Planty et al., 2009). Many of these children (44%) are concentrated in the early instructional years (between pre-K and third grade), and the majority of these students (68%) are classified as low income. The intersection of ELL status and low income amplifies these children's risk for reading failure (Snow et al., 1998) and poor language skills (Tabors, Paez, & Lopez, 2003), puts them at greater risk than monolingual students of being placed in special education (Bennet, 1999; Oviedo & Gonzalez, 1999), and increases the likelihood that they will drop out of school. Of major concern is proper training of pre-K teachers so that they are adequately equipped to address the unique needs of ELL students regardless of programmatic concerns such as language of instruction (e.g., English immersion, bilingual instruction with 90/10 models or 50/50 models) or service delivery center (e.g., child care, school district, Head Start).

In 2008, the State Center at CLI received funding from the Texas Education Agency to test a comprehensive PD model that more rigorously met the needs of ELL children and bilingual teachers. Our first step in creating the comprehensive ELL PD model was to update the web-based PD (eCIRCLE) course offerings. Before 2008, the eCIRCLE course content demonstrated only effective teaching practice examples in English with expert commentary concentrating mainly on effective teaching practices in English. Staff at CLI updated and extended all eCIRCLE courses to include teaching examples and expert commentary to specifically address the unique learning needs of ELL children. These additions were meant to be extensions of the already existing web-based PD programs utilized in previous studies and already being implemented across the state with pre-K teachers. Our ELL model also included the critical pieces of the comprehensive PD model that had been previously researched: in-class mentoring and child progress monitoring. A bilingual mentor implemented our in-class mentoring so that he or she could mentor teachers in both their English and Spanish teaching practices. In addition, progress-monitoring data were collected in both English and Spanish so that teachers could use the data in both languages to group students and provide appropriate instruction across languages. Finally, the ELL PD program provides teachers with classroom resources such as bilingual classroom management kits, texts for reading aloud, and a bilingual version of the CIRCLE manual that includes curriculum supplement activities in English and Spanish for children with different skill levels, as determined from the progress-monitoring assessments.

The ELL PD model was tested in a randomized treatment control study between 2008 and 2010. Teachers were randomly assigned to a treatment condition in which they received the comprehensive ELL PD model or a control condition in which they continued their practice as usual ($n =$ 84 teachers; $n = 672$ students). Teachers were observed in the fall and spring of the academic year using a bilingual version of the TBRS (B-TBRS). We observed significant differences between target and control teachers' behaviors in overall classroom environment and in quality and quantity of oral language instruction and literacy instruction. Child data demonstrated that children who were most at risk at the beginning of the year benefitted more from the program than children who were in average ranges at the beginning of the year. For the children whose teachers had the ELL PD program, effects were observed for both literacy and oral language measures.

Initiative 3: Advancing the Mentoring Model to Increase Reflective Teaching

Increasing evidence demonstrates the importance of moving teachers to more reflective knowledge and practice in order to have an effect on students' learning (Snow, Griffin, & Burns, 2005). As the program has expanded to serve more classrooms, the PD model has continued to encourage reflective teaching by providing mentors with new formative assessment tools. These mentoring tools enhance the quality of in-class mentoring and increase the use of classroom observation data to improve teaching quality.

The first of these tools is the Classroom Observation Tool (COT), a 140-item mentor observation checklist based on items from the TBRS, which has been linked across multiple studies with gains in child literacy and social skills (Assel et al., 2007). Mentors complete the COT at the beginning of the year during a 2-hour classroom visit and update it during subsequent mentoring visits using the COT Report. COT Reports display the date a behavior was first observed in the classroom, along with the date a particular behavior was set as a goal for the coming weeks. These dates allow teachers, mentors, and program managers to monitor progress and plan for additional PD in areas of greatest need. The most critical component in the COT process is the Short-Term Goals Report (STGR), which is reflected upon and revised at the close of each mentoring visit. A STGR displays a set of goals, selected from the COT Report, along with item level links to the Texas Prekindergarten Guidelines, CIRCLE manual activities, and in-depth background information and mentoring strategies from the TSR! Technical Assistance Guide. Mentors and teachers select goals through collaboration and formalize an action plan detailing which of these goals the teacher can begin to work toward on his or her own, and which goals will require more support from the mentor. Action plans include specific information about the mentoring strategies that will be used during the next mentoring visit, including modeling, side-by-side coaching, and video playback and reflection. STGRs provide a clear focus for the coming weeks and can be used as a quick reference to activities and strategies teachers and mentors can use to support their goals. By linking mentoring goals with behaviors from the COT, we ensure alignment with program objectives while still allowing mentors and teachers considerable flexibility to collaborate and set goals that fit the needs and interests of each teacher. Mentors can generate each of these reports in real time in the classroom using their netbooks. When Internet access is limited, mentors complete paper-and-pencil versions and then generate reports once Internet access is available.

Research shows the value of repeated opportunities to reflect and receive feedback on one's own practices through video recordings of adult–child interactions (e.g., Landry, Smith, Swank, & Guttentag, 2008; Mendelsohn et al., 2011; Pianta et al., 2008). In response to these studies, each mentor has been provided with a pocketsize video camera for use during classroom visits. Mentors are trained to link video-recording opportunities with a teacher's short-term goals. Using two basic approaches, mentors may provide teachers either: 1) quick video playback and reflection immediately during the in-class visit, such that 30 seconds to 1 minute of video is played back on the spot (e.g., while children are working in learning centers) and the teacher is encouraged to improve an observed behavior or try a different approach than used in the video during that same that in-class coaching session; or 2) immediately following the in-class coaching, and typically when students are napping or with another teacher, a more extended video playback (e.g., a few 5–7-minute segments of instruction) and reflection or problem-solving discussion occurs. The first quick type of video playback is referred to as "in-flight" video reflection, and the second, more extended playback is called "reflective follow-up." We have found that teachers often respond well to the in-flight playback, because it gives them an opportunity to see exactly how students respond to their moves and they can adjust their approach soon after viewing the video and while their mentor is by their side to support or model the behavior. During the reflective follow-up discussions, mentors and teachers use what they have seen in the videos to select new goals for the STGR and write their action plan for the coming weeks.

The use of video in the classroom has also allowed for the development of new learning opportunities for program mentors. A sampling of teacher clips used during mentoring sessions, along with footage of mentors conducting reflective follow-ups with their teachers, are uploaded and used during mentors' monthly web-conferencing meetings as a form of PD for mentors, who also need ongoing training (Gallucci, Van Lare, Yoon, & Boatright, 2010). These meetings are held at the community level and are facilitated by regional technical assistance specialists and program managers at the State Center. During these meetings, mentors are provided opportunities to practice scoring teacher clips using the COT, participate in group discussions concerning next steps for mentoring teachers in the videos, as well as opportunities to reflect and receive feedback about their own mentoring practices during their video recorded follow-up meetings with teachers.

These web conferences are designed to support mentors in making specific observations using ideas from the COT, increase mentors' self-efficacy, and ensure adherence to the mentoring philosophy across all regions.

Initiative 4: Implementing a Prekindergarten Response to Instruction Framework

After the 2008–2009 academic year, statewide trends in students' progress-monitoring data revealed that students whose teachers were participating in the comprehensive PD program were making solid progress in literacy skills, but the typical trajectory for language skills was less robust. Researchers often report that language skills of at-risk children can be more difficult to improve than other domains, perhaps because they receive language input in the home and at school that is not consistently rich and well matched to their developmental needs (Chapman, 2007; Dickinson, Golinkoff, & Hirsh-Pasek, 2010; Hart & Risley, 1995).

In response to these national reports and our statewide data, staff at the State Center started exploring innovative approaches to enhancing the oral language components of the PD program, with a specific focus on improving vocabulary and listening comprehension skills that are known to be important to later reading achievement (NELP, 2008; Storch & Whitehurst, 2002; Vellutino, Tunmer, Jaccard, & Chen, 2007). In the spring of 2010, we piloted new components to the program designed to systematically enhance pre-K teachers' oral language instruction using a tiered, data-driven approach that follows a Pre-K Response to Instruction (P-RTI) framework while maintaining developmentally appropriate beliefs and practices in early childhood. P-RTI approaches represent a relatively new methodology in pre-K that is supported by a growing body of evidence (see Coleman, Roth, & West, 2009). In the fall of 2010, we implemented a P-RTI framework for supporting oral language with all teachers in the second year of the PD program. (Teachers in the first year of the PD program continue using the already developed courses on oral language instruction.)

Specifically, the PD format we created includes a new eCIRCLE course entitled P-RTI with a corresponding curriculum supplement called Developing Talkers: Pre-K in English or Hablemos Juntos: Pre-K in Spanish. The English version is designed for use with monolinguals or ELLs, whereas the Spanish version is designed for bilingual classrooms. The rationale behind these new components was that a P-RTI framework could improve prevention of learning difficulties at an early age, but preschool teachers would require their own scaffolding and support to implement P-RTI approaches that we felt would be best achieved by providing a curriculum supplement that followed a P-RTI framework. Similar to the CIRCLE Manual provided to first-year teachers, this supplement is designed to extend instructional supports to second-year teachers, but it does not replace their core curriculum. We targeted teachers in the second year of the PD program because they should be well positioned to use more explicit, systematic, and data-based instruction as delivered in Tier 1 and Tier 2 of P-RTI frameworks after the sustained period receiving the comprehensive PD in the first year of the program.

The eCIRCLE course on P-RTI enhances second-year teachers' use of the progress-monitoring assessment and small-group instruction that they began using in their first year of the program. Similar to the other eCIRCLE courses, facilitators use discussion-based activities, video examples, expert video commentary, role play, and classroom practice activities to help teachers learn the basics of a P-RTI approach. For example, during the 7-hour course, teachers practice analyzing sample data and their own classroom data to identify children who need Tier 2 or 3 instruction. Then, teachers work together on skill-building activities to practice using components of evidence-based Tier 1 and Tier 2 instruction in their own lesson planning.

The major components of the P-RTI framework are similar to Response to Intervention (RTI) in elementary with the focus on three tiers of increasingly intensive and targeted instruction delivered to students who do not make expected progress as measured with screening/progress-monitoring measures given three times per year at Tier 1 and with monthly or weekly Curriculum Based Measures (CBM) at Tier 2. Nonetheless, the P-RTI framework in preschool is unique in that it focuses on prevention rather than using RTI as a method for identifying learning disabilities, which typically does not occur until kindergarten or later in Texas. Moreover, in preschool, the delivery of Tier 2 interventions is typically conducted by the classroom teacher, because many programs are private child cares or Head Starts that do not have regular access to reading specialists, speech-language pathologists, or other specialists who often deliver higher tiers of instruction in elementary schools. One of the greatest challenges in P-RTI is determining what services can be realistically provided at Tier 3. Many preschools do not have the schoolwide infrastructure and resources to provide one-to-one instruction at sufficient intensity at Tier 3; therefore, mentors work with teachers to use a problem-solving protocol for children who are not responding to Tier 2 instruction that focuses on finding creative ways to deliver more intensive instruction to these students.

The Developing Talkers, Pre-K or Hablemos Juntos, Pre-K curriculum supplements follow a P-RTI framework and include books, activities, simple lesson plans, and CBMs to support teachers in developing children's vocabulary and listening comprehension skills. Teachers learn to use these materials in a 3-hour eCIRCLE course. Tier 1 instruction is delivered through a whole-group read aloud with instruction before, during, and after reading to address important comprehension questions and six target vocabulary words per book. Tier 2 instruction is delivered to groups of four students and includes review of the text used earlier in the day and more explicit and extended vocabulary instruction. Tier 3 instruction is determined at each school because of the variability in resources at the preschool level. The curriculum supplements were developed to be planful, purposeful, and playful, instructional characteristics that are central to the larger PD model. Lessons are planful because they follow a systematic sequence and provide sample teacher language that includes scripted components and components with more flexibility. Lessons are purposeful in that evidence-based techniques are used to deliver instruction targeted to students' individual skill levels and to use language-scaffolding techniques that range from minimal, moderate, to intense. Finally, lessons are playful because science topics are included in all texts, and young students are curious about exploring the natural world around them. The curriculum supplements contain extension activities that teachers can use in science, writing, computer, and library centers. In the fall of 2010, these new components were introduced statewide to all teachers in the second year of the PD program. We are collecting data on the effectiveness of the new components and feedback from teachers to improve these approaches.

LESSONS LEARNED IN BRINGING THE PROGRAM TO SCALE

During this 13-year process of piloting, evaluating, and bringing this PD program to scale across various pre-K service delivery settings in Texas, we have learned several lessons that support effective implementation and sustainability. To conclude this chapter, we outline some of the obstacles to change we have encountered and some key beliefs we have identified that are likely to be relevant to others who have long-term goals of bringing their own programs to scale.

- **Advance shared priorities.** Any type of education reform should be driven by demand from the stakeholders who will actually implement and be affected by the reform, because people must want to change in order to do so (Healey & DeStefano, 1997). Data can be a tool for generating a belief that change is needed and for developing a vision of shared priorities. To get pre-K teachers and community leaders to buy into the reform, we have learned to involve communities in developing and taking credit for their own unique contributions to the PD program, including identifying ways to integrate the program into existing local priorities and practices.

- **Adapt practices within a well-articulated framework.** When educators are given a deep conceptual understanding behind the program's framework, instead of simply a set of activities or skills, they are more likely to implement the program effectively and appropriately modify the practices to fit the classroom environment more closely (McIntosh, Filter, Bennett, Ryan, & Sugai, 2010). We have learned that when aspects of the model are too rigid, they are unlikely to be sustained after the formal training years conclude. Therefore, we have sought to articulate a cogent model that allows room for educators to modify many components while ensuring the integrity of the most key components. In this way we can encourage a sustained, flexible fidelity to the practices within the program.

- **Continue improving and refining the model.** We have encountered many naysayers who tell us these ideas and practices will never work in their classroom or with their students. Yet many teachers are astonished when their mentor supports them in trying new practices and they see a positive response from their students. However, other critical feedback has signaled a need to refine or extend the program to meet the demands of educational realities. For example, in response to calls for more effective supports of ELL or better use of data, we have implemented new initiatives designed to continually improve the PD program. We have learned that critical feedback about the program should be carefully considered to determine whether it signals a need for additional mentoring support or a need to improve the program.

- **Ensure effective local partnerships.** State education policy in Texas gives sizable local control to effective districts and programs. Therefore, we knew from the outset that our PD model must include local partnerships within regions or proximal communities. One of the largest challenges of this effort was to get buy-in and cooperation in communities across the three types of service delivery programs. At the beginning of the implementation of the statewide program, very few communities were working together across the three types of service delivery programs. A goal was to have state-funded certified teachers assigned to subsidized child care classrooms in which a minimum of 15 children were being served who were eligible for state public school pre-K. Many of the programs achieved this goal by the second year. Building partnerships was challenged by differences in program cultures, philosophies, student entry criteria, and staffing patterns. With the exception of one community, at the outset of this project, these types of partnerships were not in place in the communities. In some cases there was not even goodwill among some of the programs. Thus, the initiative involved changing teachers' practices as well as changing the culture of pre-K service delivery in the state, which we have learned is best achieved with honest, timely communication that relies on data as the impetus for change.

- **Build capacity to sustain implementation.** To support teachers in implementing these practices after their formal training concludes, we attempt to build resources and knowledge within the school and community. In the third year of the PD program, teachers no longer receive coursework and mentoring but more limited technical assistance to ensure that key components are available and implemented. The goal is to shift the reliance in the third year to regionally based resources with less support from the university-funded staff, using a similar approach to regional scaling as has occurred with other successful education interventions operating at scale (e.g, Slavin & Madden, 2004). We have learned that this third year of minimal support is sufficient for many, but not all, schools and classrooms to maintain practices, and we continue to investigate ways to bolster sustainability.

To conclude, we firmly believe that national concern and urgency are still needed to provide pre-K children across the nation with the experiences they need to be successful in kindergarten. This chapter chronicles how we have sought to make progress toward this goal in one state. We remain committed to identifying and extending effective PD programs for early childhood teachers that ensure all children enter school ready to learn.

REFERENCES

Assel, M.A., Landry, S.H., & Swank, P.R. (2007). Are early childhood classrooms preparing children to be school ready? The CIRCLE Teacher Behavior Rating Scale. In L. Justice & C. Vukelich (Eds.), *Achieving excellence in preschool literacy instruction* (pp. 120–135). New York, NY: Guilford Press.

Assel, M.A., Landry, S.H., Swank, P.R., & Gunnewig, S. (2007). An evaluation of curriculum, setting, and mentoring on the performance of children enrolled in pre-kindergarten. *Reading and Writing Quarterly, 20,* 463–494. doi:10.1007/s11145-006-9039-5

Bennet, C.I. (1999). *Comprehensive multicultural education: Theory and practice.* Needham Heights, MA: Allyn and Bacon.

Bierman, K.L., Domitrovich, C.E., Nix, R.L., Gest, S.D., Welsh, J.A., Greenberg, M.T., … Gill, S. (2008). Promoting academic and social-emotional school readiness: The Head Start REDI program. *Child Development, 79,* 1802–1817. doi:10.1111/j.1467-8624.2008.01227

Blau, D.M., & Mocan, N. (2002). The supply of quality in child care centers. *Review of Economics and Statistics, 84,* 483–496.

Bodily, S.J., Glennan, T.K., Jr., Kerr, K.A., & Galegher J.R. (2004). Introduction: Framing the problem. In T.K. Glennan, S.J. Bodilly, J.R. Galegher, & K.A. Kerr (Eds.), *Expanding the reach of education reforms: Perspectives from leaders in the scale up of educational interventions* (pp. 1–40). Arlington, VA: RAND Corporation.

Bowman, B.T., Donovan, M.S., & Burns, M.S. (2001). *Eager to learn: Educating our preschoolers.* Washington, DC: National Academy Press.

Bransford, J., Brown, A., & Cocking, R.R. (2000). *How people learn: Brain, mind, experience, and school.* Washington, DC: National Academy Press.

Bronfenbrenner, U., & Morris, P.A. (2006). The bioecological model of human development. In R.M. Lerner & W. Damon (Eds.), *Handbook of child psychology: Vol. 1, Theoretical models of human development.* (6th ed., pp. 793-828). Hoboken, NJ: John Wiley & Sons, Inc.

Brownell, R. (2000). *Expressive One-word Picture Vocabulary Test Manual.* Novato, CA: Academic Therapy Publications.

Chapman, R.S. (2007). Children's language learning: An interactionist perspective. Mahwah, NJ: Lawrence Erlbaum.

CIRCLE *Preschool Early Language and Literacy Including Mathmatics; Teachers Manual.* (2009). Children's Learning Institute publication, University of Texas, Houston, Texas.

Cohen, D.K. & Ball, D.L. (2007). Educational innovation and the problem of scale. In B. Schneider & S.K. McDonald (Eds.) *Scale up in education: Ideas in principle* (pp. 19–36). Lanham, MA: Rowman & Littlefield.

Coleman, M.R., Roth, F.P., & West, T. (2009). *Roadmap to pre-K RTI: Applying response to intervention in preschool settings.* New York, NY: National Center for Learning Disabilities.

Crosser, S. (1992). Managing the early childhood classroom. *Young Children, 47,* 23–29.

Dawson, G., Klinger, L., Panagiotides, H., Hill, D., & Spieker, S. (1992). Frontal lobe activity and affective behavior of infants of mothers with depressive symptoms. *Child Development, 63*(3), 725–737. doi:10.2307/1131357

Diamond, A., Barnett, W., Thomas, J., & Munro, S. (2007). Preschool program improves cognitive control. *Science, 318*(5855), 1387–1388. doi:10.1126/science.1151148

Dickinson, D.K., Golinkoff, R., & Hirsh-Pasek, K. (2010). Speaking out for language: Why language is central to reading development. *Educational Researcher, 39*(4), 305–310. doi:10.3102/0013189X10370204

Dumas, J.E., Martinez, A., & LaFreniere, P.J. (1998). The Spanish version of the Social Competence and Behavior Evaluation (SCBE)—Preschool edition: Translation and field testing. *Hispanic Journal of Behavioral Sciences, 20,* 255–269. doi:10.1177/07399863980202008

Dunn, L., Beach, S.A., & Kontos, S. (1994). Quality of the literacy environment in day care and children's development. *Journal of Research in Childhood Education, 9,* 24–34. doi:10.1080/02568549409594950

Early, D.M., Maxwell, K.L., Burchinal, M., Bender, R.H., Ebanks, C., Henry, G.T., Iriondo-Perez, J., ... Zill, N. (2007). Teachers' education, classroom quality, and young children's academic skills: Results from seven studies of preschool programs. *Child Development, 78*(2), 558–580. doi:10.1111/j.1467-8624.2007.01014

Elmore, R.R. (2002). *Bridging the gap between standards and achievement. The imperative for professional development in education.* New York, NY: The Albert Shanker Institute.

Gallucci, C., Van Lare, M., Yoon, I., & Boatright, B. (2010). Instructional coaching: Building theory about the role and organizational support for professional learning *American Educational Research Journal, 47.* doi:10.3102/0002831210371497

Girolametto, L., Weitzman, E., Lefebvre, P., & Greenberg, J. (2007). The effects of in-service education to promote emergent literacy in child care centers: A feasibility study. *Language, Speech, and Hearing Services in Schools, 38*(1), 72–83. doi:10.1044/0161-1461(2007/007)

Hart, B. & Risley, T. (1995). *Meaningful differences in the everyday experience of young American children.* Baltimore, MD: Paul H. Brookes Publishing Co.

Healey, F., & DeStefano, J. (1997). *Education reform support: A framework for scaling up school reform* (Policy Paper Series). Raleigh, NC: Research Triangle Institute.

Hindson, B., Byrne, B., Fielding-Barnsley, R., Newman, C., Hine, D.W., & Shankweiler, D. (2005). Assessment and early instruction of preschool children at risk for reading disability. *Journal of Educational Psychology, 97,* 687–704. doi:10.1037/0022-0663.97.4.687

Howes, C. (1997). Children's experiences in center-based child care as a function of teacher background and adult-child ratio. *Merrill-Palmer Quarterly, 43,* 404–425.

Howes, C., Burchinal, M., Pianta, R., Bryant, D., Early, D., Clifford, R., & Barbarin, O. (2008). Ready to learn? Children's pre-academic achievement in pre-kindergarten programs. *Early Childhood Research Quarterly, 23*, 27–50. doi:10.1016/j.ecresq.2007.05.002

International Reading Association & National Association for the Education of Young Children. (1998). *Learning to reading and write: Developmentally appropriate practices for young children.* Newark, DE: International Reading Association.

Killen, M., & Smetana, J. (1999). Social interactions in preschool classrooms and the development of young children's conceptions of the personal. *Child Development, 70*(2), 486–501. doi:10.1111/1467-8624.00035

Kontos, S., Howes, C., & Galinsky, E. (1996). Does training make a difference to quality in family child care? *Early Childhood Research Quarterly, 11*, 427–445. doi:10.1016/S0885-2006(96)90016-2

Kotler, J.C., & McMahon, R.J. (2002). Differentiating anxious, aggressive and socially competent preschool children: Validation of the Social Competence and Behavior Evaluation-30 (parent version). *Behaviour Research and Therapy, 40*, 947–959. doi:10.1016/S0005-7967(01)00097-3

LaFreniere, P.J., & Dumas, J.E. (1996). Social competence and behavior evaluation children ages 3 to 6 years: The short form (SCBE-30). *Psychological Assessment, 8*(4), 369–377. doi:10.1037/1040-3590.8.4.369

Landry, S.H. (2008). Effective early childhood programs: Turning knowledge into action. In A.R. Tarlov & M.C. Debbink (Eds.), *Investing in early childhood development* (pp. 67–84). New York, NY: Palgrave Macmillan.

Landry, S.H., Anthony, J., Swank, P.R., & Assel, M.A. (2011). An experimental study evaluating professional development activities within a state funded pre-kindergarten program. *Reading & Writing: An Interdisciplinary Journal, 24*, 971-1010. Doi:10.1007/s11145-010-9243-1

Landry, S.H., Anthony, J., Swank, P.R., Monsegue-Bailey, P. (2009). Effectiveness of comprehensive professional development for teachers of at-risk preschoolers. *Journal of Educational Psychology, 101*, 448–465. doi:10.1037/a0013842

Landry, S.H., Crawford, A., Gunnewig, S., & Swank, P.R. (2002). The CIRCLE-Teacher Behavior Rating Scale. Center for Improving the Readiness of Children for Learning and Education, University of Texas Health Science Center at Houston: Unpublished research instrument.

Landry, S.H., Smith, K.E., Swank, P.R., Assel, M.A., & Vellet, S. (2001). Does early responsive parenting have a special importance for children's development or is consistency across early childhood necessary? *Developmental Psychology, 37*(3), 387–403. doi:10.1037//0012-1649.37.3.387

Landry, S.H., Smith, K.E., Swank, P.R., & Guttentag, C. (2008). A responsive parenting intervention: The optimal timing across early childhood for impacting maternal behaviors and child outcomes. *Developmental Psychology, 44*(5), 1335–1353.

Landry, S.H., Swank, P.R., Assel, M.A., & King, T. (2009). *The circle phonological awareness, language and literacy system + (C-PALLS+): Technical manual.* Children's Learning Institute. Unpublished research.

Landry, S.H., Swank, P.R., Smith, K.E., & Gunnewig, S. (2006). Enhancing cognitive readiness for pre-school children: Bringing a professional development model to scale. *Journal of Learning Disabilities. 39*(4) 306–324.

LoCasle-Crouch, J., Konold, T., Pianta, R., Howes, C., Burchinal, M., Bryant, D., … Barbarin, O. (2007). Observed teaching quality profiles in state-funded pre-kindergarten programs and associations with teacher, program, and classroom characteristics. *Early Childhood Research Quarterly, 22*, 3–17.

Lonigan, C.J., & Whitehurst, G.J. (1998). Relative efficacy of parent and teacher involvement in a shared-reading intervention for preschool children from low-income backgrounds. *Early Childhood Research Quarterly, 17*, 265–292.

Mashburn, A.J., Pianta, R.C., Hamre, B.K., Downer, J.T., Barbarin, O.A., Bryant, D., … Early, D.M. (2008). Measures of teaching quality in prekindergarten and children's development of academic, language, and social skills. *Child Development*, *79*, 732–749.

McConnel, S. R., McEvoy, M. A., Priest, J. S., & Missal, K.M. (2000). *Individual growth and development indicators—Early Literacy (IGDIs-EL)*. Minneapolis: Center for Early Education and Development, University of Minnesota.

McIntosh, K., Filter, K., Bennett, J., Ryan, C., & Sugai, G. (2010). Principles of sustainable prevention: Designing scale up of school-wide positive behavior support to promote durable systems. *Psychology in the Schools*, *47*(1), 5–21. doi:10.1002/pits.20448

National Early Literacy Panel. (2008). *Developing early literacy: Report of the National Early Literacy Panel*. Washington, DC: National Center for Family Literacy.

National Research Council. (2001). *Eager to learn: Educating our preschoolers*. Washington, DC: National Academy Press.

Neuman, S., & Cunningham, L. (2009). The impact of professional development and coaching on early language and literacy instructional practices. *American Educational Research Journal*, *46*(2), 532. doi:10.3102/0002831208328088

Oviedo, M.D. & V. Gonzalez. (1999). Standardized and alternative assessments: Diagnosis accuracy in minority children referred for special education assessment. In V. Gonzalez (Ed.), *Language and cognitive development in second language learning: Educational implications for children and adults* (pp. 227–268). Needham Heights, MA: Allyn and Bacon.

Peisner-Feinberg, E.S., Burchinal, M.R., Clifford, R.M., Culkin, M.L., Howes, C., Kagan, S.L. & Yazejian, N. (2001). The relation of preschool child-care quality to children's cognitive and social developmental trajectories through second grade. *Child Development*, *72*, 1534–1553. doi:10.1111/1467-8624.00364

Phillips, D.A., Voran, M., Kisker, E., Howes, C., & Whitebook, M. (1994). Child care for children in poverty: Opportunity of inequity. *Child Development*, *65*, 472–492. doi:10.2307/1131397

Pianta, R.C., Mashburn, A.J., Downer, J.T., Hamre, B.K., & Justice, L.M. (2008). Effects of web-mediated professional development resources on teacher-child interactions in pre-kindergarten classrooms. *Early Childhood Research Quarterly*, *23*, 431–451. doi:10.1016/j.ecresq.2008.02.001

Planty, M., Hussar, W., Snyder, T., Kena, G., KewalRamani, A., Kemp, J., Bianco, K. & Dinkes, R. (2009). *The Condition of Education 2009* (NCES 2009-081). National Center for Education Statistics, Institute of Education Sciences, U.S. Department of Education., retrieved from http://nces.ed.gov/pubsearch/pubsinfo.asp?pubid=2009081.

Putnam, R.T. & Borko, H. (2000). What do new views of knowledge and thinking have to say about research on teacher learning? *Educational Researcher*, *29*, 4–15. doi:10.2307/1176586

Raver, C., & Knitzer, J. (2002). *Ready to enter: What research tells policymakers about strategies to promote social and emotional school readiness among 3- and 4-year-old children*. National Center for Children in Poverty, Mailmain School of Public Health, New York, NY: Columbia University.

Reynolds, A.J., Mavrogenes, N.A., Bezruczko, N., & Hagemann, M. (1996). Cognitive and family-support mediators of preschool effectiveness: A confirmatory analysis. *Child Development*, *67*, 1119–1140. doi:10.2307/1131883

Rovee-Collier, C. (1995). Time windows in cognitive development. *Developmental Psychology*, *31*(2), 147–169.

Slavin, R., & Madden, N. (2004). Scaling up Success for All: Lessons for policy and practice. In T.K. Glennan, S.J. Bodilly, J.R. Galegher, & K.A. Kerr (Eds.), *Expanding the reach of education reforms: Perspectives from leaders in the scale-up of educational interventions* (pp.135–174). Arlington, VA: RAND Corporation.

Smylie, M.A., Allensworth, E., Greenberg, R.C., Harris, R., & Luppescu, S. (2001). *Teacher professional development in Chicago: Supporting effective practice.* Chicago, IL: Consortium on Chicago School Research.

Snow, C.E., Burns, M., & Griffin, P. (1998). *Preventing reading difficulties in young children.* Washington, DC: National Academies Press.

Snow, C.E., Griffin, P., & Burns, M.S. (2005). *Knowledge to support the teaching of reading: Preparing teachers for a changing world.* San Francisco, CA: Jossey-Bass.

Storch, S.A., & Whitehurst, G.J. (2002). Oral language and code-related precursors to reading: Evidence from a longitudinal structural model. *Developmental Psychology, 38*(6), 934–947. doi:10.1037/0012-1649.38.6.934

Sullivan, B. (1999). Professional development: The linchpin of teacher quality. *ASCD Infobrief No. 18.*

Tabors, P.O., Páez, M.M., & López, L.M. (2003). Dual language abilities of Spanish-English bilingual four-year olds: Initial finding from the early childhood study of language and literacy development of Spanish-speaking children. *NABE Journal of Research and Practice, 1,* 70–91.

Texas Education Agency. (1998). *Texas primary reading inventory, technical manual.* Austin, TX: TEA.

Texas Education Agency. (2002). *Tejas LEE, technical manual.* Austin, TX: Author.

Vellutino, F., Tunmer, W., Jaccard, J., & Chen, R. (2007). Components of reading ability: Multivariate evidence for a convergent skills model of reading development. *Scientific Studies of Reading, 11*(1), 3–32. doi:10.1207/s1532799xssr1101_2

Vygotsky, L.S. (1978). *Mind in society.* Cambridge, MA: Harvard University Press.

Wasik, B.A., Bond, M.A., & Hindman, A. (2006). The effects of a language and literacy intervention on Head Start children and teachers. *Journal of Educational Psychology, 98,* 63–74. doi:10.1037/0022-0663.98.1.63

Whitehurst, G.J., Epstein, J.N., Angell, A.L., Payne, A.C., Crone, D.A., & Fischel, J.E. (1994). Outcomes of an emergent literacy intervention in Head Start. *Journal of Educational Psychology, 86,* 542–555. doi:10.1037//0022-0663.86.4.542

Whitehurst, G.J., & Lonigan, C.J. (1998). Child development and emergent literacy. *Child Development 69,* 848–872. doi:10.2307/1132208

8

Scaling
Up Effective
Professional Development

Robert C. Pianta, Bridget K. Hamre, and D. Sarah Hadden

It is widely recognized that a key challenge facing early education in the United States is increasing the quality and effectiveness of teaching and teachers' interactions with children. It is also well known that most of the models in use for improving quality and impact through teacher professional development (PD) have very little evidence of benefits for teachers or children. This gap between the needs of the early childhood workforce and scalable, effective PD is a tremendous impediment to improving young children's learning and closing skills gaps. Even with federal funding pouring into initiatives that emphasize measurement and improvement of early childhood program impacts (and emphasizing teachers)—including the Race to the Top Early Learning Challenge, longitudinal data systems that connect prekindergarten to K–12, and funding for Quality Rating and Improvement Systems—the lack of effective, scalable PD and training leaves most states and programs in a quandary.

There are two overarching features of a scalable system of effective PD. First, the specific PD training and support experiences offered to teachers must actually improve practice and student learning. Second, a proven effective model must be replicable and fit within systems of incentives, management, and evaluation that enable high levels of participation and fidelity. Without either of these two conditions—a proven effective model *and* a system for scaling with fidelity—the status quo will remain ineffective, one-time experiences that have little hope of impact. The present chapter presents information gleaned from analysis of implementation of two forms of effective PD studied in the National Center for Research on Early Childhood Education (NCRECE)—a college course and a model for coaching. Because the NCRECE PD study implemented and evaluated these two PD supports with a large number of teachers across a wide range of auspices, it has the potential to shed light not only on the question of impact, but also on factors related to implementation at scale.

PROFESSIONAL DEVELOPMENT IN EARLY CHILDHOOD

Despite well-founded concerns about the quality and impact of PD in early childhood education, there are suggestions from a variety of sources regarding features of PD that tend to be related to improved practice and student learning (Zaslow, Tout, Halle, Whittaker, & Lavelle, 2010). The best focus on providing teachers with 1) relevant information on students' skill targets and progressions, 2) support for learning to skillfully use instructional and social interactions to promote student engagement and learning, and 3) to effectively implement curricula. These approaches have in common a clear focus on specific teaching practices in a specific teacher's classroom setting, with a specific curriculum. Evidence suggests that when such targeted and aligned supports are available to teachers, student skill gains can be considerable—on the order of a half a standard deviation on average, and as much as a full standard deviation. Unfortunately, teachers are rarely exposed to multiple field-based examples of objectively defined high-quality practice and they receive few, if any, opportunities to receive feedback about the extent to which their classroom interactions and instruction promote these skill domains.

The absence of PD impact is in part due to a lack of both a coherent theory of action (e.g., Why should this work?) and a direct linkage with a system for assessing teacher practice (e.g., What does good practice look like?) that explicitly aligns the PD with classroom practice. PD approaches (e.g., courses, workshops, coaching, professional learning communities) need a clear and strong basis for why that specific experience should change teachers' practice or student learning, and those courses and workshops need to directly produce the skills that can be measured as best practices (such as through an existing teacher observation system). Then comes the challenge of scale up. Because even for PD approaches that work with a few dozen teachers or a couple of schools, there is little evidence that they can be implemented in a standardized manner across teachers so that many thousands can improve their work systematically at district or state levels.

The NCRECE PD study draws from a model of PD designed to improve teacher–student interactions and in turn increase student learning and development. This program of research has involved developing standardized descriptions and measures of teachers' practices (e.g., the Classroom Assessment Scoring System™, or CLASS™; Pianta, R.C., La Paro, K.M., & Hamre, B., 2008) that we have used in thousands of classrooms and experimental studies of different approaches to PD (MyTeachingPartner, or

MTP) designed to improve teacher practices and interactions. We planned the NCRECE PD study with an interest in engineering and evaluating a scalable approach to supporting early childhood teachers in classrooms. Standardized observation of teachers' classroom interactions is the leverage point of this work, largely because of the premise that if one could observe (across many classrooms) practices of teachers proven to contribute to children's learning gains, then those observed behaviors could and should become the "target" of PD. That is, if we can see what teachers do that matters, then effective PD should produce those behaviors. This coupling of observation with effective PD satisfies the first task in building a scalable system of effective supports for teachers—a model that works (Hamre, Pianta, Burchinal, & Downer, in press; Mashburn, Downer, Hamre, Justice, & Pianta, 2010; Pianta et al., 2008).

Then the challenge becomes scaling up of a proven effective model. In the NCRECE PD study, we did this in two ways. First, we considered the importance of higher education as a mechanism for scale up, and so we developed a version of MTP that could function as a standard college course, and then we implemented this course in 10 different institutions. Second, we moved MTP coaching from a model in which coaches were centralized and located (and supported) in the university setting, to a model in which coaches were local—in the districts in which the teachers and classroom were located—and coach supports were centralized. We then evaluated this distributed model of coaching in 10 sites across the country. In the pages that follow we share some of the lessons learned and results gleaned from this multisite study that have implications for scale up.

EFFECTIVE PROFESSIONAL DEVELOPMENT IN HIGHER EDUCATION: COURSES AND DEGREES

Studies of the primary mechanism through which early childhood teachers are prepared in the United States—teacher preparation programs in institutions of higher education—show little or no influence of teacher training on teacher–child interactions or on child outcomes (Early et al., 2007; Kontos, Howes, & Galinsky, 1996). Despite these dismal results regarding impacts, 36,000 early childhood educators are trained each year in teacher preparation programs in higher education (Maxwell, Lim, & Early, 2006). Given that more than half of a trainee's credit hours in higher education are occupied by coursework, courses that are proven effective for positive impacts on classroom practice could be an important leverage point for wide-scale change and improvement in the early childhood workforce, and a way to make a degree matter.

In an effort to develop effective PD for early childhood educators' skills in the classroom and address the need for applications that work in higher education, NCRECE developed a college-level course focused on two primary aims: 1) effective teacher–child interactions, and 2) the connection between interactions and children's language and literacy development. More specifically, the course was designed to increase teachers' knowledge and skills in identifying effective interactions and the actual quality of their interactions in classrooms. Designed as a for-credit college course, this PD intervention has the potential to be scalable through existing delivery systems for teacher preparation (i.e., higher education), and may also address a critical gap created by policies requiring early childhood educators to earn a college degree (Improving Head Start Act of 2007, H.R. 1429, 2007).

With the reauthorization of Head Start that includes mandates for 50% of lead teachers to have a bachelor's degree and all teaching assistants to have a Child Development Associate (CDA) credential by 2013 (Improving Head Start Act of 2007, H.R. 1429, 2007), and with states expanding their prekindergarten programs that link teacher qualifications to the K–12 system, the demand for teachers to engage with higher education institutions for PD and advanced training is quite evident. According to a 2006 national report (Maxwell et al., 2006), there are more than 1,200 higher education institutes that offer some kind of degree program in early childhood education, and the majority of their training involves coursework.

An effective course as the method of PD delivery has several advantages related to use at scale. Coursework, which can be delivered for cohorts of preservice and/or in-service teachers, is likely to be considerably less expensive than an intervention such as coaching or mentoring, which are typically delivered one-on-one or in small groups. Furthermore, effective courses have the potential of being folded into existing teacher preparation programs in higher education, in which a considerable level of infrastructure already exists, in contrast to mentoring approaches, which are typically supplemental supports that require significant additional resources from programs (Maxwell et al., 2006). And, given their modular nature within a program, courses can be standardized in ways that accommodate the challenges of large-scale implementation across multiple institutions.

Despite the potential for coursework in higher education to leverage improvement on teacher impacts, in an examination of the relation between teachers' education and classroom quality across seven major studies, Early and colleagues (2007) found that there was no consistent link between the two. Teacher education alone was not an effective training asset for ensuring the quality of preschool classrooms. In the few studies that have systematically tested the effects of a specific course on teacher–child interactions or child outcomes (Dickinson & Caswell, 2007; Howes, Galinsky, & Kontos, 1998; Kontos et al., 1996; Neuman & Cunningham, 2009), however, there have been promising results. Thus, a course that exposes participants to and trains them in effective approaches to enhance teacher–student interactions is potentially a viable way to improve child outcomes.

IMPACTS OF THE NATIONAL CENTER FOR RESEARCH ON EARLY CHILDHOOD EDUCATION COURSE

As previously described, the NCRECE course focused on teacher–child interactions academic growth, specifically in the areas of language and literacy. The course concentrated on the three domains of interactions as assessed by the CLASS™ (Pianta et al., 2008): Emotional Support, Classroom Organization, and Instructional Support, and the specific dimensions of interaction defined within these domains. Through the use of videos of actual prekindergarten classroom interactions, and facilitated in-class discussions, teachers were taught to describe and identify *observable* teacher–child interactions in specific, objective, and behavioral terms, as well as to identify how those interactions influence keys areas of language and literacy. Class discussions fostered teachers' analysis of their own classroom interactions in light of specific linkages among teacher–child interaction as specified by the CLASS and children's language and literacy development. As a final project, teachers presented a brief videotape of their own classroom interactions highlighting a particular dimension within Instructional Support (concept development, quality of feedback, language modeling) and an area of language and literacy.

In intent-to-treat analysis, Hamre et al. (in press) demonstrated that the NCRECE course did improve the quality of teachers' interactions with children. Compared with teachers in a control condition, those who took the NCRECE course reported more intentional teaching beliefs and demonstrated greater knowledge of and skills in detecting effective teacher–child interactions. Teachers in the NCRECE course also reported stronger beliefs about the importance of teaching children early literacy and language skills and demonstrated greater knowledge about these skills. It is important to note that teachers who took the NCRECE course demonstrated more effective emotional and instructional practices in their actual practice with children. In a follow-up analysis of course effects in the next academic year, Downer et al. (2011) report that teachers receiving the course continued to demonstrate changes in knowledge and beliefs, and they were also observed to demonstrate more effective feedback and language stimulation in their interactions with children. These results add to the growing literature on effective interventions for early childhood professionals that documents the effectiveness of explicit efforts to change teachers' classroom practices that actually works (Bierman, Nix, Greenberg, Blair, & Domitrovich, 2008; Domitrovich et al., 2009; Hsieh, Hemmeter, McCollum, & Ostrosky, 2009; Pianta et al., 2008; Raver et al., 2008). We then examined what we learned from implementation across many different institutions and settings.

IMPLEMENTING COURSES WITH
FIDELITY IN HIGHER EDUCATION CONTEXTS

An effective course is unlikely to have a considerable effect on the pressing demands for PD in early childhood education without also attending to issues of how to deliver these opportunities with high degrees of implementation fidelity at a larger scale. A major challenge when increasing intervention scale involves maintaining high levels of implementation fidelity and quality in the delivery. Impacts of any putatively successful treatment usually erode when the treatment is turned over to a large number of new implementers, often because of a lack of fidelity to the original protocols (Dane & Schneider, 1998; Neuman & Cunningham, 2009; Resnicow et al., 1998; Taggart, Bush, Zuckerman, & Theiss, 1990).

Field experiments should involve specifying ahead of time the critical components and processes necessary for high implementation (O'Donnell, 2008). In addition, measures should indicate how the intervention is maintained consistently across multiple groups over time or describe parameters under which variation in implementation may occur. Building off of Dane and Schnieder's (1998) fidelity work, Berkel, Mauricio, Schoenfelder, and Sandler (2011) proposed a comprehensive model of implementation that focuses on both facilitators of an intervention and the participants. More specifically, facilitator implementation considers fidelity that addresses whether the core components of the intervention are delivered and quality that assesses whether they were delivered in a clear, comprehensible, and enthusiastic manner.

Given the results from intent-to-treat analysis of the course impacts, and evidence demonstrating its benefits for observed classroom practices, as well as knowledge and observation skills (Hamre et al., in press), we examined the supports needed that made it possible to deliver the course in 15 sections, with sufficient fidelity to support these impacts (LoCasale-Crouch et al., 2011). We examined implementation fidelity in which the key supports aimed to ensure that the NCRECE course instructors felt confident to deliver the course material, and the extent to which they were delivered consistently and appropriately. In the following section, we present the architecture of this multi-institution effort to implement a common course with a high degree of fidelity.

National Center for Research on Early
Childhood Education Course Instructors

Course instructors were hired, trained, and received ongoing support from the NCRECE course coordinators (to be described in more detail). Instructors were required to have a minimum of a master's degree in early childhood education or a related field, experience in early childhood education and teaching college-level students from diverse backgrounds, as well as proficiency with technology. As new sites came on board, the instructor position announcements were distributed through a local university, community colleges, and the partnering agency to identify a pool of qualified candidates.

Course instructor candidates were interviewed by the NCRECE course coordinators (see below) to ensure a good conceptual fit with the NCRECE course and to assess their ability and willingness to implement the NCRECE course as delineated. This is important because most instructors in higher education have nearly complete freedom to design and implement a course as they choose; so imposing a common approach that had to be implemented with fidelity was a considerable deviation from the norm.

To deliver the course across 10 higher education settings and 15 sections, 14 instructors were hired: six of the instructors held a master's degree, five held an additional specialist degree beyond their master's degree, and three instructors held a Ph.D. Eleven of the instructors were Caucasian, two were African American, and one was Cuban. Instructors ranged in age from 25 to 61, with the average around 45. On average, they had 6 years teaching in early childhood and approximately 4 year's experience teaching college courses, with a range on both experiences of 0–19 years.

Course Instructor Training and Ongoing Support

Two NCRECE course coordinators were responsible for providing training and implementation supports to the NCRECE course instructors. Course instructors were trained as to reliability on the CLASS and on course content and implementation, so that consistent delivery could be ensured across course sections. Responsibilities of the instructor included implementing the course in accordance with the content and sequence delineated by NCRECE so that the course was taught consistently across sections. To support this, prior to teaching each unit, instructors and the NCRECE course coordinators met to review implementation activities, including review of the PowerPoint, instructor's manual, readings, in-class activities, homework assignments, and exams. Instructors then completed a written assignment related to each unit, showing evidence of their understanding of and comfort with the material. In addition, instructors participated in weekly phone calls with the NCRECE study team related to these assignments, course implementation, and issues that arose while teaching the course.

Course coordinators then held weekly individual support calls and periodic group calls with course instructors, focused on clarifying content, implementation issues, and sharing successes and challenges to teaching the course. A key focus was on consistent delivery of the course materials and consistent approaches to scoring teachers' work. During each call, the upcoming unit was reviewed to ensure delivery was on track and that the instructor felt comfortable with the material. Five times during the NCRECE course, course instructors videotaped themselves teaching the planned lesson. The course instructor then sent the videotape to the individual NCRECE course coordinator support person, who reviewed the delivery of the NCRECE course material using a standard review process. The course coordinators provided both written feedback to course instructors concerning implementation and also discussed the feedback in detail during the scheduled weekly call. A checklist of the specific course instructor behaviors observed with explanatory notes was shared with the instructor (see Instructor Quality measure in the following section).

Offering the NCRECE course in multiple higher education sites was a test-case in using the higher education system as a means for scaling a standardized, effective model of PD. If the NCRECE course could be delivered with some degree of consistency across 14 instructors, in 15 sections, in 10 sites and still be effective, then it would appear that scaling is feasible and the supports we designed were somewhat useful in ensuring consistency and impacts. Of particular interest in this study was examining similarities and differences in implementation across sites and course sections.

Despite the need to make scheduling adjustments with each site, the core components of the course remained intact, though the delivery format changed. Regardless of the varied formats, instructors implemented the components of the session 95% of the time. On occasion, instructors did not complete an in-class activity, but otherwise the content was consistently provided across all sites. Instructors also reported high levels of confidence in their teaching and with their knowledge of the material.

Related to implementation quality, instructors demonstrated moderate quality at the start of the course. However, quality of implementation rapidly increased across sessions. Thus, as a group, instructors improved and became more consistent in their objectively observed implementation as the course went on. In short, across 15 sections, at 10 different institutions, with widely varying participants, 14 different instructors delivered a common course in ways that displayed high degrees of skill, fidelity to the course design, high levels of implementation quality, and in the end had a significant impact on teachers' practices in the classroom (Downer et al., 2011; Hamre et al., in press; LoCasale-Crouch et al., 2011).

HIGHER EDUCATION AS A SCALE UP MECHANISM FOR EFFECTIVE PROFESSIONAL DEVELOPMENT

Findings from the randomized control trial evaluation of the course (Hamre et al., in press) show that teachers randomly assigned to take the NCRECE course, compared with those not enrolled, exhibited positive differences in beliefs and knowledge related to interactions among teachers and were observed to use more effective teacher–child interactions. These results suggest that coursework explicitly targeting improvements in teacher–child interactions is a viable avenue to support enhancing EC effectiveness.

Analysis of the system designed to support the implementation of the course indicates that, indeed, a standardized course can be effectively delivered in a wide range of sites with fidelity to the protocol and consistent implementation (as perceived by a number of reporters) and with sufficient intensity of dosage to produce results. Moreover, it appears that variation in implementation declined across the period of delivery, suggesting that supports made available to instructors could have added to consistency of delivery. Overall, these results suggest that there is promise in delivering a proven effective PD course across many sites and that, using the considerable infrastructure available in the higher education system, could eventually lead to the reliable impacts of a degree on teacher performance and student outcomes (Early et al., 2007).

High implementation fidelity and quality did not happen by chance—course developers invested extensive time and effort into training and providing ongoing support to the course implementers. As part of their regular interactions, support staff helped instructors evaluate their practice and look for ways to enhance it. As a result, the course quality and delivery was high initially and then improved over time. Such results increase confidence in the extent to which course impacts can be attributed to the course design itself and not to varying elements of dosage or adherence by instructors.

This expansion of fidelity to include examination of training of the instructor and delivery of the intervention (Berkel et al., 2011; Resnick et al., 2005) provides helpful insight into the resources needed to support well-designed interventions to maximize their effectiveness. The NCRECE course was intended to be implemented in a standardized manner. Instructors, however, were also coached to provide individualized support and to be responsive to students. The training and support allowed the instructors to have a depth of knowledge and comfort with the material to be able to answer questions and explain content further. The regular, ongoing support offered helped instructors have a deep understanding of the material and its importance in shaping teachers' practice. This allowed the instructors to feel confident in exploring further ways to help individual participants be more engaged, and subsequently be more effective in learning the material and, ultimately, changing their teaching practices.

One possible extension of this concept of a common, effective course delivered to a wide range of participants is a highly interactive online course, perhaps with a heavy asynchronous component that could accommodate individuals' time demands and schedules. Such a learning experience, properly designed, might permit high-quality implementation of a course at scale while reducing some costs associated with maintaining consistent implementation across a large number of instructors. The use of online learning "holds great promise as a tool for early childhood teacher education" (Donohue, Fox, & Torrence, 2007, p. 7), and could be developed in a systematic way as to ensure that both course goals and learner needs were being met during implementation. Many studies show that learners who are exposed to online content in well-designed courses demonstrate the same or better content knowledge gains than their counterparts who are exposed to content in a more traditional (i.e., in-person) setting (Lebec & Luft, 2007; O'Dwyer, Carey, & Kleiman, 2007). This model is worth considering as a way to advance the intervention field moving forward.

If early education programs are going to achieve high quality programming on a large scale, then the mechanisms of training teachers must be examined and tested not only at the in-service level, but also at the preservice level (Birman, Desimone, Porter, & Garet, 2000; Borko, 2004; Clifford & Maxwell, 2002; Cochran-Smith & Zeichner, 2005; Pianta et al., 2005; Whitebook, Bellm, Lee, & Sakai, 2005). Results from the NCRECE study indicate that it is feasible to implement a predeveloped, standardized course in different teacher preparation programs (Scott-Little et al., 2011), and this needs to be an avenue explored to support the next generation of future early childhood teachers.

IMPROVING TEACHER–STUDENT INTERACTIONS IN THE CLASSROOM: MYTEACHINGPARTNER COACHING

The suite of MTP PD supports also contains two approaches to supporting teacher–child interactions that are most often delivered in the "in-service" sector of PD, which is teachers working in programs to receive these supports as part of their ongoing efforts to improve. These resources include a video library and web-mediated coaching, and they are implemented as a function of teachers' own self-selection and use of resources (the video library) or through an established relationship with a trained coach.

The MTP web video library is an opportunity to observe others' effective interactions, and it provides more than 400 video clips of teachers' effective interactions with students from pre-K to high school, as they implement a wide range of instructional activities in various context areas. Each clip is accompanied by a very detailed and specific description of the behaviors in which the teacher in the clip is engaging that defines that interaction as effective for fostering student learning and development. These 1- to 2-minute videos are organized (and searchable) by the CLASS dimensions, and each one includes an explicit, behavioral description of what was happening in the video footage that reflected a high quality teacher–child interaction. The idea behind the MTP video library was to provide opportunities for teachers to learn more about what types of interactions were important for student learning (knowing) and to understand exactly what these interactions look like when enacted by others (seeing).

MTP coaching involves observation-based analysis and feedback enacted through a regular cycle of web-mediated interaction (both synchronous and asynchronous) between a teacher and a coach. Teachers videotape their instruction and send this footage to their coach, who edits the tape into three segments that focus on a specific CLASS dimension (e.g., concept development). These edited clips are posted to a secure web site in which teachers view the segments and comments and respond to prompts. The prompts focus attention on specific aspects of teacher–child interaction, such as "What did you do here to help 'J' pay attention, and what did he do in response?" and include links to clips of "high quality" exemplars from the video library. This MTP coaching cycle is spread over two weeks and repeated across the school year, gradually deepening the reflective analysis around interactions that are more difficult to detect and enact.

In the first evaluation of these PD resources, we tested the MTP video library and coaching in a randomized controlled trial with more than 240 state-funded pre-K teachers to determine impacts on improved instruction and child outcomes. Two MTP resources were implemented and compared: 1) teachers had access to the MTP video library and 2) and some received MTP coaching and access to the video library. Teachers assigned to coaching made significant gains compared with the video library teachers in reading and responding to students' cues, using a variety of formats to actively engage children in instruction and intentionally stimulating language development. These impacts were roughly on the order of one scale-point on the CLASS rating system; for example, moving from a rating of 3 to 4 in one academic year. In classrooms in which 100% of the children enrolled were from economically disadvantaged families, there were remarkable differences in the teachers' rates of changes in sensitivity and responsiveness and in their facilitating engagement and enthusiasm in learning, in favor of those receiving coaching having increased the quality of their interactions roughly 1.5 rating points on the CLASS scale. In addition, comparisons of child outcomes indicated that children in MTP coaching classrooms made greater gains in receptive vocabulary, task orientation, and prosocial assertiveness, scoring approximately 4–5 percentile points higher than children in the other conditions on standardized tests.

Clearly, the evidence was in favor of the coaching condition. However, there were hints in follow-up analyses to suggest that teachers who only had access to video exemplars and made regular use of these exemplars were observed to be more sensitive and responsive to children's needs, proactive and effective at managing behavior, and skilled at maximizing children's learning time. In short, for some teachers, just watching examples of effective teaching on the video library made a difference for improving their practices. Those teachers who spent more time watching video exemplars online also had children who experienced greater gains in social development during the pre-K year. It is interesting to note that teachers who spent more time watching and analyzing their own classroom video footage online as part of coaching also had children who experienced greater gains in vocabulary development during the pre-K year, with gains equal to approximately 5 percentile points.

We then sought to expand the implementation and evaluation of MTP coaching (this time better integrating coaching with the video library), using a larger and more diverse sample of teachers and programs. In the NCRECE PD study, we tested the MTP coaching model with 450 pre-K teachers in 15 sites served by local consultants trained and supported by our team (all using standardized and manualized procedures), in a prototype model of how this PD support could be expanded at a larger level of scale. When evaluated in a randomized controlled trial, the benefits of MTP coaching were confirmed. Teachers (in pre-K programs) who received MTP coaching improved in nearly every feature of interaction assessed by the CLASS, particularly the dimensions of instructional support, with effect sizes averaging .5–.75 SD units. This study not only replicated the value of MTP coaching for teachers, but also demonstrated that the model of coaching can be replicated and extended through standardized training and support protocols (Downer et al., 2011).

SUPPORTING MYTEACHINGPARTNER COACH FIDELITY AND QUALITY

Coaching offers an opportunity for teachers to get direct feedback about their practices from knowledgeable experts who engage with the teachers in collaborative work. Although there are a number of coaching programs that have demonstrated efficacy in small trials, there are very few examples of these programs being delivered at scale. We know very little about how best to support local coaches to deliver evidence-based coaching models at scale.

Training and Support Procedures

Coaches were all hired locally through postings at universities and local early childhood agencies. Requirements included a master's degree in education or a related field and experience as an early childhood teacher. The weeklong training focused on the CLASS, the MTP coaching model, and use of the MTP website for supporting teachers. Coaches completed a CLASS reliability assessment, and all coaches became reliable on the CLASS instrument. A 2-day booster training was held in January. NCRECE staff and coaches participated in a weekly support phone call, lasting approximately 30 minutes. In addition to the weekly calls, coaches placed group calls as well. These calls were an hour long and took place every two weeks, providing coaches with a forum for sharing successes and challenges of the job.

Coaches completed a survey following their initial MTP coach training that included information regarding demographics, as well as questionnaires regarding their beliefs about early childhood education and their preparedness to be MTP coaches. Fidelity of implementation was assessed through research staff weekly review of coaches' cycles, using a 25-item checklist that assessed the degree to which each cycle conformed to the

MTP model. Coaches reported information about each MTP cycle, including which CLASS dimension was the focus of the coaching session. Quality of implementation was assessed through teacher ratings. Four times during the year, teachers reported on the quality of MTP experience and their relationship with the coach.

Coach review forms revealed high levels of fidelity across the year. However, there were significant differences among coaches, with one coach in particular demonstrating difficulty during much of the year. There were also significant differences in the average number of cycles completed per teacher and the content (CLASS domains) on which coaches tended to focus. Teachers were overwhelmingly positive about their experiences with MTP, rating both the video/prompts process and the conferences very highly. They were also overwhelmingly positive about their relationships with coaches at the end of the year. Very few coach characteristics were related to fidelity or quality of implementation, although the small number of coaches greatly reduced our power to detect these associations. Coaches with more time teaching early childhood (0–5) were less likely to focus on instructional support, while coaches' end-of-training ratings of preparedness were the most consistent predictor of later fidelity.

SCALING UP COACHING WITH A
HIGH DEGREE OF FIDELITY—AN EXAMPLE

The findings from the NCRECE coaching phase of the PD study showed not only that local coaching can be an effective tool for improving teacher–child interactions (Downer et al., 2011), but also that local coaches can be trained to deliver the MTP coaching model with a high degree of fidelity and quality, although coaches do vary on some important aspects of fidelity. In particular, some coaches appeared better able to engage teachers in more MTP cycles. This is important, as previous work demonstrates that teacher dosage to MTP is associated with gains in teacher performance. Coaches also differed in the content on which they focused with teachers. Although there were not many significant predictors of coach fidelity or quality, coaches' beliefs about a teacher's role in the classroom and their self-ratings of MTP readiness following training may be good ways to identify coaches early in the process who are in need of more support.

In a recent larger scale implementation of CLASS observations with nearly 700 preschool classrooms in an urban setting, approximately 68 teachers were enrolled in MTP and began working one-on-one with coaches. This specific program was implemented as closely as possible to the original research-tested model. Coaches worked one-on-one with up to 15 teachers each and aimed to complete a coaching cycle with each teacher every two weeks. Coaches also received support from an MTP specialist on a biweekly basis. Support consists of one-on-one phone calls, group conference calls, and webinars designed to help coaches implement the MTP program with fidelity. Every two weeks, the MTP specialist reviews a cycle for each coach and provides the coach with feedback on implementation of the MTP program.

Many aspects of the implementation were successful. Nine coaches, all employees of the local family services department, were trained to deliver the MTP program and were given coaching loads ranging from 3 to 14 teachers each. Sixty-six percent of the teachers completed five or more MTP cycles during the first five months of program implementation, with 13% completing 10 or more cycles. As of the end of the academic year, 79% of teachers had completed a cycle within the previous month, indicating ongoing, active involvement with the program. Coaches, in turn, actively participated in coach support activities. During the program start-up period and the first five months of the program (eight months total), coaches participated in an average of 17 one-on-one calls, six conference calls, and four webinars with the MTP specialist. In cycle reviews, coaches received an average of 20 out of 22 possible points on a program implementation rating scale, indicating high fidelity to the MTP model.

Several challenges arose in this more locally driven model of implementing the MTP program. Technological difficulties caused delays for both coaches and teachers: Coaches needed practice and support to learn how to edit videos, and some teachers had difficulty accessing computers with high-speed internet, which was necessary to watch their videos through the online MTP system. MTP staff and technology support personnel worked closely with coaches and teachers to resolve these problems. Some teachers were initially resistant to participating in MTP, due to the perception that MTP was being provided to lower-performing teachers. Coaches worked closely with teachers to increase buy-in to the program, listening to teachers' concerns and highlighting the potential benefits of the program for teachers and children. Coaches also brought these issues to their one-on-one calls.

Furthermore, several modifications were made to the MTP model. The largest was that coaches were asked by city staff to conduct the bi-weekly coach–teacher conferences in person, rather than over the phone; in the research-tested MTP model, conferences took place remotely. The face-to-face conferences increased the time it takes coaches to complete each cycle, as they had to drive to various locations throughout the city in order to hold each conference. This effectively resulted in an increased workload for coaches in respect to the original program model.

Overall, it is apparent that coaching, using a standardized model such as MTP, can be a highly effective method for improving teachers' practices in the classroom, a conclusion borne out not only in the MTP PD study, but in extensions of the work on MTP in more locally designed implementations, as well as in studies of larger-scale implementations of other coaching models (Bierman et al., 2008; Cunningham, Zibulsky, & Callahan, 2009; Dickinson & Caswell, 2007). It is also clear that although larger-scale implementations can be supported to attain a high degree of fidelity and impact, there is considerable need for maintaining ongoing support and feedback to the direct service staff (e.g., coaches) and, importantly, that when such feedback and support is provided with regularity and intensity, that coach fidelity is maintained across time and between-coach variability is constrained. In short, it appears from these early stage larger-scale implementations across multiple sites that coaching can be delivered at larger levels of scale, if sufficient attention is paid to supervision, adherence to standardized protocols, and use of a model that enables teachers and coaches to feel effective and motivated to participate.

The section that follows describes the work of a new organization, Teachstone, as a more formal, self sustaining mechanism for scaling up some of the effective PD models presented earlier.

SUPPORTING SCALE UP OF EFFECTIVE PROFESSIONAL DEVELOPMENT

Moving from implementing and evaluating PD in research studies, even when such studies involve a large number of teachers and sites, to responding to the aims, requirements, and constraints of local program decision makers (e.g., community agencies, Head Start grantees, states, quality rating improvement system) requires a major shift in focus and infrastructure—from design and evaluation of an intervention to development of infrastructure that supports implementation and decision making under widely varying circumstances and constraints. This shift entails a knowledge base and skill set that is different from that of the investigator seeking to test models and understand theories; rather, it requires skills in building self-sustaining organizations and financing models that can closely couple proven effective supports to teachers with the features of the implementation context in ways that ensure a tight linkage among goals, supports, and existing resources and policies so that implementation can be achieved with a high degree of fidelity, quality, and intensity. At all levels, the complexity of this process undermines the impacts of the original effective PD approach.

In engineering and biosciences, the familiar framework for this shift is "tech-transfer," in which university-based researchers patent new innovations, which in turn triggers the creation of start-up companies or licensing to established businesses for scale. The overall frame for tech-transfer is that to be implemented at some level of scale, an innovation must be supported by some market-driven financing system, whether in the for-profit or nonprofit sector, that provides resources for implementation. In the educational and social sciences, there is not often much explicit attention paid to tech-transfer, other than the copyrighting of material to vendors who in turn distribute materials and PD resources. The primary concern with this model is that very often attention to high-fidelity implementation is not a focus of the vendor.

In an effort to address these aims of tech-transfer, high-fidelity implementation, and self-sustaining resource model, Teachstone, was formed to develop the infrastructure necessary to achieve these aims for the MyTeachingPartner suite of PD resources (coaching, video library, and course). The next sections present information gleaned from the early phases of work as they illustrate some of the parameters and challenges of scaling up. Over the past several years, Teachstone has focused on scaling up two of the proven effective PD programs described earlier.

Teachstone offers MTP coaching as a PD program, providing both direct teacher support in which a Teachstone coach works directly with a cadre of teachers, as well as training and support for site-based coaches who do not work for Teachstone, but rather are employed or contracted by the program requesting MTP. In this second model of support, MTP staff from Teachstone train coaches at other organizations (e.g., Head Start or other early care and school-based programs) and provide regular, systematic support to help them hone both their knowledge of the CLASS and their understanding of the MTP coaching model to ensure that the site-based coaches implement the MTP model with a high degree of fidelity.

Teachstone, as of 2011, is providing direct teacher support for 43 teachers in a Head Start program, as well as in a few smaller programs. More notably, they are providing support to 65 site-based coaches in a variety of programs around the country, who will in turn support approximately 575 teachers. In general, the on site coaches have extensive experience working in early childhood settings, and many have advanced degrees in early childhood education or a related field (e.g., speech-language pathology, ECSE). In order to work as a coach, individuals had to attend a CLASS observation training and pass reliability and then attend the MTP training.

The second program being scaled up by Teachstone is titled Making the Most of Classroom Interactions (MMCI). MMCI is based on the semester-long college level course that was developed though NCRECE. Teachstone revised the course for wider distribution and is now supporting this PD program in one urban district–wide location and in a statewide implementation. To meet demands, Teachstone trained 13 MMCI instructors across these two sites. One site offered nine sections to 180 teachers, while the other site is launching with 50 teachers this school year.

Over the 2 years that Teachstone has been scaling up these programs, both successes and challenges have been evident. One success simply is the fact that infrastructure, independent from research funding, has been developed to support expansion of effective PD in the form of MTP coaching from a research project implemented in 150 preschool classrooms in one state, to a standardized program that is being delivered to approximately 575 teachers in seven states, with additional sites expressing interest in adopting the program. Similarly, MMCI has grown from being a course offered as a part of a research study to a course that is being implemented at a community level with plans to repeat in local settings and expand.

In short, Teachstone is a "proof of concept" that research-based PD for teachers can be exported, or transferred, to the field and can meet a growing demand with high fidelity in a model that provides capacity for organizational sustainability with a high emphasis on quality and impact.

The expansion of these programs necessitated that Teachstone develop new infrastructure to support this growth, including ongoing support systems to ensure that the on site coaches and instructors deliver the programs as intended. Professional roles of coach specialist position and specialists who deliver support to the on site MMCI instructors were formed. The creation, professionalization, and standardization of these roles were also complemented by the creation of a web infrastructure to link individuals at all levels of implementation—teachers, on site deliverers of PD supports, and centralized specialists providing support to field staff. All of these roles and their functions had to be linked to key implementation metrics and systems for regular feedback and calibration. Not surprisingly, Teachstone also encountered some challenges in scale up. These included organizational and participant buy-in, the hiring, training, and supervision of site-based coaches and instructors, fidelity of implementation, workload, and technology.

A considerable challenge to the adoption of a proven effective model for PD is the existence of local models that often have advocates, which can lead to problems with participation and buy-in. If organizational decision makers choose to adopt a new program, oftentimes the program provider has no control over the information the district or grantee provides to teachers regarding their participation. For example, in one implementation of MTP, some teachers were told that they were assigned to a specific PD option because they had low CLASS scores, which led to resentment and negativity on their part, and which was not accurate.

Although Teachstone provides guidelines for the hiring of local staff, it has no control over who is hired in order to implement these PD programs. This means that there are potential concerns about the qualifications of the individuals who have been hired to deliver intervention. This turned out not to be the case in one site in which they opted to train their cadre of early childhood specialists to deliver their programs and ensured that they were well trained. For example, each coach or instructor attended a CLASS observation training and became reliable on the tool. They later attended a CLASS Train the Trainer program to hone their knowledge base. In addition, the early childhood specialists who are involved in this project are ensuring ongoing CLASS reliability by double coding with

Teachstone observers and participating in quarterly calibration sessions. In contrast, the coaches and facilitators in a different site, while reliable on CLASS and trained to deliver their respective programs, were hired as consultants and have not participated in double coding or calibration programs.

There is also little to no control over direct service staff that is implementing these PD programs; they are accountable to their local site, not to Teachstone. For example, at Teachstone a coach specialist guides the work of a coach, but they are not the supervisor of that coach from an HR perspective. This can cause challenges when a site-based coach or instructor fails to complete something that is in the protocol. In addition to being an issue of hiring and supervision, this challenge has the potential to have an impact on fidelity.

PD programs can sometimes be delivered locally in a manner that is different than designed and also different from what the research has shown to be effective. This decoupling of the ingredients of a proven effective model as it gets used in practice is routine in education. Sometimes these modifications are driven by disconnects between the intended implementation strategy and the reality of practice settings. For example, the course modules developed in MMCI were designed to be delivered once a week. However, rules governing the hiring and use of substitute teachers at one MMCI site forced them to divide each course session into two sessions that were delivered in the same week. This delivery model forced instructors to rush through some material and also did not give teachers enough time to digest and study information from one session before having to attend the next.

Thus for an organization to ensure high fidelity and quality of implementation in a complex and often localized system of decision making, there is a considerable need for developing a suite of supports that can recognize and validate, as well as guide and shape, local decision making, policy, and implementation toward aims of high fidelity to an effective model. This dedicated function is the work of a scale up organization. In sum, even when a separate organization is established to attend to the unique demands of scaling up proven effective PD, a whole new set of challenges and questions emerges. Local authority, decision-making structures, personnel and roles, focus, and aims all intersect even with well-designed and supported implementation systems and supports as challenges to high fidelity implementation at scale.

CONCLUSIONS: TAKING EFFECTIVE PROFESSIONAL DEVELOPMENT TO SCALE

A lot of resources are being deployed to improve teachers' effectiveness, not only in early childhood but in K–12 as well. In fact, one way to look at the landscape of expenses and activity suggests that we are actually very good at going to scale with *something*, as shown in the sheer amount of money and activity devoted to PD and quality improvement (including preservice and in-service investments), maybe reflecting the problem being that there are not enough proven effective models. We believe the challenges lie in the gap among proven effective models, such as MTP, and systems that exist for scaling, such as higher education or teacher certification. The problem is not as much a lack of capacity for scaling or for effective models, but in a gap that deals with fidelity, local decision-making, local financial allocation, and local policy.

One could argue that the costs per teacher for PD, estimated to be between $3,000 and $9,000 annually, produce little to no impact on practice or student learning, and the real task is to shift existing funds to high fidelity implementation of proven effective programs. This cost-shifting strategy is borne out by the pre-K scale up study of MTP coaching using local personnel as coaches. Although teachers could access MTP coaching through web-based interactions with coaches located remotely in which all costs are "new," it is now clear that local coaches can be trained to deliver MTP coaching with similar, if not greater, impacts on practice. These results open the potential for existing personnel involved in supervision or coaching (school districts already employ many of these individuals at considerable expense) to be trained to use an MTP coaching model (or other proven effective model) in the context of their existing roles. Thus existing resources can be readily redeployed to implement proven effective PD models at considerably lower costs. But, what localized decision-making or policy constraints exist to impede this strategy?

It is also the case that existing resources could be redeployed to cover costs associated with the MTP course. It is no surprise that courses and degrees have been the primary mechanism through which state and federal investments in the capacity of the teaching workforce have been made. And courses and degrees are the primary means through which teachers advance on a career and salary scale. Each year millions of dollars are being spent on courses, both preservice and in-service, for teachers to acquire degrees, certificates, or move up a career ladder. In early childhood, Head Start has required that system-wide, more than 50% of its lead teachers have a bachelor's degree at a time when the majority have an associate's degree. This policy requires much course taking by Head Start teachers. Over a 5-year period, First 5 California and local county First 5 commissions spent more than $157 million dollars providing incentives for more than 58,000 early childhood providers, much of it going to coursework—equaling an average of more than $2700 per teacher. And many states' QRIS devote a significant amount of their total resources to workforce development (e.g., courses, degrees). What local or state or institutional decision making, resource allocation, or policy-making processes make it difficult to achieve a more widespread adoption of effective PD?

In short, the consideration of costs for proven effective PD must be made in light of local policies and local incentives for delivery of proven effective models. In this regard, states could be far more active in requiring evidence of impacts from PD providers, higher education settings, and product vendors before any of their resources could be posted on an "approved" list. States could also be more prescriptive in their directions to localities, where much of the choice regarding the allocation of PD funds resides. But, if states want localities to retain control over expenditures, then they must ramp up considerably the supports and training available to local decision makers so that they choose wisely from effective programs. Just requiring localities to spend money on "research-based" or "evidence-based" programs is not enough in a world in which most anything can be labeled as such.

There is widespread acknowledgement that the production of effective teaching (and teachers) is perhaps the critical component of education reform and innovation for improvement of student learning. This aim requires a serious investment of time, rigor, and evaluation to produce PD programs that actually work and the development of entire organizations and systems to support implementation with high fidelity at scale. This chapter has described the conceptual, operational, and evidentiary basis of one such model, the CLASS-based MyTeachingPartner suite of PD resources. In so doing, we present a proof of concept, an illustration of the features of a model with some evidence of success. There are other models for which evidence of impacts is also available; these models share several common elements—a strong conceptual framework that provides the basis for expecting impacts; clear alignment and linkages that connect input to teachers to inputs from teachers to children, to children's learning; strong metrics and manualized protocols that support standardization and high fidelity of implementation; and dedicated organizations for scale up. The future for scaling up effective early education PD is very bright but will require careful and dedicated attention to capacity, training, decision-making, and implementation supports.

REFERENCES

Berkel, C., Mauricio, A., Schoenfelder, E., & Sandler, I. (2011). Putting the pieces together: An integrated model of program implementation. *Prevention Science*, *12*(1), 23–33. doi:10.1007/s11121-010-0186-1

Bierman, K., Nix, R.L., Greenberg, M.T., Blair, C., & Domitrovich, C. (2008). Executive functions and school readiness intervention: Impact, moderation, and mediation in Head Start REDI program. *Development and Psychopathology, 20*, 821–843. doi:10.1017/S0954579408000394

Birman, B.F., Desimone, L., Porter, A.C., & Garet, M.S. (2000). Designing professional development that works. *Educational Leadership*, *57*(8), 28–33.

Borko, H. (2004). Professional development and teacher learning: Mapping the terrain. *Educational Researcher, 33*(8), 3–15. doi:10.3102/0013189X033008003

Clifford, D., & Maxwell, K. (2002, April). *The need for highly qualified prekindergarten teachers.* Paper presented at the Preparing Highly Qualified Teachers Symposium. Retrieved from http://www.fpg.unc.edu/~npc/pdfs/need.pdf

Cochran-Smith, M., & Zeichner, K.M. (2005). *Studying teacher education: The report of the AERA panel on research and teacher education.* Washington, DC: American Educational Research Association.

Cunningham, A.E., Zibulsky, J., & Callahan, M. (2009). Starting small: Building preschool teacher knowledge that supports early literacy development. *Reading and Writing, 22*(4), 487–510. doi:10.1007/s11145-009-9164-z

Dane, A.V., & Schneider, B.H. (1998). Program integrity in primary and early secondary prevention: Are implementation effects out of control? *Clinical Psychology Review, 18*(1), 23–45. doi:10.1016/S0272-7358(97)00043-3

Dickinson, D., & Caswell, L. (2007). Building support for language and early literacy in preschool classrooms through in-service professional development: Effects of the Literacy Environment Enrichment Program (LEEP). *Early Childhood Research Quarterly, 22,* 243–260. doi:10.1016/j.ecresq.2007.03.001

Domitrovich, C.E., Gest, S.D., Gill, S., Bierman, K.L., Welsh, J., & Jones, D. (2009). Fostering high quality teaching with an enriched curriculum and professional development support: The Head Start REDI program. *American Educational Research Journal, 46*(2), 567–597. doi:10.3102/0002831208328089

Donohue, C., Fox, S., & Torrence, D. (2007). Early childhood educators as eLearners: Engaging approaches to teaching and learning online. *Young Children,* 34–40.

Downer, J.T., Pianta, R.C., Burchinal, M., Field, S., Hamre, B.K., LoCasale-Crouch, J., … Scott-Little, C. (2011). *Coaching and coursework focused on teacher-child interactions during language/literacy instruction: Effects on teacher beliefs, knowledge, skills, and practice.* Manuscript in preparation.

Early, D., Maxwell, K., Burchinal, M., Alva, S., Bender, R., Bryant, D., … Zill, N. (2007). Teachers' education, classroom quality, and young children's academic skills: Results from seven studies of preschool programs. *Child Development, 78*(2), 558–580. doi:10.1111/j.1467-8624.2007.01014.x

Hamre, B.K., Pianta, R.C., Burchinal, M., & Downer, J.T. (in press). A course on supporting early language and literacy development through effective teacher-child interactions: Effects on teacher beliefs, knowledge and practice. *American Educational Research Journal.*

Howes, C., Galinsky, E., & Kontos, S. (1998). Child care caregiver sensitivity and attachment. *Social Development, 7*(1), 25–36. doi:10.1111/1467-9507.00048

Hsieh, W., Hemmeter, M.L., McCollum, J.A., & Ostrosky, M.M. (2009). Using coaching to increase preschool teachers' use of emergent literacy teaching strategies. *Early Childhood Research Quarterly, 24,* 229–247. doi:10.1016/j.ecresq.2009.03.007

Improving Head Start Act of 2007, H.R. 1429, 110th Cong. (2007). Retrieved March 14, 2011, from http://www.govtrack.us/congress/bill.xpd?bill=h110-1429

Kontos, S., Howes, C., & Galinsky, E. (1996). Does training make a difference to quality in family child care? *Early Childhood Research Quarterly, 11*(4), 427–445. doi:10.1016/S0885-2006(96)90016-2

Lebec, M., & Luft, J. (2007). A mixed methods analysis of learning in online teacher professional development: A case report. *Contemporary Issues in Technology and Teacher Education, 7*(1), 554–574.

LoCasale-Crouch, J., Kraft-Sayre, M., Pianta, R., Hamre, B., Downer, J., Leach, A., … Scott-Little, C. (2011). Implementing an early childhood professional development course across 10 sites and 15 sections: Lessons learned. *NHSA Dialog, 14*(4), 275–292.

Mashburn, A.J., Downer, J.T., Hamre, B.K., Justice, L.M., & Pianta, R.C. (2010). Consultation for teachers and children's language and literacy development during pre-kindergarten. *Applied Developmental Science, 14,* 179–196. doi:10.1080/1 0888691.2010.516187

Maxwell, K.L., Lim, C.-I., & Early, D.M. (2006). *Early childhood teacher preparation programs in the United States: National report.* Chapel Hill: The University of North Carolina, FPG Child Development Institute.

Neuman, S., & Cunningham, L. (2009). The impact of professional development and coaching on early language and literacy instructional practices. *American Educational Research Journal, 46*(2), 532–566. doi:10.3102/0002831208328088

O'Donnell, C.L. (2008). Defining, conceptualizing, and measuring fidelity of implementation and its relationship to outcomes in K–12 curriculum intervention research. *Review of Educational Research, 78,* 33–84. doi:10.3102/0034654307313793

O'Dwyer, L., Carey, R., & Kleiman, G. (2007). The Louisiana algebra online initiative as a model for teacher professional development: Examining teacher experiences. *Journal of Asynchronous Learning Networks, 11*(3), 69–93.

Pianta, R.C., Howes, C., Burchinal, M., Bryant, D., Clifford, R., Early, C., & Barbarin, O. (2005). Features of pre-kindergarten programs, classrooms, and teachers: Do they predict observed classroom quality and child-teacher interactions? *Applied Developmental Science, 9*(3), 144–159. doi:10.1207/s1532480xads0903_2

Pianta, R.C., La Paro, K.M., & Hamre, B.K. (2008). *Classroom Assessment Scoring System,*™ *(CLASS),*™ *Pre-K Manual.* Baltimore, MD: Paul H. Brookes Publishing Co.

Raver, C.C., Jones, A.S., Li-Grining, C.P., Metzger, M., Smallwood, K., & Sardin, L. (2008). Improving preschool classroom processes: Preliminary findings from a randomized trial implemented in head start settings. *Early Childhood Research Quarterly, 23*(1), 10–26. doi:10.1016/j.ecresq.2007.09.001

Resnick, B., Bellg, A.J., Borrelli, B., DeFrancesco, C., Berger, R., Hecht, J., ... Czajkowski, S. (2005). Examples of implementation and evaluation of treatment fidelity in the BCC studies: Where we are and where we need to go. *Annals of Behavioral Medicine, 29,* 46–54. doi:10.1207/s15324796abm2902s_8

Resnicow, K., Davis, M., Smith, M., Lazarus-Yaroch, A., Baranowski, T., Baranowski, J., ... Wang, T. (1998). How best to measure implementation of school health curricula: A comparison of three measures. *Health Education Research, 13,* 239–250. doi:10.1093/her/13.2.239

Scott-Little, C., La Paro, K.M., Thomason, A.C., Pianta, R.C., Hamre, B., Downer, J., ... Howes, C. (2011). Implementation of a course focused on language and literacy within teacher–child interactions: Instructor and student perspectives across three institutions of higher education. *Journal of Early Childhood Teacher Education, 32*(3), 200–224. doi:10.1080/10901027.2011.594489

Taggart, V.S., Bush, P.J., Zuckerman, A.E., & Theiss, P.K. (1990). A process evaluation of the District of Columbia "Know Your Body" project. *Journal of School Health, 60*(2), 60–66. doi:10.1111/j.1746-1561.1990.tb05907.x

Whitebook, M., Bellm, D., Lee, Y., & Sakai, L. (2005). *Time to revamp and expand: Early childhood teacher preparation programs in California's institutions of higher education.* Berkeley, CA: Center for the Study of Child Care Employment.

Zaslow, M., Tout, K., Halle, T., Whittaker, J., & Lavelle, B. (2010). *Toward the identification of features of effective professional development for early childhood educators: Literature review.* Washington, DC: U.S. Department of Education, Office of Planning, Evaluation, and Social Development.

CONCLUSION

Moving Evidence-Based Professional Development into the Field

Recommendations for Policy and Research

Bridget K. Hamre and Bridget E. Hatfield

The professional development (PD) programs described in this volume offer clear evidence that intensive, well-designed PD, targeting evidence-based teaching strategies, can improve early childhood teachers' practice and promote positive child development. Not only is there have a growing body of evidence regarding PD programs that work (Fukkink & Lont, 2007; Zaslow, Tout, Halle, Whittaker, & Lavelle, 2010), leaders in the field are beginning to push beyond these efficacy trials to think about *why* these programs work and *for whom* (Downer et al., Chapter 6; Justice & McGinty, Chapter 4; Raver et al., Chapter 5). These programs have been implemented with a broad spectrum of early childhood teachers in diverse settings, and a few even have evidence of effectiveness at scale (Landry et al., Chapter 7; Pianta, Hamre, and Hadden, Chapter 8.)

Readers of this volume may walk away with a rosy picture of the state of early childhood PD. Unfortunately, a quick examination of PD for the

The research reported here was supported by the Institute of Education Sciences, U.S. Department of Education, through Grant R305A060021 to the University of Virginia—funding the National Center for Research on Early Childhood Education (NCRECE)—and by the National Institute of Child Health and Human Development and the Interagency Consortium on School Readiness. [The opinions expressed are those of the authors and do not represent views of the funders.]

nation's early childhood work force in 2011 brings us quickly back down to a less inspiring reality. The typical early childhood teacher working in state pre-K, Head Start, or child care programs is still most likely to be engaged in brief workshops that fail to target the types of teaching we in the field now know are critical to producing positive outcomes for children (Garet, Porter, Desimone, Birman, & Yoon, 2001). Not surprisingly, this disconnect is not apparent only at the program and classroom levels, but at the policy level as well. Some of the largest policy initiatives targeting improvements in the quality of teaching in early childhood programs, such as quality rating and improvement systems, state-funded PD systems, or federally funded Training and Technical Assistance (T/TA) networks, provide little evidence to suggest effectiveness, and there are very few examples of these systems implementing evidence-based PD programs.

Of course this disconnect should be of no surprise; it is consistent with the well-established failures to move evidence-based programs into practice (Fixen et al., 2005). However, if practitioners are unable to quickly address this disconnect within the world of early childhood PD, an important opportunity will be lost. Several interrelated policy reforms are providing a unique opportunity to invest PD resources in ways that could actually lead to meaningful changes in the nature, quality, and impact of our early childhood programs. First, there is a growing consensus regarding the significance of the early childhood years for setting children on a positive social and academic trajectory (Blair, 2002; Shonkoff, 2010). Though budget shortfalls have led to some reductions in federal and state spending on early childhood programs, there are many other examples of continued or increased funding of these programs, even in these challenging fiscal times (Barnett et al., 2010). Second is the new and intense focus on teacher effectiveness. The Obama administration has pushed forward a number of initiatives, including Race to the Top and the Investing in Innovation funds, that are leading states and districts to pay more attention than ever before to the systems that are in place to ensure that teachers are effective. It is important to note that these efforts have moved beyond simply categorizing teachers as "qualified" based on education and credentials and pushed states and districts to assess teacher performance in quantifiable ways, including measures of student achievement and observations of teaching quality.

The intersection of these two policy streams is most apparent in the Early Childhood Challenge Grant competition, which is jointly administered by the Department of Education and the Department of Health and Human Services, HHS. This competition has the potential to push states to more strategically invest public dollars in evidence-based PD for early childhood teachers. The question is: Are we ready for that push? How can researchers, policy makers, and practitioners work together to help ensure that an opportunity for meaningful reform is not lost?

The goals of this chapter are to 1) outline the opportunities for connection between research and policy in early childhood PD; 2) examine barriers at the research, practice, and policy levels; and 3) offer recommendations for ways to address these barriers.

OPPORTUNITIES FOR CONNECTIONS BETWEEN RESEARCH, PRACTICE, AND POLICY

For many years, disconnects between research, policy, and practice made it difficult for effective PD programs to be developed and implemented at scale. Although barriers remain, there are a number of factors that can facilitate the types of effective PD programs described in this volume being integrated into federal, state, and local PD initiatives. As we discuss in detail, there is general consensus among researchers and policy makers around a set of child outcomes and teaching practices that should be a target of PD programs. There are also federal, state, and local initiatives that offer financial and structural resources to support the implementation of these PD programs. In addition, there is strong consensus around the general parameters of effective (and ineffective) PD programs. Thus well-designed, intensive PD programs that target teaching strategies we know promote positive social and early academic development have the potential to lead to meaningful improvements in children's school readiness.

Despite ongoing debate about the most appropriate outcomes for early childhood programs, there is increasing agreement among policy makers and researchers regarding appropriate targets for children's development within these programs. The newly revised Head Start Early Learning Framework and state- and district-level early childhood learning standards incorporate a broad set of outcomes, such as self-regulation, social relationships, phonological awareness, math, and language. These newer documents represent a shift from earlier versions that predominantly focused on language and cognitive domains (Scott-Little, Kagan, & Frelow, 2006), and they reflect the wealth of research regarding the skills and knowledge young children need to succeed in school and in life (e.g., Blair & Diamond, 2008; Ginsburg, Boyd, & Sun Lee, 2008; Shanahan & Lonigan, 2010).

There is also converging evidence around teaching practices that we know help children develop these skills. As reflected in this volume, there is greatest consensus with regard to the teaching strategies that are effective for supporting early literacy, language, and social development (e.g., Hemmeter, Santos, & Ostrosky, 2008; Shanahan & Lonigan, 2010). Most of the projects in this volume focused on these domains, and there is a high degree of alignment in the very specific teaching strategies targeted in each of these different PD programs. Children in a variety of settings benefit from interactions with teachers characterized by warmth, sensitivity, and proactive management (Howes et al., 2008). Children develop stronger early academic skills in classrooms when they receive ongoing feedback and teachers engage them in stimulating conversations and provide explicit instructional opportunities in phonological awareness and print knowledge (Shanahan & Lonigan, 2010). These learning opportunities cannot be simply incidental but must be intentionally designed and implemented by teachers (Hamre, Downer, Jamil, & Pianta, in press). There is somewhat less consensus on effective teaching practices in other domains, such as math and science, but this research base is growing rapidly (Ginsburg et al., 2008; Kinzie et al., Chapter 2; National Research Council, NRC, 2009).

To achieve desired outcomes for children, PD programs must target evidence-based teaching practices specifically. The projects represented in this volume provide a nice example of the benefits of taking this approach, with many projects documenting effects on evidence-based teaching strategies as well as corresponding development in children's skills.

Although evidence regarding elements of effective teaching in early childhood contexts has accumulated over the past several decades, the inclusion of these elements in federal and state early education policy is new. Quality rating and improvement systems and Head Start monitoring have placed a greater emphasis on the important role of evidence-based teaching practices as a primary indicator of the quality of early childhood programs (Hamre, Goffin, & Kraft-Sayre, 2009; Improving Head Start Act of 2007, H.R. 1429, 2007; Tout et al., 2010). These policy systems have helped make programs accountable not just for the materials and environment they provide for children, but also for the ways in which early childhood programs foster and support learning and development through positive and cognitively engaging teacher–child interactions. Policies that hold programs accountable for demonstrating effective teaching may help push programs to adopt PD programs with evidence for improving these practices.

There are positive signs on the funding front as well. Despite budget shortfalls, there are many examples of significant investments in PD for early childhood teachers. The Early Learning Challenge Fund will provide states more than $500 million to improve early childhood program quality, with an emphasis on effective teaching. Both the Office of Head Start and the Child Care Bureau have invested significant resources in new national centers intended to disseminate evidence-based practices to programs and teachers across the country. There are significant state-level investments as well. First 5 California is just beginning a new round of its quality improvement initiative, Comprehensive Approaches to Raising Education Standards (CARES) Plus program, with state funding of $36 million and additional resources invested in each participating county. States such as Georgia are using Race to the Top funds to support new PD opportunities for state pre-K programs. Thus resources are available to support the implementation of effective PD programs.

One final factor that should enable the implementation of effective PD programs at scale is increasing evidence regarding the elements of effective

PD. Although we still have much to learn and there is a need for greater specificity with regard to these common elements of effective PD, they do provide an initial roadmap for how the resources devoted to PD should be allocated. Zaslow et al. (2010, pp. xii–xiv) summarize the common elements of good PD programs:

- There are specific and articulated objectives for PD.

- Practice is an explicit focus of the PD, and attention is given to linking the focus on early educator knowledge and practice.

- There is collective participation of teachers from the same classrooms or schools in PD.

- The intensity and duration of the PD is matched to the content being conveyed.

- The educators are prepared to conduct child assessments and interpret their results as a tool for ongoing monitoring of the effects of PD.

- It is appropriate for the organizational context and aligned with standards for practice.

Not surprisingly, most of the PD programs described in this volume include these elements.

Given these factors—alignment between research evidence and policy standards for teaching and learning; federal, state, and local resources devoted to PD; agreement on common elements of effective PD—it seems that we would find many examples of evidence-based PD being used in practice. However, beyond a few examples described in this volume of use of these programs at scale (Landry et al., Chapter 7, Pianta et al., Chapter 8), examples of large-scale implementation of effective early childhood PD programs are scarce. In the next sections, we describe some of the barriers to large-scale implementation of the types of programs described in this volume.

BARRIERS TO LARGE-SCALE IMPLEMENTATION OF PROFESSIONAL DEVELOPMENT

As policy makers and program administrators select and implement PD for their teachers, they are faced with myriad decisions: On which teacher skills should they focus? In what types of PD should they engage (e.g., workshops, coaching)? To whom should they look to provide the PD—internal resources (e.g., coaches, education mangers, directors), affiliated but external sources (T/TA networks), or outside organizations (e.g., consultants, not-for- and for-profit PD purveyors)? Perhaps most important, which programs are most likely to produce outcomes? There are few resources available to help programs answer these questions. In the following sections, we discuss barriers related to both the selection and implementation of effective PD.

Selection of Effective Professional Development

One of the first decisions to be made in the selection of PD programs concerns the content on which the PD should focus. With movement toward greater "academic" content in early childhood programs, these decisions have become increasingly complicated. For example, the 2011 revision of the Head Start Early Learning Framework highlights 10 areas for focus at the child outcome level, nested in five broad domains. At the teacher level, the CLASS, now being used as a part of quality rating and improvement systems in several states, describes 10 dimensions of teaching practice, nested within three broad domains. Landry and colleagues (Chapter 7) describe five areas of teacher practice. So, despite the alignment between researchers and policy makers on targets for PD (at the child and teacher levels), there are few resources available to help programs make decisions about the areas of practice on which to focus. Ideally we would like to see programs engaging in developmentally appropriate, systematic assessment of children and/or teachers to help determine the areas of greatest need within their programs. If, for example, child assessments demonstrated low math skills at the end of the preschool year or classroom observations revealed that teachers were struggling with behavior management, programs could invest in PD programs that target these areas specifically. Unfortunately, few programs have the capacity to enact and utilize this kind of data effectively (Snow & Van Hemel, 2008).

Regardless of how decisions are made regarding the targets of PD, there is also often a fundamental mismatch between the resources (time and money) available for PD and the costs and complexities of most evidence-based PD models. Programs are often looking to fill workshop slots in a 1-day in-service meeting of staff, whereas the programs described in this volume require significant investment of time and money. There is likely a need for movement on both sides. States and programs need to move toward selecting and supporting the kind of PD that we know works—PD that is intensive, coherent, and focused on areas of teaching practice that matter most. However, there is also a need to develop and test less intensive and costly models.

Most of the programs described in this volume are quite time and resource intensive. Many rely on coaching, which is among the most costly of PD interventions. Justice, McGinty, Cabell, Knighton, and Huffman (2010) argue that we need to work to create more feasible, sustainable options for curriculum and PD that are not as complicated and costly to deliver. They provide evidence of a language and literacy curricular supplement that can be delivered with high fidelity by a range of early childhood teachers with very low levels of support. Zaslow et al. (2010) make a similar point in their review of EC PD programs:

> As a whole, the studies seem to suggest that intensive and extensive administration of professional development for language and literacy practices tends to be associated with positive educator and child outcomes, but there were several examples in which even a small dosage of professional development (e.g., 10 hours in one case, 30 minutes in another) was associated with positive child outcomes (Neuman 1999; Whitehurst et al., 1999). Our examination of the studies for which this was the case suggests that short-term or brief dosages of professional development may suffice when a *discrete set of skills* is targeted (such as joint book reading), but professional development that has a *broad, comprehensive focus* (such as a combined focus on phonological awareness, print knowledge, and oral language skills) may require more long-term and intensive professional development activities. (p. 48)

The implications of this observation are that we need programs to be more intentional in their selection of PD—focusing short-term PD resources (e.g., 1-day workshop slots) on discrete skills and focusing greater resources on PD focused on broader and more comprehensive skills.

Even if administrators successfully select targets for PD and have the resources to implement evidence-based programs, there is not accessible information regarding which PD programs are effective and even less to suggest which programs are effective for particular populations of teachers or children. The type of research represented in this volume is relatively new. Research reviews on early childhood PD, such as the seminal work conducted by Zaslow and colleagues (2010), provide an initial synthesis of some of this information but may not be in a format that is accessible for most administrators who are making decisions about how to invest PD resources.

Because so much of this research is new, we simply do not know enough about how effective these programs are at scale or with a diverse population of teachers and children. For example, we know little about the extent to which these PD programs, which are typically tested with volunteer teachers in efficacy trials, will translate when delivered at a population level. Evidence from other fields suggests important effects of volunteerism on efficacy of programs (Gordon, 1976). Also, most of the PD programs with evidence of efficacy, including those cited in this volume, have been conducted in Head Start or state pre-K programs with fewer examples of effective programs for early childhood teachers working in child care or family child care settings. Landry and colleagues (Chapter 7) describe working with a broader spectrum of early childhood teachers, and Pianta et al. (Chapter 8) cite examples of MyTeachingPartner (MTP) being delivered more broadly. However, less is known about the efficacy of programs in these settings.

One exception comes from Quality Interventions for Early Care and Education (QUINCE; Bryant et al., 2009), which was conducted in center-based child care and family child care settings. The study tested the Partnerships for Inclusion (PFI) model of assessment-based, individualized, on site consultation (Palsha & Wesley, 1998; Wesley, 1994). Results indicated some effects of treatment on classroom quality, as measured by the Early Childhood Environment Rating Scale-Extension, ECERS-E (Sylva, Siraj-Blatchford, & Taggart, 2003) and PFI, did result in increases over time on the language measure for children in child care centers, compared with control children in centers. There were, however, no effects of the intervention in family child care settings. Study authors cite a multitude of implementation issues, such as staff turnover and low levels of fidelity, as potential contributing factors. Thus, although the aforementioned PD programs provide evidence of efficacy, early childhood program directors and policy makers need to be aware of the limitations of our knowledge and make sure to evaluate programs as implemented.

Implementation of Effective Professional Development

If policy makers or administrators make it through the myriad issues related to the selection of effective PD, a number of issues related to implementation remain. A primary barrier at the implementation level concerns the simple question of whether evidence-based PD, such as those described in this volume and the Zaslow et al. (2010) review, are available for broad dissemination. There is a tendency for researchers to hold back interventions from the practice community, because they are constantly striving to revise the program to achieve the greatest effects on teachers and children. Although this is a laudable goal, we also need to consider when programs are good enough to be disseminated more broadly. This question needs to be answered while simultaneously considering the status quo, in which most early childhood programs offer their teachers very few PD options that are likely to lead to meaningful change in practice.

On the research side, there are often attitudinal and organizational barriers to implementation as well. Many academics have little interest in issues of large-scale implementation; they are interested in research and would prefer to turn implementation over to others. In addition, few universities are prepared to handle these implementation efforts. Thus, in most cases, there is a need for an outside organization to be created or accessed in order to broadly disseminate the types of programs described in this volume. Fixen et al. (2005) discuss at length how critical these "purveyors" are to the successful implementation of evidence-based programs. Yet there are few examples of these organizations in the early childhood PD world.

Another important barrier to the successful implementation of effective PD programs concerns the lack of available data on the critical ingredients or issues of dosage. Thus, as practitioners look to implement effective programs, they have little guidance on exactly which components of the intervention are most important to ensure effectiveness or how true to the model they need to stay in order to achieve good results. Fixen et al. (2005) suggest that programs tend to be implemented more successfully if there is more known about the core intervention components. For example, teachers who participate in MTP improve their teaching and children in their classrooms learn more (Downer, et al., 2011; Mashburn, Downer, Hamre, Justice, & Pianta, 2010; Pianta, Mashburn, Downer, Hamre, & Justice, 2008). However, we are uncertain how much of this change is attributable to the coaching versus the teachers viewing and reflecting on videos highlighting their own and others teaching practices. In regard to dosage, we do not yet have clear evidence regarding how many cycles of MTP are needed to produce change. Untangling these core components and dosage issues is often a challenge. Teachers who participate actively in one component of an intervention (e.g., workshop attendance) tend to also participate highly in other components (e.g., viewing of online resources), so it is difficult to determine which pieces may be most critical. Another common challenge is that teachers who are struggling most ask for and receive the highest dosage (Li-Grinning, Raver, Champion, Sardin, & Metzger, 2010), which can sometimes lead to negative or null associations between dosage and outcomes (Brennan, Bradley, Allen, & Perry, 2008).

A final barrier to effective implementation concerns the limitations of the work force delivering PD in the early childhood field. A review of programs in this volume and Zaslow et al. (2010) suggests that the implementers of effective PD programs are often highly educated (i.e., master's degree), highly specialized, and intensively trained in the models they are delivering. With the exception of those programs that have been implemented at scale (Landry et al., Chapter 7; Pianta et al., Chapter 8), almost none of these programs use existing staff in programs or existing T/TA providers in the community. There are thus clear questions about the successful implementation of these programs at scale, in which existing staff need to be accessed.

Existing data suggest there is great variability in the skills and abilities of those who are actually responsible for delivering support to teachers and programs (Hong, Walters, & Mintz, 2011). There are, however, examples of attempts to use federal and state T/TA dollars in more systematic ways, such as the redesigned Office of Head Start and the Child Care Bureau T/TA networks and national centers previously described. At the state level there are many examples of attempts to increase the quality of T/TA and PD providers. At least 23 states have developed tracking systems for these providers (National Child Care Information and Technical Assistance Center, 2009). Some states have moved beyond tracking and have developed comprehensive training and certification requirements. For example, Pennsylvania uses QRS dollars to support the Pennsylvania Quality Assurance System. Anyone who receives funding from the state to provide training has to participate in this system, which includes online coursework and a review of PD activities (Hong et al., 2011). Unfortunately we have little data regarding the effectiveness of these efforts in ensuring high-quality PD and effects on teacher practices or child outcomes.

RECOMMENDATIONS FOR MOVING EVIDENCE-BASED PROFESSIONAL DEVELOPMENT INTO THE FIELD

Given the opportunities and barriers discussed previously, we have several recommendations for helping move the types of PD programs described in this volume into the field more broadly.

1. **Stop delivering professional development that does not work.** Briefs workshops do not promote meaningful change for teachers or the children in their care (Bullough, 2009). It is known that effective PD is explicitly focused on teachers' everyday work in classrooms, not on abstract child development theory in isolation (Fuligni, Howes, Lara-Cinisomo, & Karoly, 2009). For PD to have any hope of leading to improved outcomes for children, PD investments must be absolutely aligned with evidence-based teaching practices. PD has to target practices that we know make a difference for children. But most PD resources will be spent on workshops on workshops and other programs with no evidence for effectiveness.

   Discontinuing current PD practices will not be easy. There is a powerful force of the status quo that pushes federal, state, district, and program PD systems and T/TA networks to develop more of the things programs and teachers are used to: 1– 2-hour workshops, one pagers for teachers, and so forth. When given choices, teachers may be drawn to PD opportunities that are fun and easy, rather than selecting those that are challenging and focused on children's learning. Moving away from the status quo will require changes at the policy level. Programs need to be held accountable for how they spend their PD resources and demonstrate evidence that these investments lead to improvements in teachers' practice and children's development and learning.

2. **Invest in evidence-based options that are ready to be used at scale.** Although there are not enough examples of evidence-based options for PD that are ready for scale up to fit all PD needs, policy makers should not shy away from investing resources in those that are ready. A shift is needed in the tendency to develop new programs that exactly meet local needs and shy away from endorsing particular evidence-based programs. Grossman (2009) takes a strong stance in suggesting that greater emphasis needs to be placed on replication:

Society does need to discover or create new programs in areas where there are no proven ones. However, the bias in the nonprofit world is for everything to be home grown and local. Given how hard it is to engineer change in the natural courses of people's lives, we should invest more in successfully spreading proven programs than we do now. (p. 12)

There are nice examples from other areas of social service that have leveraged federal and state resources to adopt and implement evidence-based programs to great success (Olds, Hill, O'Brien, Racine, & Moritz, 2003; Schoenwald & Hoagwood, 2001).

3. **Provide policy- and practice-friendly information on evidence-based programs.** If policy makers enact the type of reforms suggested here they need access to clear and concise information on effective PD options. There are good models for how to communicate this kind of information. The U.S. Department of Education's What Work's Clearinghouse and companion site for Doing What Works is one example, though as of 2011 there are not any reports on PD on these sites. The Center for Academic and Social Emotional Learning's (SEL) Safe and Sound Guide (2005) is another example. This summary of more than 80 SEL programs uses a *Consumer Reports* approach to quickly and clearly communicating information about each programs design and cost, the student outcomes targeted, evidence regarding effectiveness, and availability of implementation supports. For the early childhood PD community, such a product should include alignment and crosswalks of existing programs with major targets at the child (e.g., Head Start Outcomes Framework) and teacher (evidence-based teaching practices) level. Such a tool would help address many of the barriers discussed related to program selection.

4. **Use existing and new communication networks to build bridges between research and practice.** The Office of Head Start and the Office of Child Care have invested heavily in T/TA networks to help support the dispersion of knowledge to the field. These networks have the potential to become disseminators of evidence-based PD, but systems are not aligned to support this role. With the creation of new national centers for both the Office of Head Start and Office of Child Care, there may be an opportunity to strategically shift the role of these networks to focus more of their time on disseminating PD programs with evidence of effectiveness.

5. **Create more university–purveyor partnerships to facilitate the high-quality dissemination of evidence-based PD programs.** Moving evidence-based programs from the lab to the community is complex, and leaders in implementation research highlight the importance of creating purveyors whose sole responsibility is dissemination. As Blasé, Van Dyke, and Fixsen (2009) stated,

Purveyors and intermediaries are critical to developing efficient and effective processes to create the necessary conditions for success, and they represent new roles, functions, and structures (Olds et al., 2003). While scholars may contribute to understanding these emerging entities and functions, it is not likely that they will participate in directly providing such implementation services and expertise. Universities simply are not designed to support or reward such functions, and the skill sets required do not directly map onto the skill sets of researchers and scholars. (p. 14)

The main goal of these organizations is not to "sell" the program, but rather to ensure that programs are delivered with high fidelity and quality in ways that can help better ensure effectiveness as the programs move to scale (Schoenwald & Henngeler, 2003). These partnerships may be created through the collaboration of university researchers with existing purveyors, such as Landry's work with Wireless Generation and Teachscape to disseminate assessment tools and online coursework, as well as through the creation of new entities such as Teachstone, which, as described by Pianta et al. (Chapter 8), is dedicated solely to dissemination of evidence-based programs.

6. **Build and test sustainable models for PD.** Many of the barriers to large-scale implementation of evidence-based PD programs relate to a disconnect between program models and existing resources (e.g., staff, finances, time). The previous recommendations describe removing these barriers with a focus on implementation of programs that we know work. However, on the other side, developers need to be more cognizant of these sustainability issues from the start. There may be better ways to build effective programs that are simpler to implement.

Partnerships between practitioners and researchers may be able to develop and test models that are more feasible and thus more likely to be adopted in the long-term. For example Cappella, Jackson, Wagner, Hamre, and Soulé (in press) describe the way in which researchers and schools worked together to adapt two evidence-based coaching models to best fit the needs and resources of the local community. The end result was a coaching model that was both feasible for existing school-based mental health providers and efficacious (Cappella et al., in press). There are few examples of this type of formative, yet rigorous, partnership in early childhood PD development. The Head Start University Partnership Research Grants, which began in 2008 in seven sites across the country, and this may lead to the development and testing of sustainable models for intervention.

Effective use of technology may help reduce costs of delivering some of these programs. Examples include programs such as those described by Kinzie et al. (Chapter 2) and the CLASS video library (Pianta et al., Chapter 8), which can be delivered online for very little beyond the initial development costs. In-person and online coursework, such as that described by Pianta et al. (Chapter 8) and Landry et al. (Chapter 7) also offer potentially cost-effective and more easily scalable options.

7. **Fund research on implementation at scale.** Most of the projects described in this volume were funded by either the Institute of Education Sciences (IES) or the National Institute of Child Health and Human Development (NICHD). NICHD and the larger National Institutes of Health (NIH) have invested quite heavily in implementation research. This funding has helped to spur advances in the conceptualization, measurement, and conduct of implementation science and facilitated the successful large-scale use of numerous health-related programs. There are far fewer examples of high-quality implementation research in educational settings (Penuel, Frank, Fishman, Sabelli, & Cheng, 2009). Often these implementation studies are embedded in large scale-up projects, rather than the sole focus of research. As of 2011, there are few opportunities within the IES funding structure to facilitate real-time response to opportunities to examine the adoption and implementation of these types of programs when they do occur. Collaborative meetings focused on implementation issues between NIH, NICHD, IES, National Science Foundation, and other funders have begun this conversation, and if this interest continues, we expect that we will know much more about large-scale implementation of PD programs in coming years.

SUMMARY

We in the field, have a unique opportunity to invest in the development of the early childhood work force that will have a direct impact on program quality and children's learning. In many ways it is an optimal time for this work. There are PD programs that are proven to work and known resources to implement them. Yet it is not at all clear that these efforts will be successful. Researchers and policy makers need to work carefully together in the coming years to help ensure that 10 years from now it can be said that early childhood PD has been transformed in the United States.

REFERENCES

Barnett, W.S., Epstein, D.J., Carolan, M.E., Fitzgerald, J., Ackerman, D.J., & Friedman, A.H. (2010). *The state of preschool, 2010*. Retrieved from http://nieer.org/yearbook/pdf/yearbook.pdf.

Blair, C. (2002). Integrating cognition and emotion in a neurobiological conceptualization of children's functioning at school entry. *American Psychologist, 57*, 111–127. doi:10.1037//0003-066X.57.2.111

Blair, C., & Diamond, A. (2008). Biological processes in prevention and intervention: The promotion of self-regulation as a means of preventing school failure. *Development and Psychopathology, 20*, 899–911. doi:10.1017/S0954579408000436

Blasé, K.A., Van Dyke, M., & Fixsen, D. (2009). Evidence-based programming in the context of practice and policy. *Social Policy Report, 23*(3), 14.

Brennan, E.M., Bradley, J.R., Allen, M.D., & Perry, D.F. (2008). The evidence base for mental health consultation in early childhood settings: Research synthesis addressing staff and program outcomes. *Early Education and Development, 19,* 982–1022. doi:10.1080/10409280801975834

Bryant, D., Wesley, P., Burchinal, P., Hegland, S., Hughes, K., Tout, K.,… Joen, H. (2009). *The QUINCE-PFI study: An evaluation of a promising model for child care provider training.* Retreived from http://www.researchconnections.org/child-care/resources/18547

Bullough, R.V. (2009). The continuing education of teachers: In-service training and workshops. In L.J. Saha & A.G. Dworkin (Eds.), *International handbook of research on teachers and teaching* (pp. 159–169). New York, NY: Springer.

Cappella, E., Jackson, D., Wagner, C., Hamre, B., & Soulé, C. (in press). Bridging mental health and education in urban elementary schools: Participatory research to inform intervention development and implementation. *School Psychology Review.*

Collaborative for Academic, Social, and Emotional Learning. (2005). *Safe and sound: An educational leader's guide to evidence-based social and emotional learning (SEL) programs.* Chicago, IL: Author.

Downer, J., T., Pianta, R. C., Fan, X., Hamre, B. K., Mashburn, A., & Justice, L. (2011). Effects of web-mediated teacher professional development on the language and literacy skills of children enrolled in prekindergarten programs. *NHSA Dialog: Research-to-Practice Journal for the Early Childhood Field, 14*(4), 189–212.

Fixsen, D. L., Naoom, S. F., Blase, K. A., Friedman, R. M., & Wallace, F. (2005). *Implementation research: A synthesis of the literature* (No. Louis de la Parte Florida Mental Health Publication #231). Tampa: University of South Florida.

Fukkink, R.G., & Lont, A. (2007). Does training matter? A meta-analysis and review of caregiver training studies. *Early Childhood Research Quarterly, 22,* 294–311. doi:10.1016/j.ecresq.2007.04.005

Fuligni, A.S., Howes, C., Lara-Cinisomo, S., & Karoly, L. (2009). Diverse pathways in early childhood professional development: An exploration of early educators in public preschools, private preschools, and family child care homes. *Early Education and Development, 20,* 507–526. doi:10.1080/10409280902783483

Garet, M.S., Porter, A., C., Desimone, L., Birman B.F., & Yoon, K.S. (2001). What makes professional development effective? Results from a national sample of teachers. *American Education Research Journal, 38,* 915–945. doi:10.3102/00028312038004915

Ginsburg, H.P., Boyd, J, & Sun Lee, J. (2008). Mathematics education for young children: What it is and how to promote it. *Social Policy Report, 22*(1), 1–23.

Gordon, R.M. (1976). Effects of volunteering and responsibility on the perceived value and effectiveness of a clinical treatment. *Journal of Consulting and Clinical Psychology, 44,* 799–801. doi:10.1037//0022-006X.44.5.799

Grossman, J.B. (2009). A case for replicating proven programs. *Social Policy Report, 23*(3), 12.

Hamre, B.K., Downer, J.T., Jamil, F., & Pianta, R.C. (in press). Enhancing teachers' intentional use of effective interactions with children: Designing and testing professional development interventions. In R.C. Pianta (Ed)., *Handbook of early education.*

Hamre, B.K., Goffin, S.G., & Kraft-Sayre, M. (2009). *Measuring and improving classroom interactions in early childhood settings.* Charlottesville, VA: Teachstone. Retrieved from http://www.teachstone.org/wp-content/uploads/2010/06/CL-ASSImplementationGuide.pdf

Hemmeter, M.L., Santos, R.M., & Ostrosky, M.M. (2008). Preparing early childhood educators to address young children's social-emotional development and challenging behavior: A survey of higher education programs in nine states. *Journal of Early Intervention, 30*, 321–340. doi:10.1177/1053815108320900

Hong, S.L.S., Walters, T., & Mintz, T. (2011). Professional development systems for early childhood educators within a state and federal policy context. In C. Howes & R.C. Pianta (Eds.), *Foundations for teaching excellence: Connecting early childhood quality rating, professional development, and competency systems in states.* (pp. 117–132). Baltimore, MD: Paul H. Brookes Publishing Co.

Howes, C., Burchinal, P., Pianta, R., Bryant, D., Early, D., Clifford, R., & Barbarin, O. (2008). Ready to learn? Children's pre-academic achievement in pre-Kindergarten programs. *Early Childhood Research Quarterly, 23*, 27–50. doi:10.1016/j.ecresq.2007.05.002

Improving Head Start Act of 2007, H.R. 1429, 110th Cong. (2007). Retrieved March 14, 2011, from http://www.govtrack.us/congress/bill.xpd?bill=h110-1429

Justice, L.M., McGinty, A.S., Cabell, S.Q., Knighton, K., & Huffman, G. (2010). Language and literacy curriculum supplement for preschoolers who are academically at risk: A feasibility study. *Language, Speech, Hearing Services in Schools, 41*, 161–178. doi:10.1044/0161-1461(2009/08-0058)

Li-Grinning, C., Raver, C.C., Champion, K., Sardin, L., & Metzger, M. (2010). Understanding and improving classroom emotional climate and behavior management in the "real world": The role of Head Start teachers' psychosocial stressors. *Early Education and Development, 21*, 65–94. doi:10.1080/10409280902783509

Mashburn, A.J., Downer, J.T., Hamre, B.K., Justice, L.M., & Pianta, R.C. (2010). Consultation for teachers and children's language and literacy development during pre-kindergarten. *Applied Developmental Science, 14*, 179–196.

National Child Care Information and Technical Assistance Center. (2009). *Early childhood professional development systems toolkit.* Retrieved from http://nccic.acf.hhs.gov/pubs/pd_toolkit/index.html

National Research Council. (2009). *Mathematics learning in early childhood: Paths toward excellence and equity.* Washington, DC: National Academies Press.

Neuman, S.B. (1999). Books make a difference: A study of access to literacy. *Reading Research Quarterly, 34*, 286–310. doi:10.1598/RRQ.34.3.3

Olds, D.L., Hill, P.L., O'Brien, R., Racine, D., & Moritz, P. (2003). Taking preventive intervention to scale: The nurse-family partnership. *Cognitive and Behavioral Practice, 10*, 278–290. doi:10.1016/S1077-7229(03)80046-9

Palsha, S. & Wesley, P. (1998). Improving quality in early childhood environments through on site consultation. *Topics in Early Childhood Special Education, 18*, 243–253. doi:10.1177/027112149801800407

Penuel, W.R., Frank, K.A., Fishman, B.J., Sabelli, N., & Cheng, B. (2009). *Expanding the scope of implementation research in education to inform design.* Menlo Park, CA: SRI International.

Pianta, R.C., Mashburn, A.J., Downer, J.T., Hamre, B.K., & Justice, L.M. (2008). Effects of web-mediated professional development resources on teacher–child interactions in pre-kindergarten classrooms. *Early Childhood Research Quarterly, 23*, 431–451. doi:10.1016/j.ecresq.2008.02.001

Schoenwald, S.K., & Henggeler, S.W. (2003). Current strategies for moving evidence-based interventions into clinical practice: Introductory comments. *Cognitive and Behavioral Practice, 10*, 275–277.

Schoenwald, S.K., & Hoagwood, K. (2011). Effectiveness, transportability, and dissemination of interventions: What matters when? *Journal of Psychiatric Services, 52*, 1190–1197.

Scott-Little, C., Kagan, S.L., & Frelow, V.S. (2006). Conceptualization of readiness and the content of early learning standards: The intersection of policy and research? *Early Childhood Research Quarterly, 21*, 153–173.

Shanahan, T., & Lonigan, C. J. (2010). The national early literacy panel: A summary of the process and the report. *Educational Researcher, 19*(4), 279–283. doi:10.3102/0013189X10369172

Shonkoff, J.P. (2010). Building a new biodevelopmental framework to guide the future of early childhood policy. *Child Development, 81,* 357–367. doi:10.1111 /j.1467-8624.2009.01399

Snow, C., & Van Hemel, S. (2008). *Early childhood assessment: Why, what and how? Report of the Committee on Developmental Outcomes and Assessments for Young Children,* Washington, DC: National Academies Press.

Sylva, K., Siraj-Blatchford, I., & Taggart, B. (2003). *Assessing quality in the early years: Early Childhood Environment Rating Scale-Extension (ECERS-E): Four curricular subscales.* Stoke-on Trent, England: Trentham Books.

Tout, K., Starr, R., Moodie, S., Soli, M., Kirby, G. & Boller, K. (2010). *ACF-OPRE Report. Compendium of quality rating systems and evaluations.* Washington, DC: U.S. Department of Health and Human Services, Administration for Children and Families, Office of Planning, Research and Evaluation.

Wesley, P.W. (1994). Providing on site consultation to promote quality integrated child care programs. *Journal of Early Intervention, 18,* 391–402. doi:10.1177/105381519401800408

Whitehurst, G.J., Zevenberegen, A.A., Crone, D.A., Shultz, M.D., Velting, O.N., & Fischel. J.E. (1999). Outcomes of an emergent literacy intervention from Head Start through second grade. *Journal of Educational Psychology, 91,* 261–272. doi:10.1037//0022-0663.91.2.261

Zaslow, M., Tout, K., Halle, T., Whittaker, J.V., & Lavelle, B. (2010). *Toward the identification of features of effective professional development for early childhood educators.* Washington, DC: Child Trends. Retrieved from http://www2.ed.gov/rsch-stat/eval/professional-development/literature-review.pdf

Index

Tables, figures, and footnotes are indicated by *t*, *f*, and *n*, respectively.